ORGANIZATIONAL DIAGNOSIS:

A WORKBOOK OF THEORY AND PRACTICE

MARVIN R. WEISBORD

ADDISON-WESLEY PUBLISHING COMPANY

Reading, Massachusetts • Menlo Park, California • New York
Don Mills, Ontario • Wokingham, England • Amsterdam
Bonn • Sydney • Singapore • Tokyo • Madrid • San Juan
Paris • Seoul • Milan • Mexico City • Taipei

The publisher offers discounts on this book when ordered in quantity for
special sales. For more information please contact:

    Corporate & Professional Publishing Group
    Addison-Wesley Publishing Company
    Route 128
    Reading, Massachusetts 01867

ISBN 0-201-08357-4

22 23 24 25 26 27-CRS-97969594
Twenty-second Printing, October 1994

PREFACE

>>>

Learning organizational diagnosis is something like learning to play the piano. You can't sight read until you know the names of the notes and their location on the keyboard. As with piano playing, the more theory and practice you've had already, the easier it will be to improve your diagnostic skills.

Part I of this workbook presents a vocabulary and concepts for helping you quickly understand many things about an organization. Especially, it will help you see what it takes to make an organization perform better. Many people have applied these concepts successfully to work teams, industrial firms, government agencies, universities, medical centers, and small businesses.

The vocabulary of the "six-box model" can be learned in a few minutes. You can apply the concepts on paper, using the workbook, in a matter of hours, days, or weeks—depending on whether you do it alone or in a workshop or a course with others. You'll find that these ideas fit easily into whatever managerial, administrative, or consulting work you do now.

The concepts can be used as a "cognitive" framework for team development, management training, supervisory training courses, organizational-behavior education, or diagnostic self-studies and survey-data feedback. They can also be used as simple tools for individual management of programs, projects, and day-to-day problems.

Education is the main purpose of this workbook. It is designed to help you teach yourself some important elements about managing organizations, building on what you already know.

You are invited to do each step deliberately, slowly, and in exaggerated fashion. You will be asked to make distinctions that are not "neat", to separate issues that often blur together, to make judgments that may seem arbitrary and oversimplified. If this workbook is to help you educate yourself, it's important that you dispel any anxiety you may have about "doing it wrong."

Once you try out the concepts, you'll find that you use them easily, and naturally, in your own way, without having to strain to make distinctions, as you did in the learning phase. In addition to learning, there are four possible outcomes you might achieve:

1. Identify the strong and weak points of a particular organization you have chosen to study;

2. Identify the choices you have if you wish to improve things ("intervene") in a systematic way;

3. Become more conscious of your biases and untested assumptions;

4. Develop a more systematic way of managing organized work.

The workbook has two main features:

1. *Text*—a written description of concepts appears on the left-hand page throughout Part I.

2. *Work sheets*—brief paper-and-pencil exercises appear on the right-hand pages of Part I. These will guide you in applying each concept in turn to an organization you know well.

The workbook is designed so that you can proceed alone. If you do, take three or four sessions a few days apart; a single sitting would be too tedious. Better still, do the exercises with others, comparing notes as you go. More often than not, you'll be using this workbook as part of a course or workshop. In that case, time will be provided for discussion and consultation with others, and tasks will be assigned to help you assimilate and use the material.

Output—following each step will lead you to develop a diagnostic profile of the organization you choose—that is, an outline of its important features, both formal and informal, and how they work together to solve or block solutions to performance problems.

Start by reading the introductory text on the next few pages; then proceed with Steps 1 through 20.

Resource Readings—Part II consists of Resource Readings. In this section you'll find listed additional texts on each of the major concepts in the workbook. I suggest that unless otherwise instructed, you try doing the exercises before consulting the readings.

Wynnewood, Pennsylvania　　　　　　M.R.W.
March 1978

THANK YOU

So many people have influenced my thinking on these matters that I find it impossible to list them all. Where I can, I cite sources. However, there are friends and colleagues I want to thank personally.

I believe that this workbook could not exist but for the collaborative support and colleague-ship of Paul R. Lawrence for the past several years. Our work together, more than any literature, has taught me how to value, conceptualize, and use knowledge as a means for improving organizations.

In addition, Peter Vaill and Neale Clapp have stimulated me continually with their crea-tive ideas and by challenging my assumptions. Marguerite Schaefer and Leonard Goodstein in particular have encouraged the development of the concepts presented here. Martin P. Charns has been continually supportive.

Much of this material evolved in an organizational diagnosis "module" presented at the NTL Institute Professional Development Learning Community at Bethel, Maine. That most, if not all, of it has been tested in practice is testimony to the commitment and skill of my workshop partner, Allan Drexler.

CONTENTS

>>>>>>>>>>>>>>>>>>>>>>>>>>>>>>>>

PART I   ORGANIZATIONAL DIAGNOSIS

Introduction	2
Warm-Up Step 1	3
Action Research	4
Warm-Up Step 2: Ten Minutes of Action Research	5
"Jargon"	6
Warm-Up Step 3: Jargon Exercise	7
What to Look For	8
What to Look For	9
Defining Boundaries	10
Step 1: Boundary Definition	11
The Input/Output System	12
Step 2: Input/Output Overview	13
Formal and Informal Systems	14
Step 3: Where to Start	15
What Else Is Going On?	16
Step 4: Scanning "Everything Else"	17
Purposes	18
Step 5: Diagnosing Purposes (Part 1)	19
Step 6: Diagnosing Purposes (Part 2)	21
Structure	22
Step 7: Diagnosing Structure (Formal System)	23
Step 8: Diagnosing Structure (Informal System)	27
Step 9: Diagnosing Structure (Pseudomatrix)	29
Relationships	30
Step 10: Diagnosing Relationships	31
Rewards	36
Step 11: Diagnosing Rewards	37
Leadership	40
Diagnosing Leadership	41
Helpful Mechanisms	44
Step 13: Diagnosing Helpful Mechanisms	45
Overall Diagnosis: Building a Profile	48
Step 14: A Diagnostic Profile	49
Clarifying	50
Step 15: Clarification	51
Intervention Theory	52
Step 16: Diagnosing Your Own Knowledge of Possible Interventions	53
Examples of Strengths/Limitations of Various Interventions	55
Power—A Dynamic Concept	56
Step 17: Diagnosing Power	57
Anticipating and Acting	58
Step 18: Action	59
Building Your Own Model	60
Step 19: Building Your Own Model	61
Comparing Organizations	62
Step 20: Diagnostic Comparisons	63
References and Bibliography	64
Afterword: A Value Statement	67

PART II   RESOURCE READINGS IN DIAGNOSIS

1 **Action Research**
Action Research and Organization
Development
*Wendell L. French and Cecil H.
Bell, Jr.*   69

2 **Jargon**
An Informal Glossary of Terms and
Phrases in Organization Development
Peter B. Vaill   71

3 **Boundaries/Input-Output
Systems/Environments**
A Systems Approach
*Fremont E. Kast and
James E. Rosenzweig*   78

4 **"Everything Else":
Scanning the Environment**
Domains of Organized Action
James D. Thompson   82

5 **Formal versus Informal Systems**
Diagnosing an Informal System
Neale Clapp   86

6 **Purposes—Who Is the Customer?**
Business Purpose and Business
Mission
Peter F. Drucker   90

7 **Structure—Matrix Revisited**
The Human Side of the Matrix
*Paul R. Lawrence, Harvey F. Kolodny,
and Stanley M. Davis*   104

8 **Structure—What Lies Ahead?**
Designing Organizations to Match
Tomorrow
*Bo L. T. Hedberg, Paul C. Nystrom,
and William H. Starbuck*   115

9 **Relationships: Diagnosing Conflict
Between Individuals**
Management of Differences
*Warren H. Schmidt and
Robert Tannenbaum*   124

10 **Relationships: Diagnosing Conflict
Between Units**
Diagnosing Conflict Between Groups
in Organizations
Tony Petrella and Peter Block   136

11 **Rewards—A Far Frontier**
Overview of Reward-System
Requirements
Edward E. Lawler, III   145
Model of the Determinants of
Production Restriction
Edward E. Lawler, III   146
Overview: Reward Systems
Edward E. Lawler, III   147

12 **Leadership**
The Performance of Relationship-
and Task-Motivated Leaders in
Different Situational Favorableness
Conditions
Fred Fiedler   149

Leadership, Learning, and Changing
the Status Quo
Chris Argyris   150
Leadership: A Beleaguered Species?
Warren Bennis   151

13 **Helpful Mechanisms**
Notes on Technology
Peter B. Vaill   153

14 **Interventions**
OD Interventions—An Overivew
*Wendell L. French and Cecil H.
Bell, Jr.*   160

15 **Power in Organizations**
Who Gets Power and How They Hold
On to It: A Strategic-Contingency
Model of Power
Gerald R. Salancik and Jeffrey Pfeffer 163

16 **Comparing Organizations**
Why Organization Development Hasn't
Worked (So Far) in Medical Centers
Marvin R. Weisbord   168

No single model or conceptual scheme embraces the whole breadth and complexity of reality, even though each in turn may be useful in particular instances. This is why management remains an art, for the practitioner must go beyond the limits of theoretical knowledge if he is to be effective.

Seymour Tilles (1963)*

The importance of proper diagnosis cannot be overstressed.

Edgar F. Huse (1975)

*This and all other references are listed on pp. 64–65.

PART I

ORGANIZATIONAL DIAGNOSIS

PART I

ORGANIZATIONAL DIAGNOSIS

INTRODUCTION

There are, in my opinion, too many equally valid theories, techniques, methods, and instruments to make an exact science of organizational diagnosis. Faced with so much uncertainty, one is greatly tempted to behave like the tipsy sailor in the barroom, throwing darts at a blank wall.

"What are you aiming at?" asked the bartender.

"Easy," said the sailor, "whatever the dart hits!"

Given the blank wall called organizational diagnosis, how can a person limit the search to a few areas with confidence that they are the "right" ones? Although there is no single answer to this question, Part I of this workbook does provide a few tools for reducing uncertainty. Especially, it pushes you to think *conceptually* about your experience. This means selecting certain areas for inquiry and finding in them meaning and freedom of action toward some purposes that make sense to you. It also means testing the strengths and limits of *every* concept you wish to apply.

Probably you're using this workbook in a course or workshop. People come to workshops to learn techniques. After all, you can't practice if you don't know what to do. However, there are two questions to consider, lest the pursuit of techniques become a dart-throwing exercise.

1. Why do *you* want to learn diagnosis?
2. What *categories* should you investigate, given infinite possibilities?

Of course, only you can answer the first question. This workbook provides one answer to the second question. It offers some useful categories and a conceptual scheme for organizing each one. This workbook is based on the assumption that what you look for is what you find and that when organizational improvement is your target, some categories are more worth finding than others. Hence the "six boxes"—*structure, purposes, relationships, rewards, helpful mechanisms,* and *leadership*. I have found these categories broad enough to focus my gaze on important issues and precise enough for deciding whether I should try to do anything about what I see.

Briefly answer the following, drawing on your experience to date. (Revise or add at any time later.)

A. Why are *you* interested in diagnosis?

    1. Here?

    2. In general?

B. What concepts do you use *now* to guide you in understanding organizations? Have you a pet theory of management? Are there other theories that attract you, even if you don't know much about them?

FOCUS

ACTION RESEARCH*

Action research is one name for a form of systematic problem identification and solution in which the identifiers and solvers (the principal actors in the situation) are the same people. The term implies learning from your own situation, as you modify and seek to improve it.

Diagnosis is *one step* in the action-research process and should not be mistaken for the whole thing. Moreover, it is not the same thing as "data collection." The word "data" refers to bits and pieces of information from which a diagnosis may be built. "Data"

means clues, not hypotheses. "Diagnosis" implies conclusions about *what the data mean*. Only when a *gap* is specified (e.g., "We ought to reward teaching better if we expect it to be done well") has a diagnosis taken place. Thus "data" means assembling facts. "Diagnosis" means assigning meaning, weight, priority, and relationship to the facts.

Although this process can be written down in a neat sequence, it rarely happens so cleanly. In practice, action-research tends to be messy, incomplete, iterative (repeated over and over), with many loose ends that are never quite tucked in. Nevertheless, I find the chart below helpful for talking about these processes.

---

*A concept of the late social psychologist Kurt Lewin, who said, "There's nothing so practical as a good theory" and went on to prove it with this one.

STEPS IN ACTION RESEARCH

Data collection (facts, opinions, etc.)

    Diagnosis (identifying "gaps" between "what is" and "what ought to be" as supported by the data)

        Action (planning and carrying out steps that you predict will improve things)

            Evaluation (rediagnosis: What's the gap now?)

$\longleftarrow$ ————————— TIME LINE ————————— $\longrightarrow$

DAYS • WEEKS • MONTHS • YEARS

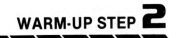
TEN MINUTES OF ACTION RESEARCH: A BRIEF DEMONSTRATION

Take ten minutes, no more, to jot down your findings and conclusions below about your present situation—here, now, in this room.

A. **Data Collection:** What data are available and relevant to the situation you find yourself in right now? Just observe, don't evaluate. What is the nature of this organization? How are you affected? Thoughts? Feelings? Body sensations? What do you see? Smell? Hear? Relations with others here? (3 minutes)

Bits of data:

B. **Diagnosis:** What does it all mean? Are there gaps between the way things are and the way you would like them to be? (2 minutes)

Your diagnosis:

C. **Action:** How might you "intervene" with yourself or others to improve things right now? Write it down. Do it if time and situation allow. (3 minutes)

D. **Evaluation:** To what extent have the few minutes you just invested helped you understand better the differences among "data," "diagnosis," and "intervention"? What clues or bits of data tell you this is so? (2 minutes)

See excerpt by French and Bell—Resource Reading 1.

BASIC CONCEPTS

"JARGON"

This workbook integrates several concepts from management, organization, and social-psychological theory. Some concepts are expressed in words which make up a special vocabulary—"jargon"—which I would like to acknowledge up front.

Having tried substitute words for many concepts in my field, I conclude that it's difficult, maybe impossible, to talk about these matters in "plain English" all the time. I think that this workbook does rather better than most texts, but it's far from jargon-free, for the cost of eliminating some words is, in my opinion, to lose important concepts for managing organizations. So I translate when I can, write jargon when I must.

Here are some terms used in this workbook which sometimes are considered jargon, starting with the title.

Diagnosis This describes a way of looking over an organization to determine the "gap" between what is and what ought to be. This gap, or "variance," suggests a deviation from what somebody considers appropriate. Unfortunately, diagnosis, a term borrowed from the field of medicine, connotes to many people the medical meaning, "to recognize symptoms of disease." Organizations have few vital signs as precise as pulse, temperature, blood pressure, and respiration which signal precisely what shape they're in.

I view people in organizations as explorers who are trying to learn how to do better, rather than as patients who are waiting for a cure. Ultimately, people who live in organizations must define what's wrong and what they wish to do about it. Moreover, whether or not anybody will share and act on a particular diagnosis depends very much on a concept called "ownership."

Ownership Who thinks that the organization has a problem? Owner? Manager? Employee? Customer? Client? Consultant? Which of these are you? How much power, authority, credibility, and commitment have you to act on your insights? Ownership usually requires that people who are expected to do something talk vigorously with one another. Ownership is rarely achieved through written documents alone.

Even when a few people "own" an insight, they will find it hard to change things, no matter what "intervention" they use, unless they can get others affected by it to share their vision.

Intervention This means a deliberate attempt to change things. Interventions can be as simple as commenting in a meeting, "It seems to me that we've been talking for hours about this situation without coming any closer to a solution," to year-long "Management By Objectives" or "job enrichment" programs. Behind every intervention lurks a diagnosis. Intervenors, consciously or not, have identified gaps between the way things are and the way they think they should be. They also have made a decision to pierce in some way the organization's "boundaries."

Boundaries An organization is better understood as having some limits, even though these are sometimes hard to see. Usually, these limits are defined as people on the organization's payroll or formally related to it in some way. Boundaries can be drawn to include employees only, employees and stockholders, employees and consumers, employees and regulators, or some combination of these, depending on what one wishes to diagnose. You can't do a usable diagnosis without specifying at the start how much of the "environment" you wish to confront at one sitting.

Environment Once boundaries are drawn, environment refers to "everything else." Usually it includes (if boundaries are drawn around those on the payroll) some combination of customers, suppliers, competitors, regulatory agencies, and (for some large corporations or agencies) the parent firm or central headquarters. In this workbook we think of "task environment"—that portion of everything else to which people in the organization must respond in order to successfully produce goods or services. It includes whatever is outside and part of the organization's "open system."

Open system This implies a recognition that organizations do not do whatever they please, independent of what's going on outside their boundaries. In fact, they take in money, ideas, and supplies ("inputs") from the environment, transform these materials in some way, and release back to the environment products, services, and new ideas ("outputs"). What they do inside, how they do it, and whether they continue to do it successfully today the way they did yesterday very much depend on their skill at making sense of clues both inside and outside ("feedback"). To the extent that a system responds appropriately to such clues, it can be said to be open. To the extent that it ignores them or dismisses them as temporary or not important, it can be said to be closed.

WARM-UP STEP 3

JARGON EXERCISE

A. Do this *after* reading the initial pages and doing Steps 1 and 2. Do you identify any words so far as "jargon," that is, special language you don't understand, or that you feel is unnecessarily obscure? If so, which?

Word(s):   *Your definition(s):*

B. If you're doing these exercises in a group, discuss with others the meanings of the terms you have flagged. Decide whether you can live with your understanding of the meanings or whether you need to have further explanation and discussions. Do *not* dismiss potential conflicts as "merely semantic." It helps to use words the same way or to find neutral terms if certain ones are too loaded emotionally.

See excerpt by Vaill—Resource Reading 2.

A SIX-BOX MODEL

WHAT TO LOOK FOR*

For several years I've experimented with "cognitive maps" of organizations. These are labels that would help me better describe what I saw and heard and understand the relationships among various bits of data. I started this endeavor when I realized that though I knew a lot of organization theory, most theories are either (1) too narrow to include everything I wished to understand, or (2) too broadly abstract to give much guidance.

These notes represent a progress report on my efforts to combine bits of data, theories, research, and hunches into a working tool which anybody can use. For want of a more elegant name, I call this tool the "Six-Box Model." This model (Fig. 1) has helped me to rapidly expand my diagnostic frame-

*Based on Marvin R. Weisbord, "Organizational Diagnosis: Six Places to Look for Trouble with or without a Theory," *Group & Organization Studies* **1**, 4 (December 1976): 430–447.

work from interpersonal and group issues to the more complicated contexts in which organizations are managed.

Figure 1 provides six labels under which one can sort much of the "funny stuff" that goes on in organizations, both formal and informal. These labels allow people to apply whatever theories they already know in doing a diagnosis and to discover new connections among apparently unrelated events.

Visualize Fig. 1 as a radar screen. "Process" issues show up as blips in one or more boxes, blocking work on important tasks. Air controllers use radar to manage relationships among aircraft—height, speed, distance apart—and to avoid heavy weather. Similarly, a blip in any one box cannot be managed independently of its relationship to the other boxes. However, six potential starting places give you several alternatives when choosing an improvement strategy.

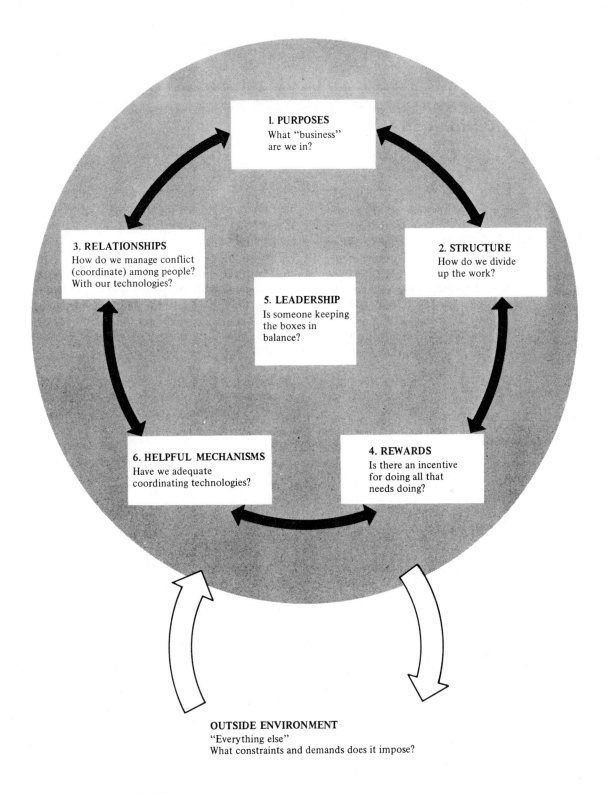

Fig. 1. A Six-Box Model.

DEFINING BOUNDARIES

The circle in Fig. 1 circumscribes the boundaries of an organization I wish to diagnose. "Environment" describes forces difficult to control from inside, but which nonetheless demand a response—customers, government, unions, students, families, friends. It's not always clear where the boundaries are or should be. Although such a system can be characterized accurately as "open," its rationality depends heavily on partially closing off infinite choices. This is an act of reason wed to values, for no great measuring rod exists in the sky for calibrating precisely such judgments (Vickers, 1975).

I find it necessary to set boundaries arbitrarily so that a diagnosis can proceed. I do this by picking a unit name (XYZ Company, Department ABC, QRS Team) and listing groups or individuals "inside" by virtue of money commitments, contract, or formal membership.

BOUNDARY DEFINITION

A. Pick an organization to diagnose. Criteria for selecting an organization: (1) you have a clear role in it; (2) size is 10 to 1000 people; (3) it's not performing as well as you would like.

Organization name _____

B. Define the organization's boundaries in any way that makes sense. In the space below, draw a chart or list important units or individuals or functions. Be clear who is inside, who out. How many levels of organization are included?

See excerpt by Kast and Rosenzweig—Resource Reading 3.

THE INPUT/OUTPUT SYSTEM

Within the boundaries, boxes interact in what is sometimes called an "input/output system." The function of this input/output system is to transform resources (e.g., people, ideas, raw materials, dollars) into goods or services. Figure 2 below expresses the six-box organization/environment in input/output terms. Another word for this concept is "open system" or "sociotechnical system" (Trist, 1969).

"Transformation process" is a term sometimes used to describe the interaction of people and technical systems in creating outputs. Now, if you imagine that this process works or doesn't work depending on what's going on in each of the six boxes and between them, you have the basis for doing an organizational diagnosis.

What do I mean by "works"? Well, I have an optimistic assumption that the "fit" between person and organization can be improved. It should be possible for an organization to do a better job of producing goods and services while creating ways for people to boost their competence and self-esteem. The problem, however, is not so simple. An organization can't "do a better job" if there's no clarity in the first place about what job it should do. Therefore, the "fit" between organization and environment—a concept of Lawrence and Lorsch (1967)—is equally important in any diagnosis.

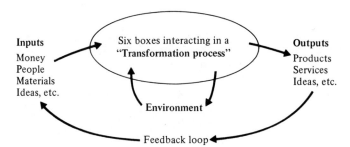

Fig. 2.   The Six-Box Model in Input/Output Terms.

INPUT/OUTPUT OVERVIEW

A. List three important environmental demands that influence your organization's strategic mission (major purpose for being):

1. _____

2. _____

3. _____

B. Imagine your organization represented by the circle below. What are your important inputs, outputs, and sources of feedback? List in the spaces below.

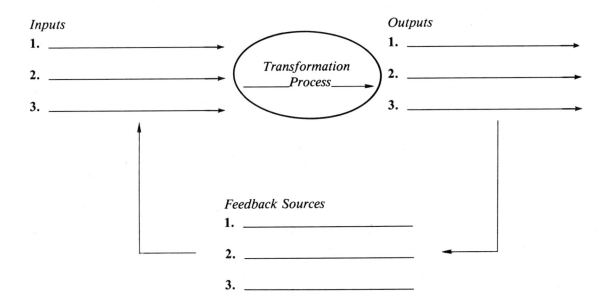

Inputs
1. _____→

2. _____→

3. _____→

Transformation Process

Outputs
1. _____→

2. _____→

3. _____→

Feedback Sources
1. _____

2. _____

3. _____

C. What name would you put on your "transformation process"? What is the thing you do that makes your organization unique?

See excerpt by Kast and Rosenzweig—Resource Reading 3.

FOCUS

FORMAL AND INFORMAL SYSTEMS

No organization has productive transactions with all parts of its environment all of the time. Some events are so unpredictable that all a manager can do is react. Most of the time, though, things inside an organization —in each of the six boxes—can be improved. One key to improvement is discovering which factors you can *do* something about. That is not always easy.

You can see quickly that each box has two potential trouble sources. One is the formal system—what exists on paper. The other is the informal system—what people actually do. Neither system is to be preferred, for both exist in any case. However, in doing a diagnosis, it helps to identify blips in each system and to see whether you can spot a relationship.

Diagnosing the formal system requires some informed guessing. The informed part is knowing what—in fact—this organization *says* in its statements, reports, charts, graphs, and speeches about how it's organized. The guessing part is comparing the organization's rhetoric to its environment and making a judgment about whether this stuff "fits." In other words, will society value and underwrite an organization that declares such-and-such a purpose and organizes itself by so-and-so means to fulfill it?

One level of organizational change is to bring the rhetoric—the system as designed —into better harmony with the rest of the world. It is this target at which much "expert" consultation is aimed.

However, in every organization there's another level of behavior—what people actually do. Diagnosing informal systems is sometimes called "normative" diagnosis. It focuses on the frequency with which people do certain things, in relation to how important they are for organizational performance. Normative behavior usually determines whether otherwise technically excellent systems succeed or fail. For the normative behavior tells you the degree to which the system as designed is meeting the needs of the people who have to operate it (Clapp, 1974). (See also Resource Reading 5.)

Sometimes norms can't be changed without formal changes; hence the need to study relationships *between* formal and informal systems. To persist in such an inquiry is to discover some new reasons why the input-output-transformation stream isn't flowing as smoothly as it could.

WHERE TO START

Start a diagnosis by considering one major output. To trace its relationship to the whole system is to understand quite a lot about gaps in this organization between "what is" and "what ought to be." Here's a simple idea borrowed from Peter Vaill (1974). Take one output and apply the "output congruity matrix" (Fig. 3) to it. Ask, "How satisfied are the *producers* with this output? How satisfied are the *consumers*?" If the answer is "neither," (cell D), the organization is in serious trouble. If one is and the other isn't (cells B or C), trouble is brewing. Either way, the situation can be diagnosed by tracing the dissatisfactions through each box, looking for a likely intervention point.

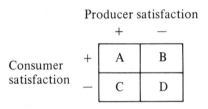

Fig. 3   The Output Congruity Matrix.

A. Major output you wish to trace: _____

B. Write a few words describing producer/consumer satisfaction right now. In which cell on the matrix would you place your organization?____A____B____C____D (Check one)

C. Circle your judgment on the scales below:

Producers

	1	2	3	4	5	

Extremely dissatisfied

1   2   3   4   5

Extremely satisfied

Consumers

WHAT ELSE IS GOING ON?

You've identified an output you wish to use as a lightning rod for understanding how your organization functions. Perhaps consumers or producers or both are dissatisfied.

Assume that there is a rational basis for your organization's existence; that is, it survives because it copes with the stresses and strains of its environment. It's doing something unique and socially useful. It has succeeded in budgeting, hiring, firing, promoting, and producing goods and/or services and is dealing in some fashion with outside groups interested in what it does.

Yet things could be improved. Listed below are some of the major sources of organizational support and restraint which constitute important pressures from outside. Organizations struggle to reduce uncertainty at each of these contact points. In a technique called open-systems planning, these contact points are known as "domains," a shorthand word for "everything else" outside (Thompson, 1967).

1. Customers (distributors and/or users);

2. Suppliers (of materials, capital, equipment, space);

3. Competitors (for both markets and resources);

4. Regulatory groups (government, unions, trade associations, certifying groups);

5. Parent organizations (central headquarters, university, etc.) (Vaill, 1976).

Another way to think about the six boxes is that each is continually being juggled to keep up with shifting—and uncertain—winds in the external domains. So in diagnosing, it helps to discover whether the fact of poor relations with one or more domains is putting a strain on internal relationships, structure, rewards, leadership, etc. Conversely, poor coping with internal issues may be straining relations with one or more important domains.

=====================================

SCANNING "EVERYTHING ELSE"

A. For each domain of your organization, name one important example.

Actual examples

Customer _____

Supplier _____

Competitor_____

Regulator _____

Parent organization_____

B. For each example, circle how satisfactory you view current transactions between it and your organization.

Transactions with:	Highly Unsatisfactory				Highly Satisfactory
Customer	1	2	3	4	5
Supplier	1	2	3	4	5
Competitor	1	2	3	4	5
Regulator	1	2	3	4	5
Parent organization	1	2	3	4	5

C. For each item you rated 1 or 2, list briefly what's wrong:

D. In what way, if any, is the output you are tracing affected?

E. Have you any influence over the situation? _____Yes _____No _____Maybe

See excerpt by Thompson—Resource Reading 4.

FOCUS: "SCANNING THE RADAR"

At this point we will put a magnifying glass on the radar screen, examining each of the six boxes in turn. The goal is to discover significant details of both formal and informal systems that might be related to consumer or producer satisfaction.

PURPOSES (PART 1)

People have all sorts of feelings (mainly anxiety) about work, which cannot be addressed rationally if an organization's goals remain obscure. Thus the two critical factors in this box are goal clarity and goal agreement (Steers and Porter, 1974). The more of each, the less anxiety.

Purposes also go by such names as "missions," "goals" or "objectives." These words have so many meanings, however, that I've tried to find a more neutral handle. "Core mission" or "core transformation process" (in open-systems planning language) comes pretty close to what I mean by purposes.

An organization's purpose results from a psychological negotiation between "what we want to do" (our values, beliefs, satisfactions, competencies) and "what we have to do" (demands of environment, survival needs, etc.). This negotiation *always* takes place, whether or not people are conscious of it and discuss it. It leads to a set of priorities. These priorities make up the organization's current agenda. If the negotiation has not been conscious, priorities can be deduced from what people spend time, energy, and/or money on—independent of what they say is impor-

tant. Such investments are likely to be a good approximation of "what we want to do" tempered by "what we have to do."

In an alert organization the agenda continually changes as some issues are resolved and others emerge. However, this doesn't mean that purposes change rapidly or often.

Naming purposes is one valuable way by which organizations cope with uncertainty. An adequate purpose statement should always permit the drawing of boundaries around which activities are or are not appropriate for this organization in this time and place. Properly stated, purposes highlight an organization's unique feature—the thing that makes it different in a formal sense from all others, including competitors in its field.

An individual's contract with an organization includes accepting its core purposes. Considerable conflict exists where purposes are vague. However, purposes (informal) can nearly always be deduced by examining the strongest programs (or projects or product lines). Programs are the helpful mechanisms by which purposes are translated into action. Ideally, an organization's programs reflect its priorities. If they don't, the organization is in (or headed for) trouble.

Ill-defined or overly broad purposes strain relations with producers and consumers alike. They work against focused activity or concentration, without which, says Peter Drucker (1974), an organization cannot be made to perform. Organizations perform well when they (1) fulfill certain functions better than anybody else, which (2) enough consumers wish to have fulfilled. Hence a diagnosis should examine the following.

1. *Goal "fit."* How appropriate is the goal to the organization's environment? Is there enough consumer support to ensure survival?

2. *Goal clarity.* Are purposes stated concretely enough to include some things and exclude others?

3. *Goal agreement.* To what extent do people exhibit in their informal behavior agreement with stated goals?

DIAGNOSING PURPOSES (PART 1)

FORMAL SYSTEM

A. What documents, if any, concretely define your organization's purposes?

B. From these documents or from other sources, what are the *formal* central purposes *supposed* to be?

C. From your knowledge of environmental demands, how congruent are the purposes in (A) and (B) above with your organization's *formal* environment? How good is the fit between stated purposes and consumer needs?

_____Excellent   _____Good   _____Fair   _____Poor

INFORMAL SYSTEM

D. To what extent do most people in the organization understand the purposes the same way you do?

| Most would agree | 1 | 2 | 3 | 4 | 5 | Most would not agree |

E. To what extent do the people in the organization see it serving in major ways purposes different from the stated ones?

| To a great extent | 1 | 2 | 3 | 4 | 5 | To no extent |

F. Note examples of behavior which tend to contradict formal purposes, showing lack of clarity or lack of agreement:

==

PURPOSES (PART 2)

Sooner or later every organization questions its purposes. Fashions change. Technology evolves. Practices become obsolete. Old markets die. New markets emerge. People gain new insight that changes the way they think about what they're doing.

One car rental company, for instance, discovered that its profits depended on its used-car sales more so than on rentals. It reconceptualized its business from "renting autos" to "turning new cars into used cars (via the rental business), then selling them." This insight radically affected the way the business was managed and with what focus.

Here are some other examples:

Organization	Old Mission	New Mission
Food service company	Provide meals	Efficient production of garbage

Organization	Old Mission	New Mission
Recreation-equipment manufacturer	Leisure products, e.g., bowling balls, sailboats	"We make weekends"
Womens liberal arts college	Well-rounded liberal education	Educate for new career opportunities for women
Health clinic	Treating sickness	Teaching people to take care of themselves

In diagnosing an organization, consider how it conceptualizes its work. Are there other ways it might think about what it does that would:

1. Improve the fit with the environment?
2. Clarify its goals?
3. Gain higher goal agreement?

DIAGNOSING PURPOSES (PART 2)

When an organization has a bad "fit" with the environment or low goal clarity and/or commitment, it's tempting to say "we have no goals" or "we mean all things to all people." Every organization, however, serves *some* purpose, even if the purpose isn't clear.

A. Consider how your organization is now being managed. In the space below, brainstorm as many endings as possible to the statement: "This organization is being run as if its objective were. . . ."

B. Do your answers surprise you? Now, consider how the purposes might be reframed. What statement of purpose might gain you:

1. a better "fit" with environment?

2. greater goal clarity?

3. higher commitment? (your own, or others)

See also excerpt by Drucker—Resource Reading 6.

STRUCTURE

In organizations, as in architecture, form follows function. Every structure is good for something; none is good for everything. There are three main ways to organize (Gulick and Urwick, 1937):

1. By function—specialists work together;
2. By product, program, or project—multiskill teams work together;
3. Mixture of both—two homes for everybody.

None of these structures is hassle-free. Each just makes for different hassles.

FUNCTIONAL ORGANIZATION

Take, for instance, the *functional* organization (Fig. 4).

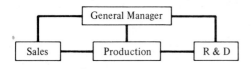

Fig. 4. The Functional Organization

1. Division of labor, budgets, promotions, and rewards are all based on special competence.
2. Functional bosses have the most influence.
3. Functions seek to maximize their own goals—not those of the organization as a whole.

Drawbacks (1) Intergroup conflict is more predictable. (2) Big decisions pile up at the top. (3) Few members have the "big picture." (4) It's tough to shift directions quickly.

Strengths (1) There is support for in-depth competence—many people in each function "talk the same language." (2) There is freedom to specialize while others do coordination—chance to maximize what you do best. (3) People are stable, and secure in environments in which change is slow and quick response not essential.

Highlight Functional organizations resist rapid change. Functionalism and bureaucracy make fine marriage partners.

DIAGNOSING STRUCTURE (FORMAL SYSTEM)

A. Draw another organization chart below, showing the most significant units or functions. Keep in mind that *your* organization may *not* be functional in structure, but rather product line (program, project team, etc.) or mixed.

B. Is the chart above of a: ____mainly functional organization? ____mainly product line (program, project)? ____mixture of both? ____not sure yet how to tell.

PRODUCT ORGANIZATION

Now consider the product line (or program, or project team) organization (Fig. 5). This form is better suited to fast-changing environments and technologies. People do several tasks, and they seek to integrate their skills around a single product or the solution of one class of problem.

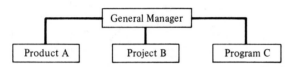

Fig. 5. The Product Organization

1. Coordination with other teams is minimal.
2. Rewards, promotions, and influence go to those who can integrate resources to innovate, produce, and deliver a product or service quickly.
3. Team managers have most influence.

Drawbacks (1) In-depth competence erodes rapidly in each specialty, for generalists can't keep up with everything. (2) Specialists become harder to attract. (3) Innovation is restricted to existing areas. (4) Teams may compete for pooled staff resources such as computers, purchasing, etc.

Strengths (1) This type of organization is responsive to rapid change in environment or technologies. (2) It is less likely to have intergroup conflicts. (3) It is easier for all team members to see the total organization's goals. (4) It provides a chance for members to learn broader skills and have wider responsibilities.

Highlight When organizations "decentralize," they often change from functional to product-line structure; this may improve the informal system in the short run at an (eventual) cost to formal needs.

C. Rate of change in:

Rate of change in:	√ Fast	Medium	Slow
Overall environment			
Your field's technology			
Subunits (name them): A			
B			
C			

(*Note:* Various units of the organization may experience *different* rates of change, thus requiring *different* structural features.)

D. Overall, how would you rate the structures you have in terms of their "fit" with the environment?

Excellent fit   1   2   3   4   5   Poor fit

E. If you have a *mixed* organization, can you identify examples of each type of organizational unit?

Functional Units   *Product (Project, Program)*

F. Have you reorganized in recent years? If so, how?

G. What problem was the reorganization supposed to solve?

H. Did it? _____Yes _____No _____Maybe _____Don't know

MATRIX ORGANIZATION

Some organizations try to have the best of both worlds. This requires a *matrix,* or a *mixed model,* which was developed in the aerospace industry when projects required both diverse state-of-the-art expertise and focused efforts on each project. In a matrix, people have two or more formal locations on the chart (see Fig.6).

No organization could neatly arrange itself from top to bottom as in Fig. 6. This might better be called a *mixed model*, in which some units of a company, university, or medical center are functional and others programmatic; some people wear two hats and some only one; and all of these differences are based on various environments surrounding each subunit.

A mixed model provides maximum flex-ibility. It can shrink or expand with need. It provides multiple career paths, rewarding both special and integrative skills. However, there are serious drawbacks, which might be summarized as "human limitation." Conflict management is time-consuming, for an effective mixed organization requires two budget lines, contracts with two bosses, dual reward systems, etc. Such mechanisms are expensive. Moreover, they are not well understood, for few of us have the experience or training to prepare us for life in such complex relation-ships.

In mixed models, people must invent/dis-cover new procedures and norms. This is dif-ficult and seems justified only when the stakes are high (e.g., saving lives or getting to the moon). It's hardly worth the energy if simpler forms will serve, for it greatly complicates relationships at every turn.

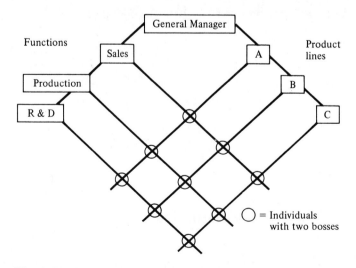

Fig. 6. The Matrix Organization

===

DIAGNOSING STRUCTURE (INFORMAL SYSTEM)

I. Structure is supposed to solve division-of-labor problems. Are there any important organizational tasks falling through the cracks—that is, not being done by somebody?

_____Many _____A few _____None Name one _____

What's the reason?

J. To what extent are those *without* formal responsibility taking on tasks in order to keep things moving?

　　　　　　　　Not at all　　1　　2　　3　　4　　5　　A great deal

What effect does this have?

K. Go back to your list of environmental demands (Step 2). For each, identify where the response is being managed:

Environmental Demand	*Location/Person Managing*	*Adequacy of Response*

L. Can you find a relationship between the structure as it *is* and degree of consumer and/or producer satisfaction? _____No _____Yes

If yes, what do you make of it?

The "Pseudomatrix"

Some managers assume that the existence of ad hoc committees, task forces, or representative project teams in addition to functions constitutes a "matrix." When these groups fail to solve the problems that brought them into being, managers conclude that the matrix is an illusion, another "impractical" idea. Before blaming the concept, check out the following points. It is not a *true* matrix when:

1. The ad hoc or project group has no budget of its own.

2. The group has no clear purpose tied to larger purposes of the organization.

3. No formal mechanism exists for making the output of the "matrix" group input to the rest of the organization.

4. The leader of a committee, task force, or project has less authority than functional managers have.

5. People are not given released time from functional tasks to work on the program tasks.

6. Successful task force or committee work does not figure in raises, bonuses, or promotions.

Thus in diagnosing what people identify as a "matrix," look to see whether any or all of the conditions above are present. Any one of these situations is enough to seriously compromise the potential effectiveness of this organizational form.

DIAGNOSING STRUCTURE (PSEUDOMATRIX)

A. Does your organization use the word "matrix?" ____Yes ____No ____Don't know

B. If yes, to what sort of organization(s) is it applied?

C. Take one unit that represents the project, or program or product side of your matrix. (You can look at task forces or committees this way, too, if they are not performing as well as they should.)

Unit name: _____

1. Does it have its own budget? ____Yes ____No
2. Are its formal purposes consistent with those of the organization as a whole? ____Yes ____No
3. Does its output become input to the rest of the organization in an effective way? ____Yes ____No
4. Has the leader enough authority vis-à-vis other people in authority? ____Yes ____No
5. Are people given regular work time to do this unit's tasks? ____Yes ____No
6. Do people recognize multiple bosses? ____Yes ____No
7. Does task force, committee, or program work figure in promotions? ____Yes ____No
   In bonuses? ____Yes ____No   In raises? ____Yes ____No

D. How close is your organization to a true matrix? Where does it fall short?

E. How important is it that you *have* a matrix? Does the work/environment require it?

See excerpts by Lawrence, Kolodny, and Davis—Resource Reading 7—and Hedberg and Starbuck—Resource Reading 8.

RELATIONSHIPS

Blips show up here in three sectors—between (1) people (peers or boss-subordinate); (2) units doing different tasks; and (3) people and their technologies (i.e., systems, equipment, methods). In the formal system, such relationships should be diagnosed in terms of how much interdependence is *required* to get the work done. There are two possible dysfunctions:

1. People need to work together and don't do it well;

2. People *don't* need to work together, but try to force collaboration (e.g., in the name of "good human relations" or because they "should").

A second level of relationship diagnosis relates to the degree of built-in conflict. Some units—sales and production, for instance —will fight as naturally as they eat. Such conflict is legitimate, for each unit needs to see things differently in order to do good work. This conflict is potentially useful and should be managed rather than suppressed (Lawrence and Lorsch, 1967).

Highlight Quality of relations between units (or people) matters more to an organization's performance the more they *must* work together to achieve results. Thus a relationship is "good" to the extent that it:

1. Carries forward an organization's purposes; and

2. Enhances (or at least doesn't undercut) the self-esteem of the people involved.

DIAGNOSING RELATIONSHIPS

A. Limit your diagnosis to one set of relationships, such as three units, each doing a different task, or three people on a work team, or two groups interacting with a particular system or equipment. Name the units, functions, people, and/or technologies whose relationships you wish to diagnose:

1. _____ **2.** _____ **3.** _____

B. Required interdependence How much do they *need* to work together to satisfy their consumers and/or environmental demands? For each pair, place a check ($\checkmark$) mark beside the phrase that best describes the situation as you see it right now:

1&2	1&3	2&3	
___	___	___	High interdependence: Each depends on other for survival.
___	___	___	Medium: Each needs some things from other.
___	___	___	Low: Can function okay without each other.

C. Quality of relations Now, how well do they actually get along with each other (informal system) as you see it:

1&2	1&3	2&3	
___	___	___	Excellent: Full cooperation evident.
___	___	___	Good: Often cooperative, understanding.
___	___	___	Average: Get by okay, with some friction.
___	___	___	Poor: Frequent misunderstandings, low trust.
___	___	___	Worst possible: Serious problems not solved.

D. For a pair having high or medium interdependence, how do you account for conflict or the lack of it? ____Structural differences ____Poor interpersonal skills ____Combination of both ____Absence of coordinating person/mechanism

Comment:

E. To what extent does conflict hurt performance?

Great extent   1   2   3   4   5   Not at all
Comment:

See excerpts by Schmidt and Tannenbaum—Resource Reading 9—and Petrella and Block—Resource Reading 10.

CONFLICT MANAGEMENT

Conflict can be legitimate and inevitable. How conflict is *managed* often makes the difference between high and low performance. This is a matter for normative, or informal system, diagnosis.

Some people fight openly for what they want. Others manipulate, fake, pull strings, and do everything but burn down the building, thus helping themselves and (perhaps) hurting the organization. Here's a simple classification system of conflict-management norms (Lawrence, Weisbord, and Charns, 1973).

1. *Forcing.* More powerful people get their way;

2. *Smoothing.* People either pretend that there are no differences or minimize their importance;

3. *Avoiding.* It's disloyal to raise disagreements openly;

4. *Bargaining.* People negotiate, holding some cards in hole, narrowing the issues, playing for own maximum advantage;

5. *Confronting.* People open all issues and data to inspection by both parties. An effort is made to create mechanisms that surface differences, examine disagreements, initiate problem solving.

Highlight When interdependence is *high* and the quality of relations is *poor*, note the mode of conflict management. *Whatever* it is, it is inappropriate, and people need to experiment with new styles.

Sometimes, a new formal mechanism is needed in order to change the informal mode —a monthly problem-solving meeting, for example, in which the ground rule is to heighten and explore differences.

LOOKING AT CONFLICT-MANAGEMENT NORMS

F. Using the descriptions at the left, compare your pairs of units in terms of their normative conflict-management behavior. *Rank order* the modes from 1 to 5, based on *how often* you judge that each is used between pairs. Try to tell it like it is and not as you wish it were.

	1&2	1&3	2&3
Forcing			
Smoothing			
Avoiding			
Bargaining			
Confronting			

1 = "Most often used"   2 = "2nd"   5 = "Least used"

G. Consider only the two major modes (ranks 1 and 2) in use between each pair. How *appropriate* do you judge these norms are to the situation?

Between	Quite Appropriate			Not at all Appropriate	
1&2	1	2	3	4	5
2&3	1	2	3	4	5
1&3	1	2	3	4	5

H. For any pair you rated 4 or 5 above, why is the conflict-management mode not appropriate?

I. What or who maintains the status quo?

J. Some conflicts are built in and necessary. Where that is the case above and you feel that conflict is *not* well managed, what is the major problem? _____Mainly poor behavior _____Mainly lack of mechanisms _____Combination of both

CAN CONFLICT BE MANAGED BETTER?

Here's the worst situation:

1. High interdependence;
2. Worst possible relationships;
3. Smoothing or avoiding differences.

Given this situation, what are possible causes? Lawrence and Lorsch name some frequent ones that are easy to spot:

1. No one is charged with responsibility for managing the conflict. There is no "integrator," or person accountable for getting units to resolve their differences.
2. The person formally charged with integration lacks the knowledge or skills needed to do it effectively.
3. No mechanisms exist which can be used dependably for coordination. (By mechanisms, I mean a formally accepted procedure—a monthly problem-solving meeting, for example, in which airing differences is encouraged.)

One useful finding: Effective integrators tend to have certain characteristics *not found* in ineffective ones:

1. People accept them more for their competence and knowledge *of the situation* than for their formal authority.
2. They have a balanced orientation—between the units they seek to have work together—and will not consistently favor one orientation (such as sales *or* production, teaching *or* research) over the other.
3. Their rewards are based on the total performance of the system, not just their individual work.
4. They have the skills to resolve conflicts between departments.

LOOKING AT HOW CONFLICT IS MANAGED

K. Pick a *major* unresolved conflict between two units, persons, programs, or departments.

Nature of conflict _____

Units _____

1. Who has formal responsibility for resolution? _____No one

   Name of person _____

2. Who has the required knowledge/skill to manage the situation? _____No one

   Name of person(s) _____

3. If you've named *different* persons in 1 and 2 above, to what extent do both participate in helpful procedures for resolving conflict?

   _____Not at all   _____Somewhat

   What do they do?

4. What mechanisms or procedures are presently available for managing conflict between the two units?

5. Does the informal system (normative behavior) support the units' getting together?

6. Summarize what you've learned: Is your diagnosis of the situation a (a) lack of person to do it; (b) lack of skills/knowledge; (c) lack of mechanism; (d) all? Other:

(Your answer above provides clues to whether interpersonal-skills training or structural change or both are called for.)

REWARDS

Having a reward system (formal) in no way guarantees that people will feel and act as if they are rewarded (informal). Maslow (1954) explained the problem in terms of a "hierarchy of needs," which, once satisfied, become essential. Herzberg (1959) showed that meeting basic needs ("hygiene factors") is necessary for morale, but not sufficient for motivation to carry out creatively the tasks an organization needs done.

The chart below expresses a relationship between Maslow's theory and Herzberg's research findings (Maddox, 1965).

Both lists reinforce the point that "fit" between person and organization improves when there's a chance for growth, responsibility, and achievement. A reward system that

Maslow's Needs Hierachy:		Herzberg's Factors:
Personal growth Esteem	Motivators	Work itself, achievement, advancement, recognition
Belongingness Safety Physiological	Hygiene factors	Interpersonal, supervisor relationships, technical supervision, working conditions, company policies, salary

pays off in fringe benefits and salary alone may be inadequate if people do not value their work and see in it a chance to grow.

DIAGNOSING REWARDS

A. Measure the existing system—formal and informal—against Maslow's hierarchy. What exists now that fulfills each need:

Need	*Formal System*	*Informal System*
Personal growth		
Esteem		
Belongingness		
Safety		
Physiological		

B. Now, try the same thing with "motivators" versus "hygiene factors."

		Formal Example	*Informal Example*
Motivators	Work itself Responsibility Achievement		
	Advancement Recognition		
Hygiene Factors	Interpersonal and supervisor relations		
	Technical supervision		
	Working conditions Policies Salary		

C. For your reward system, what are its main:

Strengths	*Weaknesses*

The trick is translating reward theory into organizational practices. Some folks still believe that salary and fringe benefits "motivate," although there is considerable evidence to support the idea that once a need is satisfied, it no longer motivates. Thus salary and benefits stimulate performance only when given as symbols of worthy work which is needed and valued by the organization ("recognition").

A second important issue is "equity," or fairness among members. Informal feelings or beliefs determine whether or not people *act* as if rewarded, independent of how much they actually receive. Herbert Meyer (1975), for example, has made a convincing argument that "merit" pay may undermine self-esteem and reduce commitment to the work itself—because most of us feel that we *always* are worth more than our supervisors judge, especially in comparison to others.

Moreover, especially in industrial systems where "incentive" pay is based on individual production, the informal norm of peer approval frequently outweighs the economic benefits of rate busting. This functions to hold down production to a level below what people are capable of doing (Whyte and Miller, 1957).

In knowledge work the case is more complex. Take the well-known "publish or perish" norm of higher education. Creating rewards for teaching as psychologically potent as those for research is a critical dilemma, especially when research funds dry up.

Thus the diagnosis:

1. What does the organization need to reward ("fit")?

2. What does it pay off for, both actually and psychologically (formal system)?

3. What do people *feel* rewarded or punished for doing (informal system)?

D. To check out the *formal* system, list at left some important activities of your organization. Then identify rewards people get for doing each thing:

Important Activities	Rewards

E. If you named a "task falling through the cracks" in your structural diagnosis (Step 8), think now, is it being rewarded? ____Yes ____No If yes, how do you account for the gap?

F. To check out the *informal* system, can you name:

1. A payoff for *not* doing something important? Why does it pay off?

2. Punishments or sanctions against *harmful* behavior?

3. A payoff for doing something *against* the organization's best interests? Why does it pay off?

4. Punishments or sanctions against *useful* behavior?

See excerpts by Lawler—Resource Reading 11.

LEADERSHIP

"O, it is excellent,
To have a giant's strength,
  but it is tyrannous
To use it like a giant."

—From Shakespeare's *Measure for Measure*
(Act II, Scene II)

Much leadership theory focuses on interpersonal style—the informal system. One popular approach sorts behavior on an autocratic/democratic continuum. Likert (1967) found that "System 4" managers (participative) exhibited high support, high standards, and used group methods. They also were more productive than "System 1" autocrats. Blake and Mouton (1964) hypothesize that the best managers are those who can emphasize production and/or people as the situation requires.

Both notions suggest development through training. "Pseudodemocrats" can learn to stop asking others for answers they already have and be more decisive; autocrats can learn to collect more data before plunging ahead. Both can learn to solicit and use feedback to find out how they're doing.

Fiedler (1967) takes a different approach. He sorts leaders by task or relationship orientation, suggesting that each style is good in some situations, neither is good in all, and that changing one's orientation is difficult to do. Thus rather than training, he recommends either (1) fitting leaders to the task/situation, or (2) changing the task to fit the leader's style. (See his article in Part II.)

Unfortunately, this notion takes in so many contingencies that it seems to me hard to use. However, it does highlight an issue we don't understand very well, especially in non-industrial organizations. That is the growing evidence that interpersonal skills are most functional in unstructured, ambiguous, and/or high-anxiety situations. Moreover, although a leader can use such skills to smooth ruffled feathers, they contribute little to organizational performance in the absence of goal clarity and goal agreement.

No one knows for sure what makes for good leadership in every situation. The best you can do is try to understand *your* organization and its requirements and then judge the extent to which your leadership norms contribute or block and the extent to which leaders can learn new skills if needed.

DIAGNOSING LEADERSHIP

A. Using whatever leadership theory you know, characterize the *informal* behavior of the organization you are diagnosing. That is, are most people "task-oriented" or "relationship-oriented" or both? Participative? Autocratic? What?

B. How appropriate is the behavior to purposes? _____Very _____Not very

C. How would you characterize the style of the top-management group?

D. The top person?

E. Do you see any common threads in your answers above? _____Yes _____No _____Not sure

F. Characterize the strengths and weaknesses of your organization's leadership norms, as you see them:

Strengths	*Weaknesses*

There remains a formal dimension of leadership which may make the difference between having and not having an organization that "works." Selznick (1957) names four leadership *tasks* which if not done seriously undermine organizations:

1. Defining purposes;
2. Embodying purposes in programs;
3. Defending institutional integrity;
4. Ordering internal conflict.

Much turmoil in organizations—especially among "knowledge" workers—stems from lack of structure which only somebody doing the tasks above can provide.

Thus a unique task of leadership might be seen as responsibility for scanning the six-box radar screen, looking for blips both formal and informal, and doing something about them. This task can be shared, but it can't be delegated. This is especially true in functional organizations, where if specialists look out for their *own* tasks, they can't be expected to be responsible for the whole thing.

I'm not saying that leaders should know and do everything. I *am* saying that they should know where the trouble spots are and how these affect the whole. This requires systematic monitoring and the initiation of corrective action ("interventions") whenever the radar reveals a blip that threatens performance.

The main leadership dilemma is getting others to share the risk. They won't do it if they think that a leader has defective vision, for normative behavior tends to be reinforced from the top down, and few people get out ahead of the boss.

Leadership, then, requires, in addition to behavioral skill, an understanding of environment and a will to focus purposes, especially when there's a blip on the radar screen. Look for a leader's formal understanding of his or her role and the extent to which it results in mechanisms designed to keep formal and informal systems in balance.

Nobody does this high-wire act exactly right; to the extent that it's not done at all, a formal organization may in practice be (informally) leaderless.

G. To what extent does leadership make a *formal* effort to monitor and keep the boxes in balance?

Great extent	1	2	3	4	5	To no extent

What effect does this have on the organization?

H. To what extent does the leader or leadership group show an interest in relating *formal* systems and procedures and how well they work to *informal* behavior?

Great extent	1	2	3	4	5	To no extent

What consequences does this have?

I. What help and/or helpful mechanisms do you know of for improving the organization's scanning ability?

1.

2.

3.

4.

For each item, why is it not being used more or better?

See excerpts by Fiedler, Argyris, and Bennis—Resource Reading 12.

HELPFUL MECHANISMS

I intend for this category to be broad, simple, and a stimulus to creative thinking. Mechanisms are "helpful" when they:

1. Assist in the *coordination* or *integration* of work; they help people do things together which require joint effort.

2. Assist in *monitoring* the organization's work; they help people keep track of whether things are going well or badly.

3. Are created to deal with a blip on the radar screen for which no existing procedure is adequate.

Management systems, whether complex like MBO and performance appraisal or simple like weekly staff meetings, are intended to *coordinate* activities which *should* be coordinated. They are *helpful* when in fact they do what they are intended to do.

Think of helpful mechanisms as cutting across the other boxes—useful ways to work on purposes, structure, relationships, rewards; methods or procedures for improving the scanning of all boxes; inventions to improve the quality of working life. Here are three classes of (potentially) helpful mechanisms:

1. Policies, procedures, agendas, meetings—"formal" events, activities, and tools which have been found to *help* people work together.

2. Informal devices, ad hoc solutions, inventions, creative adaptations which people devise spontaneously to solve problems not envisioned by the formal mechanisms.

3. Traditional management systems; the four important ones, in my opinion, are planning, budgeting, control, and measurement (information). Each, of course, *can* be a helpful mechanism, but the fact that a system exists does not automatically make it helpful.

Examples from my recent experience:

Helpful (business)
1. Weekly problem-solving meetings in customer service.
2. Shared filing among entire department.
3. Scheduling on-the-job training.

Helpful (medical school)
1. Faculty retreat to discuss program budgeting.
2. Weekly coordination meeting between dean and hospital director.

Not Helpful (business)
1. Counting orders three times for three purposes (all of which could be served by same count).
2. Referring all nonroutine problems to a common boss (causing bottlenecks).
3. Single file clerk.

Not Helpful (medical school)
1. Distribution of procedures book without discussion.
2. Faculty "effort" report on how time is spent.

==

DIAGNOSING HELPFUL MECHANISMS

A. Identify examples of mechanisms which you see as genuinely *helpful* to people working together in your organization.

Formal Examples	*Informal Examples*

B. Diagnose your management systems. Below, give an example, formal or informal, of how it's done, who's in charge, and whether you consider the mechanism adequate to be helpful for coordination.

	Formal Mechanism	*Informal Mechanism*	*Person*	*Adequate?*
Planning				
Budgeting				
Control				
Measurement				

HELPFUL VERSUS NOT HELPFUL

What makes a mechanism "helpful"? Certainly not the fact that it exists. In my view, a mechanism is helpful when it enables people to do work they and others consider valuable. Thus work must be consistent with purposes, divided up reasonably (structure), with decent relationships, and adequate rewards.

A frequent error in running organizations is to mistake the *availability* of a system, policy, or procedure for the solution to a persistent problem. Formal systems have no lives of their own and don't care whether they make things better or worse. Availability always signals a potential problem as well as a potential solution, for neither is independent of the skill and will of people to use what's available.

Sometimes mechanisms exacerbate the problems they were intended to solve. At worst, they create new problems more irritating than the old ones. When this happens, that too is a signal that some new helpful mechanism is needed.

One way to think of "interventions" is as the creation of vehicles which make possible the solution of problems not solvable within the current formal/informal setup. I use the word "problem" here not just to mean technical dysfunction, but rather *any* situation with which producers or consumers are dissatisfied (e.g., use of time, punitive atmosphere, etc.).

C. Identify some obviously *unhelpful* formal mechanisms. What makes them unhelpful?

Formal Mechanism	*Why Unhelpful?*

D. Identify some *unhelpful* informal mechanisms, e.g., norms or practices. What makes them unhelpful?

Informal Mechanism	*Why Unhelpful?*

E. Consider one or two blips on your radar screen so far in other boxes. Is the situation an *unhelpful* mechanism? A *lack of* any mechanism?

Blip/Box	*Unhelpful?*	*Missing?*

F. What new mechanisms might you create that you predict would improve the situation? Consider both formal and informal, simple and complex.

G. Which of the above is most doable?

See excerpt by Vaill—Resource Reading 13.

FOCUS

OVERALL DIAGNOSIS: BUILDING A PROFILE

The six-box notion makes a useful "early-warning system" in trying to decide where and whether to attempt corrective action. Overall, there are three levels of diagnosis which provide clues to appropriate interventions:

1. Does the organization fit its environment? If not, it can't be developed until the fit can be rationalized and supported.

2. Is it structured to carry out its purposes? If not, work on structure is required before an examination of interpersonal and group processes can take on meanings in addition to personal growth.

3. Are the norms out of phase with the intent? That is, how much discrepancy exists between formal and informal systems? If this is the main problem, as it often is in otherwise successful businesses, most of the organization development tool kit will apply.

Any diagnostic questions you ask about any of the boxes will yield useful data. You can use questions similar to the ones here or make up your own. The profile guide on the next page, backed up by your notes so far, should allow you to make judgments about each level of diagnosis.

There are as many ways to use these notions as there are managers. I've used the six boxes as the basis for starting new work teams, task forces, and committees and for helping existing teams decide what they need to do next. Others have used these questions to screen prospective employers, evaluate management literature in terms of which issues it illuminates, write job descriptions, and organize research findings.

Once you complete the profile and final steps, you'll be in a good position to decide whether and how this framework can be made to assist you.

A DIAGNOSTIC PROFILE

It's time to reach some conclusions. The profile below will help you integrate your thinking. Circle one number for each item:

To What Extent:

1. Do customers honor and support *purposes*?	Completely	1 2 3 4 5	Not at all
2. Is *structure* flexible enough for environment?	Too loose	1 2 3 4 5	Too rigid
3. Is conflict managed to optimize *relationships*?	Well managed	1 2 3 4 5	Badly managed
4. Are systems a source of *relationship* conflict?	No systems conflict	1 2 3 4 5	Serious conflict
5. Are *rewards* adequate for *purposes*?	Adequate rewards	1 2 3 4 5	Inadequate rewards
6. Do people feel *motivated* to perform?	High motivation	1 2 3 4 5	Poor motivation
7. Is *leadership* style appropriate to issues?	Highly appropriate	1 2 3 4 5	Not at all appropriate
8. Are existing *mechanisms* actually *helpful*?	Quite helpful	1 2 3 4 5	Quite hindering
9. Is the *formal system* adequate in your opinion?	Quite adequate	1 2 3 4 5	Quite hindering
10. Is the *informal system* adequate?	Quite adequate	1 2 3 4 5	Not at all adequate

Now make a couple of global judgments. *Overall*, how good is the "fit" of organization with environment?

Excellent fit   1   2   3   4   5   Poor fit

How good is the "fit" of individual and organization?

Excellent fit   1   2   3   4   5   Poor fit

Draw a straight line from circle to circle in the first ten items. The more items show to the left, the healthier the situation; the more to the right, the more difficulty in managing. Take a minute to visualize how the issues reinforce one another.

FOCUS

CLARIFYING

"For the organization as a totality, the important question is not what it has accomplished but its fitness for future action."

—James Thompson (1967)

By now you have a pretty good fix on what is and isn't being done in your organization. One way to deepen your understanding is to use the six-box categories to identify "gaps" between formal and informal systems.

The chart on the next page gives you a chance to reexamine each category in these terms. It also provides an extra box in case you have an issue that doesn't sort easily into other categories. Finally, it invites you to be prescriptive—to say what you think is needed for your organization to improve its performance.

CLARIFICATION

Now, boil down your understandings to some succinct, manageable definitions. Organize issues in terms of how much they require attention. Make statements about the "gaps" or lack of same you see.

Box	What We SAY We Have (Formal)	What We DO Have (Informal)	What We Need
Purposes			
Structure			
Relationships			
Rewards			
Leadership			
Helpful mechanisms			

FOCUS

>>>>>>>>>>>>>>>>>>>>>>>>>>>>>>>>>>>>>

INTERVENTION THEORY

Here are some hypotheses, based on the six-box model, about whether, where, and how to intervene to improve things. These are "practice theories," meaning that they work for me much of the time, but so far as I know are very difficult to prove in a formal way. Thus you must test them for yourself. Many of these points have been made in the workbook text.

1. "Process" issues *always* block work. Indeed, work stalling is a sign that something's wrong and that people will have strong feelings.

2. Such issues can nearly always be located in one or more boxes.

3. Stalled work indicates—if people don't spontaneously restart—a lack of any useful mechanism for getting back on the track.

4. Data are *clues*—internal and external—to what is blocking work.

5. Diagnosis means assigning value to the clues, that is, making predictions about what's wrong and how it might be put right.

6. Behind every intervention (action step) lies a diagnosis. The more conscious the diagnosis, the more purposeful and easier to evaluate the action step.

7. Interventions, whether simple (e.g., new formal-meeting design) or complex (Management By Objectives system) usually have as their major target one or two of the six boxes.

8. No one intervention can by itself improve *everything*.

9. Any intervention guarantees a need to intervene in other boxes, for improving one part of the system will create lags or gaps in other parts.

10. Managing/organizing is a *process* for continually scanning the six boxes, seeking to keep things in balance.

11. Interventions (formal) can be seen as tools for doing this work. They must be used together, in sequence, and without end by those who value continued improvement in organizations.

12. "Improving" an organization means diagnosing and intervening in ways that increase productivity *and* enhance people's self-esteem. An intervention that does one at the expense of the other probably is a poor one for any organization.

DIAGNOSING YOUR OWN
KNOWLEDGE OF POSSIBLE INTERVENTIONS

Consider the theories, people, and issues listed at the left. Check off the box or boxes for which you could imagine applications. Which class of problem(s) comes to mind first? Can you imagine "improbable" applications?

Theory/Intervention Models:	*Purposes*	*Structure*	*Relationships*	*Rewards*	*Leadership*	*Mechanisms*
Team building (example)	?	√	√ √		√	
Transactional analysis						
Gestalt theory						
Operations research						
Management By Objectives						
Strategic planning						
Human-relations training						
Other:						
Other:						
People/Theorists: Argyris						
Blake and Mouton						
Herzberg						
Lawrence and Lorsch						
Likert						
Other:						
Other:						
Books/Articles/Handouts:						

See excerpt by French and Bell—Resource Reading 14.

NOTES

EXAMPLES OF STRENGTHS/LIMITATIONS
OF VARIOUS INTERVENTIONS

Intervention	Intended to Influence (Box)	Can Help or Harm Most	May Not Affect
1. Management By Objectives	Purposes	Relationships Mechanisms	Structure
2. Reorganization study	Structure	Purposes Relationships Leadership Mechanisms	Rewards
3. New compensation plan	Rewards	Purposes Relationships	Structure
4. Performance appraisal	Relationships Rewards	Purposes	Structure

Note: Assumption is that all interventions are intended to improve organizational performance by improving "fit" of one or more boxes with whole. Note how often intended improvements can be undermined by unplanned consequences for other boxes.

POWER—A DYNAMIC CONCEPT

It's hard, maybe impossible, to do an exercise like this one without falling periodically into thinking about solutions. For a diagnosis to have value, it must lead to action. And action depends to a great extent on a concept which has gained wide attention recently: Power.

Who has the power to make needed changes in the organization, its environment, its outside relationships? Do *you* understand the sources and possibilities of your own power to influence change?

What do I mean by power? The ability to do what you want to do is the simplest definition of power. Power connotes action. It is not only something you have or don't have, but also something that can be acquired. Usually, people, and often organizations, have sources of power they never considered before.

Three sometimes unrecognized sources of power belong to people who:

1. Handle environmental problems critical to an organization's success (e.g., legal skills when law suits are becoming common, ability to reduce health-care costs in face of mounting outside pressures).

2. Deal with matters on which many other departments (or individuals) depend. Filing clerks and secretaries, for example, have enormous (often unrecognized) power to make life difficult or easy for supervisors and executives.

3. Understand how parts of a system fit together and how their actions, with individuals and groups, can have a profound "ripple effect," e.g., those in integrator roles.

Salancik and Pfeffer (1977) give many examples of ways organizations and people get power from their relationships to the environment and the degree to which others depend on them (see their article in Part II.)

Oshry (1976) points out that power is the ability to make waves in a system, "altering systemic conditions in ways that increase the likelihood of certain events happening." In addition it is the strength and good judgment to know when to act on behalf of oneself, another, a group, or the whole organization and the range of behavioral skill equal to that choice.

The "fit" between individual and organization depends to a great extent on one's ability to accept some responsibility for self *and* system and to be aware of the consequences of exercising, or not exercising, power.

Before deciding *what* to do, consider diagnostically where your power lies, how much you have, and how willing you are to use it.

DIAGNOSING POWER

A. For each box, consider "what we *need*" as you defined it in Step 15. Does the organization have the needed power to make changes? Which person or group could do it? What is the source of their power?

To Get What We Need vis-à-vis:	*Organization (check below)*		*Person or Group*	*Source*
	Has Power	*Does not Have Power*		
Purposes				
Structure				
Relationships				
Rewards				
Leadership				
Helpful mechanisms				

B. In which box or boxes have *you* power to act or to get others to act?

Box or Boxes	*Source of Your Power*	*Person(s) to Be Influenced*

See excerpt by Salancik and Pfeffer—Resource Reading 15.

FOCUS

ANTICIPATING AND ACTING

The six boxes finally give you an easy way of testing the extent to which an intervention seems right. I've used it to both explain and anticipate my failures, and I find that more anticipating equals less explaining. In my experience all interventions "fail" eventually for one of three reasons:

1. *They are inappropriate* to the problem or organization. A T-group, for instance, may improve relationships without surfacing serious deficiencies of purpose, structure, or technology.

2. *They deal with the wrong (less important) blip* on the radar screen. When the pressing problem is ineffective leadership, a new reward system, no matter how desirable, may not make a difference.

3. *They solve the identified problem*, thus heightening issues in other boxes they were *not* designed to solve. An organization can be restructured to better fit its environment without in any way changing norms and relationships which require other interventions.

In Step 18 see what actions you might take and whether they are likely to "fail" for the wrong reasons or the right one.

ACTION

A. Can you identify one or more blips on your radar screen that require attention? For each blip, what "interventions" or programs or steps might be appropriate?

Blip	Possible Action Step	Priority

B. Now, go back and rank order your blips in terms of priority. Can *you* do anything about any of them? _____ Yes _____ No _____ Maybe _____ Don't know

C. What? When will you start?

FOCUS

BUILDING YOUR OWN MODEL

As they work with this material, some people find themselves arguing with the text. "Where does technology fit?" or "How about values?" are common questions. "Why not call 'rewards' 'incentives' or 'sanctions'?" In Step 19 you're invited to revise this model in a way that seems more natural to you. Change the box names, add or delete boxes, and redefine issues until you have a cognitive map you can work with. (Of course, if you like this one, you may not want to fiddle with it at all.)

BUILDING YOUR OWN MODEL

A. Sketch out below any modifications you might want to make in using the concepts presented here.

B. What applications—other than diagnosing organizations—can you imagine?

FOCUS

=================================>

COMPARING ORGANIZATIONS

There is still a lot we don't know about what makes organizations tick. Much behavioral "science" is not science at all, but rather seat-of-the-pants art. We cannot account for all of the "variables." We don't always know what the best arrangements are for a given task, a given environment, or a given set of people. An increasingly large number of people don't wish to be "organized" at all, at least not in the bureaucratic sense, which is the sense in which most of us—influenced by secondary schools—learned to understand organizations.

In addition, the more parts of a system and an environment one tries to tie together and deliberately coordinate in a formal way, the more unpredictable the consequences arising.

Most theories of organizing were developed and tested in industry. Industrial firms have four structural features that permit one to tinker rationally with them:

1. Concrete goals;
2. Performance measures;
3. Formal authority;
4. Task interdependence.

Briefly translated, this means that people understand, by and large, what it is they are working together to achieve, who's in charge, what constitutes good performance, and what happens when they don't work together.

To the extent that an organization lacks any of the above, it will be less likely to perform in ways acceptable to producers and consumers alike. We have already seen the implications of purposes (goals) and interdependence (relationships) and formal authority (leadership) for accomplishing organized work.

Especially if you are studying a nonindustrial organization, e.g., a hospital, school, professional society, or university, you may also have discovered in doing this exercise that things aren't working as well as they should and you can't quite see why. Consider two diagnostic possibilities:

1. The people who are most in control of output (e.g., doctors in hospitals, professors in universities) do not *wish* to be organized at all, certainly not in the industrial sense, of systems, procedures, output measures, and so on. They work more through politics, status, and coalitions than through rational structures.

2. The work and environment of your organization do not lend themselves to high control, close coordination, and detailed planning. In these instances industrial methodologies may be inappropriate.

DIAGNOSTIC COMPARISONS

A. Name two different types of organizations, one industrial and the other not. Brainstorm a list of as many differences as you can think of, not just the ones on the previous page, but all kinds:

Organization 1 (industry)   *Organization 2 (nonindustry)*

_____   _____

_____   _____

_____   _____

_____   _____

_____   _____

B. Of the items on your list, which differences *make* a difference? In other words, which ones call for different policies, procedures, systems, rewards, and so on?

C. If you could introduce one change into each of the organizations above, what would it be? Why?

See excerpt by Weisbord—Resource Reading 16.

REFERENCES AND BIBLIOGRAPHY

Blake, Robert R., and Jane S. Mouton, *The Managerial Grid* (Houston: Gulf, 1964).

Clapp, Neale W., "Work Group Norms: Leverage for Organizational Change, I—Theory, II—Application," Organization Development Reading Series, No. 2 (Plainfield, N.J.: Block Petrella Associates, 1974).

Drucker, Peter, F., "The Dimensions of Management," *Management—Tasks—Responsibilities—Practices* (New York: Harper & Row, 1974), Chapter 4.

Fiedler, Fred E., *A Theory of Leadership Effectiveness* (New York: McGraw-Hill, 1967).

Gulick, Luther, and Lyndall F. Urwick, eds., *Papers on the Science of Administration* (New York: Institute of Public Administration, Columbia University, 1937). This commonly used analysis may have originated with Gulick's "Notes on the Theory of Organizations."

Herzberg, F., B. Mausner, and B. Snyderman, *The Motivation to Work* (New York: Wiley, 1959).

Huse, Edgar F., *Organization Development and Change* (St. Paul: West, 1975).

Kast, Fremont E., and James E. Rosenzweig, *Organization and Management: A Systems Approach* (New York: McGraw-Hill, 1970). These mechanisms are covered in many standard management texts. The Kast and Rosenzweig book integrates them in a behavioral context.

Lawrence, Paul R., and J. W. Lorsch, *Organization and Environment* (Boston: Harvard Business School, 1967).

Lawrence, Paul R., Marvin R. Weisbord, and Martin P. Charns, *Academic Medical Center Self-Study Guide*, Report to Physicians' Assistance Branch, Bureau of Health Manpower Education, National Institutes of Health, 1973.

Likert, R., *The Human Organization: Its Management and Value* (New York: McGraw-Hill, 1967).

Maddox, Robert, of RCA staff. This integration was called to my attention by Dr. Maddox, who used it in a Professional Programs notebook on motivation, 1965.

Maslow, A., *Motivation and Personality* (New York: Harper, 1954).

Meyer, Herbert H., "The Pay-for-Performance Dilemma," *Organizational Dynamics* **3**, 3 (Winter 1975): 47.

Oshry, Barry. "Power and Systems: An Overview," *Social Change* **6**, 2 (1976): 7.

Salancik, Gerald R., and Jeffrey Pfeffer, "Who Gets Power and How They Hold on to It: A Strategic-Contingency Model of Power," *Organizational Dynamics* (Winter 1977): 3–21.

Selznick, Philip, *Leadership in Administration* (New York: Harper & Row, 1957).

Steers, Richard M., and Lyman W. Porter, "The Role of Task Goal Attributes in Employee Performance" (Irvine: University of California, Graduate School of Administration; Washington, D.C.: Office of Naval Research, Report No. TR-24, April 1974).

Thompson, James D., *Organizations in Action: Social Science Bases of Administrative Theory* (New York, McGraw-Hill, 1967).

Tilles, Seymour, "The Manager's Job: A Systems Approach," *Harvard Business Review* **41**, 1 (1963): 81.

Trist, E. L., "On Socio-Technical Systems," *The Planning of Change,* 2d ed., ed. Warren G. Bennis *et al.* (New York: Holt, Rinehart and Winston, 1969).

Vaill, Peter B., "Notes on Organization Development and Strategic Planning." (Paper presented at the NTL Institute Learning Community, Bethel, Maine, 1976).

____, "Output Congruity Matrix," 1974. Another concept appropriated from the fertile writings of Vaill.

Vickers, Sir Geoffrey, *The Art of Judgment* (New York: Basic Books, 1965).

Weisbord, Marvin R., "A Mixed Model for Medical Centers: Changing Structure and Behavior," in John Adams, ed., *Theory and Method in Organization Development: An Evolutionary Process* (Arlington, Va.: NTL Institute for Applied Behavioral Science, 1974).

Whyte, William Foote, and Frank B. Miller. "Industrial Sociology," in Joseph B. Gittler, ed., *Review of Sociology: Analysis of a Decade* (New York: Wiley, 1957), pp. 289–345.

Note: Additional references can be found at the end of many of the 16 Resource Readings in Part II, providing access to a wide range of current thinking about organization behavior and development.

NOTES

AFTERWORD: A VALUE STATEMENT

I see this work as continually in transition. Especially, I see it as an imperfect link between super-rationalized textbook management systems and an evolving, uncertain, nonlinear mode no one understands very well.

For example, people put quite different meanings on the word "diagnosis." Some physicians, for example, wedded to a rational medical model, use the term to mean deviations from a "healthy" norm, based on data about symptoms. Such data, taken together, add up to an illness whose cause can be pinpointed and therefore treated through prescriptive intervention.

Increasingly, many physicians recognize the limits of this model. Yet they lack a vocabulary and conceptual framework for legitimately expressing its limitations.

In organizational diagnosis, if not medicine, I consider it extremely important that we develop such a vocabulary. There are a great many more problems in prescribing organizational "cures" for a given situation, even routine ones, than physicians routinely encounter.

Organizations have no vital signs analogous to blood pressure, pulse, and temperature which universally provide clues to their health. Although costs and production figures may offer some evidence of a system's viability, they say nothing about its ability to learn from experience or about the self-esteem of its people, both of which figure importantly in development.

In short, organizational diagnosis is only partly a rational act. Rational, sequential learning has been important to me. It has served industrial societies well for some time. I also think that our organizations are reaching the limits of rationality. We are beginning to experience stresses and strains not subject to technological solutions at all.

So this workbook is a mixture—of sequential and nonlinear concepts—and of a process for modifying them. The process, action research, or the systematic testing and modifying of ideas against first-hand experience, I value more than any particular concept. In every case, I believe, the correct answer to a specific question of organizational design is, "it depends."

What "it depends" on in my opinion is expressed partially here. I say partially because my focus is limited to *organizations*. Although I'm sensitive to individual personality differences and to interpersonal and group processes, I have tried here to fit and subordinate these to a view of what makes organizations flourish or fail. Although it may not be self-evident from the text, in any test between individual and organization, my bias is firmly on the side of individuals—at least 51 percent of the time. Successful organizations in my view are productive ones. They achieve productivity in ways which enhance the competence and self-esteem of the people they touch. By "productive" I mean *both* outputs required for an organization's survival—as defined by its leadership *and* validated by its consumers—and the development of its members—as defined by themselves.

The interplay between survival and personal development becomes clearer as you examine connections among an organization's purposes, structure, rewards, and so on. I recognize that there are many more variables than these. I also believe that these—in what seems like an era of perpetual transition—still have, despite many limitations, some helping power. It is this power I'm trying to build on.

I welcome comments, suggestions, and reactions from others concerned about these matters.

—Marvin Weisbord

PART II

RESOURCE READINGS IN DIAGNOSIS

This section contains excerpts and notes from books, articles, and papers which have influenced me. They provide:

1. Quick references for those who like to read ideas in "the original" or want another point of view on the same concepts; and

2. A stimulus to readers to go deeper into sources that attract them. The books cited here, in particular, together constitute a fairly adequate survey of current thinking in organization behavior and/or management theory and practice.

Most excerpts stand on their own; that is, they provide some independent insight into a particular box, factor, or diagnostic issue.

Those who wish to dip deeper into the literature will find references with each excerpt in addition to the bibliography at the end of Part I.

Action research is, I believe, one of the more durable and flexible concepts for managers and social scientists alike. The most comprehensive description of the term I have seen—including its history and examples of its use—comes from an excellent book in organization development by French and Bell. The excerpt from their book illustrates the way action research might be used to diagnose and improve a staff meeting. It concretely portrays the use of diagnosis in action.

ACTION RESEARCH AND ORGANIZATION DEVELOPMENT

Wendell L. French and Cecil H. Bell, Jr.

A basic model underlying most organization development activities is the action research model—a data-based, problem-solving model that replicates the steps involved in action research: data collection, feedback of the data to the clients, and action planning based on the data.[1] Action research is both an *approach* to problem solving—a model or a paradigm, and a problem-solving *process*—a series of activities and events. . . .

An example applying action research to a typical organizational problem might be helpful. Suppose that the problem is unproductive weekly staff meetings—they are poorly attended; members express low commitment and involvement in them; a low level of activity and interaction is common in them; and they are generally agreed to be unproductive. Suppose also that you are the manager in charge of both the meetings and the staff and that you desire to make the meetings a vital, productive instrument for your organization. Following the action research model,

Wendell L. French and Cecil H. Bell, Jr., *Organization Development: Behavioral Science Interventions for Organization Improvement,* © 1973, pp. 84–111. Adapted by permission of Prentice-Hall, Inc., Englewood Cliffs, New Jersey.

the first step is to gather data about the *status quo*. Assume this has been done, and the data suggest the meetings are generally disliked and regarded as unproductive. The next step is to search for causes of the problem and to generate one or more hypotheses from which you deduce the consequences that will allow the hypotheses to be tested. Say you come up with four hypotheses as listed below. Note the very important feature that an action research hypothesis consists of two aspects: a goal and an action or procedure for achieving that goal.

1. Staff meetings will be more productive if I solicit and use agenda topics from the staff rather than have the agenda made up just by me.

2. Staff meetings will be more productive if I rotate the chairmanship of the meeting among the staff rather than my always being chairman.

3. Staff meetings will be more productive if we have them twice a week instead of only once a week.

4. I have always run the staff meetings in a brisk "all-business-no-nonsense" fashion; perhaps if I (*a*) loosen up on what can be

discussed and how, (*b*) encourage more discussion, (*c*) listen to what is said more carefully, and (*d*) am more open about how I am reacting to what is being said, then staff meetings will be more productive.

Each of these action research hypotheses has a goal, or objective (better staff meeting productivity), and each has an action, or procedure, for achieving the goal. Additional work would be done to clarify and specify the goal and the actions in more detail, and then the hypotheses would be systematically tested (implemented) and evaluated for their effects through data collection.

Another distinguishing feature of action research is collaboration between individuals inside the system—clients—and individuals outside the system—change agents or researchers. Havelock, for example, defines action research as

"the collaboration of researcher and practitioner in the diagnosis and evaluation of problems existing in the practice setting. . . . It provides the cooperating practitioner system with scientific data about its own operation which may be used for self-evaluation."[13]

Elsewhere Havelock discusses "collaborative Action Inquiry," which

"is similar to 'action research.' However, this model places greater emphasis on service to the practitioner system and on the collaborative teaming of research and practitioner. The inquiry team collaborates on defining goals, on all phases of the research, and on change strategies. . . ."[14]

. . . Almost all authors stress the collaborative nature of action research, with some seeing it as the primary reason for the model's efficacy.[15]

It is a widely held belief that people tend to support what they have helped to create. Such a belief is highly congruent with the collaborative aspect of the action research model and impels practitioners and researchers alike to cooperate extensively with client system members. Such a point of view implies that the client system members and the researcher should jointly define the problems they want to address, should define the methods used for data collection, should identify the hypotheses relevant to the situations, and should evaluate the consequences of actions taken. We believe this collaboration ingredient of action research is particularly important in organization development.

NOTES

1. Richard Beckhard, *Organization Development: Strategies and Models* (Reading, Mass.: Addision-Wesley Publishing Company, 1969), p. 28.

13. Ronald G. Havelock, *Planning for Innovation through Dissemination and Utilization of Knowledge* (Ann Arbor: Institute for Social Research, The University of Michigan, 1969), pp. 9–33.

14. *Ibid.*

15. In this regard, the work of Collier (cited later in this chapter), Corey, and Lippitt (cited later) indicates a heavy emphasis on the importance of collaboration between all the individuals affected by a change project of this nature.

There's no end to special language, as the excerpt below demonstrates. Peter Vaill deals with a number of terms relevant to the understanding and practice of diagnosis. I've excerpted the ones touched on in this work. The original contains many more terms related to organization development, training, and similar subjects.

AN INFORMAL GLOSSARY OF TERMS AND PHRASES IN ORGANIZATION DEVELOPMENT

Peter B. Vaill

A Personal Statement to the Reader:

I have mixed feelings about the Glossary. In writing it I have discovered that when you try something like this, you are exposing yourself on both flanks. First there's the danger that you will insult your target audience by implying with your definitions that the reader is not very well-schooled or well-read. My target is present and future practitioners in the field known as Organization Development. I know many of these men and women well. I really hope I haven't overestimated their need for a Glossary like this one.

Second, you become aware of a shadowy assemblage called "colleagues": men of at least as much experience and erudition as yourself, for whom these terms and phrases are the everyday ingredients of conversation. You hope your definitions won't seem too hilarious to this group.

Despite these fantasies and qualms, I've thought for some time that somebody ougnt to do a Glossary like this one. I don't personally like a lot of jargon and in-group language. I think it is a very serious problem in the behavioral sciences. I can live with the terminological one-upmanship that goes on among professionals, but I don't like to see the layman and practitioners getting left out. It's a sad thing when a human being must retire from a discussion of human behavior because he doesn't know the lingo.

My hope is that this Glossary will help Organization Development move forward by speeding the training of new people and by stimulating greater precision in our concepts. These aims have led me to describe how concepts are actually being used, rather than to supply the current academic definitions which no one seems to pay much attention to anyway. At points I have editorialized on the way we use our professional language, and even, I suppose, been a little sarcastic at times.

My biggest dilemma has been what to include and what to exclude, for obviously I have barely tapped the mother-lode of b.s. (behavioral science) jargon. I have tried to include those terms and phrases, though, which I hear being used and mis-used in O.D. circles.

Reprinted from John E. Jones and J. William Pfeiffer, eds., *The 1973 Annual Handbook for Group Facilitators* (La Jolla, Calif.: University Associates, 1973). Used with permission.

Action research: a cyclical process of research-change-research-change, etc. The results of research produce ideas for changes; the changes are introduced into the same system and their effects noted through further research. The number of cycles may be infinite. Increasingly the phrase is used to describe what any action-taker in an organization does.

Adaptive: a term used to describe the behavior of many kinds of systems. Originally used mainly to describe individuals (e.g., "his adaptive behavior"), it is now also applied to groups and organizations vis-a-vis their environments. It is usually employed to summarize a number of specific actions or events (e.g., "Mr. Y has a very adaptive style"), and hence its meaning is often vague.

Back-home: the situation one has come from and will return to. It is used at *off-site* conferences and retreats as a way of importing reality into the proceedings.

Behavioral science: the currently popular phrase for the various disciplines which study human behavior. As such, all of the traditional social sciences are included. Some argue that in the singular the phrase implies a spurious unity among these various disciplines. The phrase is also often capitalized, e.g., "The floor layout is consistent with findings from Behavioral Science." However, it is probably more appropriate to capitalize the phrase only where it is a proper name, as in, "The Behavioral Science Division of the Graduate School of Administration."

Boundary: a term used to describe processes in organizations which are conceived as *systems* or as fields of interacting forces. Boundaries can be conceived in physical terms, as in a wall between two departments in an organization. More subtly, boundaries may be social processes, as in the boundaries between Blacks and Whites. Boundaries may be temporal: things done at different times can be said to be bounded from each other. Any set of forces or factors which tend to differentiate parts of the system from each other can be said to have a boundary effect.

Bridging: individual, group, or organization actions which aim to bring together elements in the system, or between the system and its environment, which are bounded from each other. An excellent example is the idea of an *intergroup* and the actions which flow from it. Groups are Bridged by considering them together as a larger entity.

Catalyst: a term applied to a person, or to his role, who is in the position of trying to make something happen without desiring and/or being able to command that it happen. This is typically a self-description, and it is often not clear what is being catalyzed.

Client system: the system (person, group, or organization, etc.) which is the object of change efforts by some other agent. Often shortened to, "the client." The client may be in the same organization as the consultant/*change agent*, as in the case of a line manager who is the client of a staff group, or the client and the consultant may be in different organizations entirely. One of the crucial ingredients of a change *strategy* is asserted to be answering the question, "Who's the client?"

Clinic, to: verb, meaning to focus on a specific problem or condition. A staff meeting may include clinicking as well as planning.

Clinical: a type of stance or orientation toward reality, usually including a desire to deal with wholes, not parts; concrete facts, not abstractions; and an intent to solve problems, not merely to analyze them.

Closed system (thinking, approach, etc.): the tendency to disregard relations between a system and its environment. This tendency often tends to be an unwitting simplification, and as such can lead to error. (See **Open system**.)

Cognitive approach (style, level): knowledge-oriented. It is a term applied to behavior which is comparatively intellectual and devoid of feeling. (See **Head level**.)

Consultant (internal, external): an internal consultant is a member of the organization he is attempting to influence. He may or may not have a job title which identifies him as an internal consultant. An external consultant is not a member of the system in any sense of employeeship. Much attention has been given lately to the problem of the distinctive opportunities and limitations of these two consulting roles. The consensus appears to be that, in the long run, effective *organization development* cannot be performed without *inputs* from both positions.

Conflict management: a class of training techniques and concepts which purport to help trainees deal more effectively with *interpersonal* conflict in organizational situations. Particular stress is placed on *confronting* and *working through* conflict rather than avoiding it or trying to resolve it by fiat.

Confront: a term referring to the process by which one person attempts to make another person aware of aspects of his behavior of which he seems unaware. It is used increasingly in the phrase, "a confronting style," to describe a person who habitually gives such *feedback* to others.

Culture: a technical term with many and various definitions. It is used typically among practitioners to refer to patterns of practices and attitudes which are, or seem to be, ingrained and difficult to change. Frequently employed in such phrases as: " . . . the company culture . . . ," or " . . . it is imbedded in the culture . . . ," etc.

Data-based intervention: specific technique in Action Research. A Data-Based Intervention follows some data collection phase and is an *input* into the system using the data that have been collected. Alternatively, it can be the act of presenting the data to members of the system, thus initiating a process of system self-analysis.

Diagnosis: among practitioners, a process of finding out what is going on in a *social system* and interpreting the findings in light of the theories to which one subscribes. It is rarely used to refer to a formal process of research and analysis but rather to a more eclectic and impressionistic approach. (See **Sensing.**)

Dynamic(s): a term used very widely for any kind of process or set of forces. Its popularity is probably caused by the common desire not to appear to think in terms of static certainties. The thing or process described as Dynamic is often left quite vague and ill-defined.

Dysfunctional: those aspects of systems which work against the goals. This term refers to the "bad" parts of systems. (See **Functional.**)

Ecological: from ecology, the study of the relations between a system and its *environment*. It is being used more and more loosely and hence is in danger of losing its meaning and becoming a camouflage for vagueness.

Entry process: jargon phrase for the highly complex set of enabling conditions by which a *consultant* begins to exert influence. It is regarded as a highly important set of actions separate from the main work the consultant intends, although they are naturally closely related. Used in such sentences as: "We will have to manage the Entry Process very carefully."

Environment: used to refer to the physical and social context within which any target system is functioning, be it a person, group or organization.

Experiential: a term for a kind of learning process in which the content of what is to be learned is experienced as directly as possible, in contrast to being read about in a book or talked about in lecture and discussion. The term applies to a wide variety of training techniques. It is often used in the phrase, "Experiential level," in contrast to *cognitive level*.

Expert power: a technical term from leadership literature, referring to the influence a person has in a situation by virtue of his technical or professional expertise.

Facilitate: a verb referring to a process by which events are "helped to happen." Facilitating is a kind of influence role which is neither authoritarian, on the one hand, nor abdicative on the other. In self-description, the term can sometimes be a euphemism for an intent to be more directive.

Feedback: technical term from systems theory, used primarily to describe one person's report to another of the effect of his behavior on the reporter. "Negative Feedback" is a disapproving report. "Positive Feedback" is the opposite. The term is also sometimes used for larger-scale systems, e.g., Feedback from the market to an organization.

Formal (leader, organization, system): a term introduced originally in the Hawthorne studies to designate the set of organizational relationships that were explicitly established in policy and procedure (i.e., the "formal organization"). Now the term Formal has been prefixed onto many types of organizational phenomena, but the reference to what is established in policy and procedure remains. *Formal leader*, the designated leader of a group, whether he has the most influence in it or not, is one of the most common phrases which derive from this term. (See **Informal**.)

Functional: describes those parts of a system that promote the attainment of its goals. The term derives from a mode of analysis in psychology and sociology (which took the approach from the biological sciences) that seeks to understand systems by understanding the effects that parts of the system have on each other and the mutual effects between the system and its environment. These effects are regarded as Functions and Dysfunctions. More informally, the two terms are used in place of "good" and "bad." This latter usage thwarts the point of view embodied in the Functional approach. Premature decisions about whether effects are "good" or "bad" will prevent the effects from being fully understood in the first place.

Influence: the effects people have on each other, intended and unintended. The term has debatable meaning, however, since personal values intrude. Influence is often seen to be at odds with a *helping relationship*, somehow not *facilitative*, perhaps somewhat Machiavellian. Others argue that Influence is a useful generic concept and as such does not deny the possibility or value of help and benevolence.

Informal (leader, organization, system): a term introduced in the Hawthorne studies to designate the set of organizational relationships which emerge over time from the day-to-day experiences people have with each other. Informal relationships are expressive of the needs that people actually feel in situations, in contrast to the needs their leaders think they should feel.

Input: a term from system theory used to describe people's contributions to a system, particularly their contributions of ideas. (Frequently misspelled, "imput").

Interaction: virtually any behavior resulting from interpersonal relationships. In human relations it includes all forms of communication, verbal and non-verbal, conscious and unconscious. Interactions speak louder than words.

Interface: jargon from the aerospace industry and systems engineering, used both as a noun and a verb to describe one or more *interactions*. It is used particularly commonly in describing work-related interactions among groups.

Intergroup: an important class of intra-organization relationships, such as between departments. It is used primarily as an adjective, although some are trying to establish Intergroup as a noun.

Interpersonal: the generic term for relations between persons, usually two. It is a prefix for many phrases, such as Interpersonal relations, Interpersonal aspects, Interpersonal conflict, etc.

Intervention: a somewhat precious term for any action on the part of a *change agent,* popular among some theorists of the organization change process. Intervention carries the implication that the action is planned and deliberate, and that presumably it is *functional*.

Intrapsychic: phenomena which occur within the person, particularly feelings. It is usually not employed to refer to "thoughts," "ideas," or "beliefs." The term is often used when the intent is to stress the invisibility and inaccessibility of events within the person.

Linking pin: a term for a role described by Likert. The key function of the person in this role is to maintain lines of communication between parts of the organization. Linking pin may operate up and down a hierarchy or across hierarchies. The role may be provided for in the *formal* organization, but more commonly it is *informal*.

Management-By-Objectives: a management strategy developed by Odiorne which makes the establishment and communication of organization objectives the central function of a manager. It is based on the assumption that supervision and leadership will work best under conditions in which both superiors and subordinates have prior "contracts" (i.e., agreements) about directions, priorities, and objectives.

Matrix: a bi-variate cross-classification system, such as a two-dimensional grid. Beyond the technical meaning of this term in mathematics and its derivations in the engineering sciences, it is being used increasingly whenever two variables and their interactions are described. The recent rash of two-dimensional theories (e.g., Blake, Herzberg, McGregor) and the temptation to express these theories in a psuedo-scientific two-coordinate geometry probably has led to this usage of the term.

Mechanistic: having a machine-like quality—predictable, artificial, contrived. It is applied to a wide range of phenomena, from a single person's style to the policies of an organization; it is virtually always denigrating.

Model: a simplification of some phenomenon for purposes of study and understanding. The concrete embodiment of a theory. Behaving in an idealized way so that others might learn or change their behavior through identifying with and adopting those behaviors displayed.

Mutual influence: the condition where all parties to an action have some control over its conduct and outcome. It is considered by many to be always preferable to unilateral influence, although research does not bear this out. (See **Communication; Ownership**.)

Need hierarchy: a particular theory about the operation of needs in the organism, introduced by Abraham Maslow. The major assertion is that classes of needs are arranged in a hierarchy, with the most basic biological needs at the bottom and the more variable psychological needs near the top. The theory says that "higher" needs cannot be activated until "lower" needs are relatively satisfied. The theory has led to a variety of shorthand phrases for describing "where a person is" in the Need Hierarchy at a given time, e.g., "esteem level," "social level," "security level," etc. This particular theory also was the basis for McGregor's *Theory X—Theory Y* formulation.

Open system: the tendency to take into account relations between a system and its environment. This concept in system theory is borrowed from the biological sciences. It refers to the nature and functions of transactions that take place between a system and its environment. (See **Closed system**.)

Organic: having a natural and real aspect—uncontrived. It is the opposite quality of *mechanistic*. It is also used to talk about particularly close and interdependent relations between people. Organic is widely employed as a desirable quality of human relationships, especially in organizations.

Organization development (O.D.): an evolving collection of philosophies, concepts, and techniques which aims at the improvement of organization performance by intervening in *social systems*. Attempted changes may be directed at individuals, *dyads*, groups, *intergroups, formal* structures, or *cultures*. O.D. is not yet a coherent applied science. It derives more from the social than the biological or physical sciences.

O.D. specialist: a nascent somewhat precious term for one who consciously practices various O.D. approaches and techniques. Many O.D. Specialists actively avoid getting tagged with this title.

Ownership: jargon for the quality of being personally committed and hence presumably entitled to influence in a situation, as in: "I feel some ownership in this program."

Participant-observer: a type of role wherein the person is involved in a *social system* as a member but is also studying and evaluating it by another set of criteria as an observer. This dual role may or may not be known to other members of the system. The Participant-Observer is widely identified as a desirable and strategic role, but it has been performed successfully by comparatively few people.

Participative: a term used to describe techniques employed by a power figure which aim to involve subordinate, lower-power persons in the decision-making process of an organization. For example, "Participative Management." The aim is to increase the sense of *ownership* at lower levels.

Planned change: the generic phrase for all systematic efforts to improve the functioning of some human system. It is defined by Bennis to be a change process in which power is roughly equal between changer and changee and in which goals are mutually and deliberately set.

Policy science: a phrase for those social sciences whose theories and research findings have implications for developing policy guidelines for the management of human systems.

Post-industrial society: a phrase applied to Europe and the U.S. in the last third of the twentieth century, in which the problems of production have been solved. By implication, it is a society now confronted with questions of priority, ecological balance, and justice.

Problem-solve: a verb used to describe a process of resolving everyday issues between people in work situations. It implies focusing on the concrete and the relevant. This is an important element in *organizational development* work, reflecting the idea that if an *O.D. specialist* can't help people in *working through* their real operating problems, his reason for existing in this role is questionable.

Process: a generic term for the way any system is going about doing whatever it is doing. "Social Process" is the way persons are relating to one another as they perform some activity. Most training techniques aim, in one way or another, to make people more sensitive to "social process." The phrase, "Process Level" refers to the events occurring within the social process, as in the phrase, "Let's work at the process level for a few minutes."

Role: a position in a *social system* with certain responsibilities and functions. A Role may be established in the *formal* system, or it may have emerged from operations and be *informal*. It is used in a huge variety of phrases, such as: "Helper Role," "Dependent Role," "Role Conflict," "Role Ambiguity."

Self-organizing system: a technical term in biology, now used more loosely to refer to any system which maintains a continuous balance of internal forces and a continuous balance with its environment without major changes in its energy sources. Also, it is a system which achieves this condition by itself without assistance from forces in its environment.

Sensing: jargon to describe a *diagnosis* process under conditions in which the needed information such as attitudes is intangible and elusive.

Sensitivity training: the collection of methods for improving the individual's sensitivity to himself and others. Although a large number of variations exist, the common ingredients seem to be: (1) the guidance of a trained person or persons; (2) intense *interpersonal* experience by the trainee; (3) a relatively protected environment, free from ordinary pressures and distractions. The *T-group* is the classical, but not the only, means of achieving these three conditions.

Social leader: the person who performs the *role* of leading a group in non-work activities (See **Group maintenance.**)

Social system: any set of persons and their relationships. More narrowly, it refers to the pattern of social relations existing within a *formal* organization. The phrases "social organization" and "social grouping" are sometimes used to refer to smaller-scale Social Systems.

Socio-technical system: this concept refers to the same concrete phenomena as *social system* but by the inclusion of the term "technical" emphasizes the physical realities of the system and the *technologies* it employs to do work.

Strategy: a term employed to discuss the larger-scale plans a *change agent* may have for changing a system, a planned sequence of *interventions*. It is also used when explaining the choice of one approach or technique over another.

Structural (focus, approach, emphasis): jargon for a change *strategy* that focuses on the *formal* organization. A Structural approach may concern itself with organization charts, job descriptions, and assigning authority to roles. It assumes that behavior change will follow. This is a particularly important class of *interventions* when the target for change is an entire organization.

Survey-feedback: a type of *data-based intervention* which flows from surveys of the members of a system on some subject and reports the results of the survey to the group. It is a useful *intervention* when problems are widely shared but when each person feels rather alone.

Synergy: originally a term for the combined and cooperative operations of the bodily organs. Now it is jargon for any process in which more is accomplished by cooperation than could be done by separate efforts.

Systemic: a jargon term meaning "in the system" or "of the system." It is often redundant, as in "Systemic Interrelationships," "Systemic Interactions," etc.

T-group: training group, a type of group which is not structured at the outset by any person or agency but which rather evolves its own structure. The task is for members to learn about themselves in a social context. The evolving structure is continuously examined by looking at the social *process* of the group. The *T-group* is helped in this by a *trainer*. Usually a series of meetings is held. The goal of such groups is behavior change on the members' parts. Evi-

dence is presently mixed about the type and degree of changes which tend to occur.

Task group: a group of people who work together.

Task leader: a role which commonly emerges in any group. The Task Leader is the person who exercises the most influence on the way the group attempts to accomplish its main task.

Task-oriented: a person who is strongly interested in accomplishing the tasks of his *social system*. When applied to a person, the phrase may be mildly critical. (See also **Achievement needs.**)

Team (building, development): the process by which work relations are improved among members of some *task group* in an organization. Various techniques from *sensitivity training* may be used. It is a major overall *strategy* in *organization development*.

Technology: a standardized, communicable process for doing work. It is identified with machinery in many instances, yet it is broader than this. It is used increasingly in *organization development* to refer to ways of making *interventions*, as in *"team building technology."*

Temporary system: a relatively new phrase which refers to *ad hoc* task forces of various sorts which are formed around specific problems in, or across, organizations. Members of a Temporary System are often relative strangers.

Theory X—Theory Y: two practical theories of human motivation in organizations, developed by McGregor. Theory-X is essentially a set of negative and diminishing assumptions about man; Theory-Y is a set of positive and enhancing assumptions. Very different managerial behaviors are presumed to follow from the two sets of starting assumptions. McGregor and many subsequent theorists have strongly advocated Theory-Y. The two approaches, per se, are now somewhat in eclipse as the degree of oversimplification they contain becomes clearer. Yet the spirit that runs through Theory-Y is still strongly present in *organization development*.

3 BOUNDARIES/INPUT-OUTPUT SYSTEMS/ENVIRONMENTS

"Open system" and "sociotechnical systems"—systems thinking in general—strikes me as the most useful approach to organizations. Kast and Rosenzweig provide a comprehensive integration of traditional and modern theories. This excerpt from their textbook succinctly summarizes the main concepts in thinking about the "whole thing."

A SYSTEMS APPROACH

Fremont E. Kast and James E. Rosenzweig

ORGANIZATION: AN OPEN SYSTEM IN ITS ENVIRONMENT

Systems can be considered in two ways: (1) closed or (2) open and in interaction with their environments. This distinction is important in organization theory. Closed-system thinking stems primarily from the physical sciences and is applicable to mechanistic systems. Many of the earlier concepts in the social sciences and in organization theory were closed-system views because they considered the system under study as self-contained. Traditional management theories were primarily closed-system views concentrating only upon the internal operation of the organization and adopting highly rationalistic approaches taken from physical science models. The organization was considered as sufficiently independent so that its problems could be analyzed in terms of internal structure, tasks, and formal relationships—without reference to the external environment.

A characteristic of all closed systems is that

From *Organization and Management: A Systems Approach* by Fremont E. Kast and James E. Rosenzweig. Copyright © 1970 by McGraw-Hill Book Company. Used by permission of McGraw-Hill Book Company.

they have an inherent tendency to move toward a static equilibrium and entropy. Entropy is a term which originated in thermodynamics and is applicable to all physical systems. It is the tendency for any closed system to move toward a chaotic or random state in which there is no further potential for energy transformation or work. "The disorder, disorganization, lack of patterning, or randomness of organization of a system is known as its *entropy*."[27] A closed system tends to increase in entropy over time, to move toward greater disorder and randomness.

Biological and social systems do not fall within this classification. The open-system view recognizes that the biological or social system is in a dynamic relationship with its environment and receives various inputs, transforms these inputs in some way, and exports outputs. The receipt of inputs in the form of material, energy, and information allows the open system to offset the process of entropy. These systems are open not only in relation to their environment but also in relation to themselves, or "internally" in that interactions between components affect the system as a whole. The open system adapts to its environment by changing the structure and processes of its internal components.[28]

The organization can be considered in terms of a general open-system model, as in Figure 5–1. The open system is in continual interaction with its environment and achieves a "steady state" or dynamic equilibrium while still retaining the capacity for work or energy transformation. The survival of the system, in effect, would not be possible without continuous inflow, transformation, and outflow. In the biological or social system this is a continuous recycling process. The system must receive sufficient input of resources to maintain its operations and also to export the transformed resources to the environment in sufficient quantity to continue the cycle.

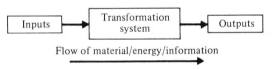

Fig. 5-1. General Model of the Organization as an Open System.

For example, the business organization receives inputs from the society in the form of people, materials, money, and information; it transforms these into outputs of products, services, and rewards to the organizational members sufficiently large to maintain their participation. For the business enterprise, money and the market provide a mechanism of the recycling of resources between the firm and its environment. The same kind of analysis can be made for all types of social organizations. Open-system views provide the basis for the development of a more comprehensive organization theory.

ORGANIZATION: A STRUCTURED SOCIOTECHNICAL SYSTEM

In addition to being considered as an open system in interaction with its environment, the organization can also be viewed as a structured sociotechnical system. This view of the organization is set forth by Trist and his associates at the Tavistock Institute. Technology is based

upon the tasks to be performed and includes the equipment, tools, facilities, and operating techniques. The social subsystem is the relationship between the participants in the organization. The technological and social subsystems are in interaction with each other and are interdependent. "Trist's concept of the socio-technical system arose from the consideration that any production system requires both a technological organization—equipment and process layout—and a work organization—relating those who carry out the necessary tasks to each other. Technological demands limit the kind of work organization possible, but a work organization has social and psychological properties of its own that are independent of technology."[29]

Under this view an organization is not simply a technical or a social system. Rather, it is the structuring and integrating of human activities around various technologies. The technologies affect the types of inputs into the organization and the outputs from the system. However, the social system determines the effectiveness and efficiency of the utilization of the technology.

Technical subsystems are determined by the task requirements of the organization and vary widely. The technical subsystem for the manufacturing of automobiles differs significantly from that in an oil refinery or in an electronics or aerospace company. Similarly, the task requirements and technology in a hospital are substantially different from those in a university. The technological subsystem is shaped by the specialization of knowledge and skills required, the types of machinery and equipment involved, and the layout of facilities.

Technology frequently prescribes the type of human inputs required. For example, an aerospace company requires the employment of many scientists, engineers, and other highly trained people. Technology also is a prime factor in determining the structure and relationships between jobs.

In addition to the technical subsystem, every organization has within its boundaries a psycho-social subsystem, which consists of the interactions, expectations and aspirations, sentiments, and values of the participants. However, it must be emphasized that these two subsystems, the technical and the social, cannot be looked at separately but must be considered in the context of the total organization. Any change in the technical subsystem will have repercussions on the social subsystem and conversely.

The organization *structure* can be considered as a third subsystem intermeshed between the technical and the social subsystems. The task requirements and technology have a fundamental influence upon the structure. Structure is concerned with the ways in which the tasks of the organization are divided into operating units and with the coordination of the units. In the formal sense, structure is set forth by the organization chart, by positions and job descriptions, and by rules and procedures. It also concerns the pattern of authority, communications, and work flow. In a sense, the organization structure provides for formalization of relationships between the technical and the psycho-social subsystems. However, it should be emphasized that this linkage is by no means complete and that many interactions and relationships occur between the technical and the psycho-social subsystems which bypass the formal structure.

One way of visualizing the organization as a structured sociotechnical system is shown in Figure 5-2. The goals and values, as well as the technical, structural, psycho-social, and managerial subsystems are shown as integral parts of the overall organization. This figure is an aid to understanding the evolution in organization theory. Traditional management theory emphasized the structural and managerial subsystems and was concerned with developing principles. The human relationists and behavioral scientists emphasized the psycho-social subsystem and focused their attention on motivation, group dynamics, and other related factors. The management science school emphasized the economic-technical subsystem and techniques for quantifying decision-making and control processes. Thus each approach to organization and management has emphasized particular primary subsystems, with little recognition of the importance of the others. The modern approach views the organization as a structured, sociotechnical system and considers *each* of the primary subsystems *and* their interactions. . . .

Boundaries

The view of the organization as an open sociotechnical system suggests that there are boundaries which separate it from the environment. The concept of boundaries helps us understand the distinction between open and closed systems. The closed system has rigid, impenetrable boundaries, whereas the open system has permeable boundaries between itself and a broader supersystem. "Boundaries are the demarcation lines or regions for the definition of appropriate system activity, for admission of members into the system, and for other imports into the system. The boundary constitutes a barrier for many types of interaction between people on the inside and people on the outside, but it includes some facilitating device for the particular types of transactions necessary for organizational functioning."[31]

The boundaries set the "domain" of the organization's activities. In a physical, mechanical, or biological system the boundaries can be identified. In a social organization, the boundaries are not easily definable and are determined primarily by the functions and activities of the organization. It is characterized by rather

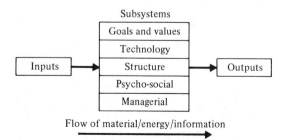

Fig. 5-2. The Organization as a Sociotechnical System.

vaguely formed, highly permeable boundaries. Frequently, in the study of social organizations, where to draw the boundaries is a matter of convenience and strategy. Thus, in the study of a small work group, we may artificially establish the boundary to include only the activities of the immediate group and may consider interactions with other groups as outside these boundaries. Or, we might set our boundaries to include an entire department, division, company, industry, or total economic system. The boundaries of a social organization are often quite flexible and changeable over time, depending upon its activities and functions.

One of the key functions within any organization is that of boundary regulation between systems. A primary role of management is serving as a linking pin or boundary agent between the various subsystems to ensure integration and cooperation.[32] Furthermore, an important managerial function is that of serving as boundary agent between the organization and environmental systems.

The concept of *interface* is useful in understanding boundary relationships. An interface may be defined as the area of contact between one system and another. Thus, the business organization has many interfaces with other systems: suppliers of materials, the local community, prospective employees, unions, custo-mers, and state, local, and federal governmental agencies. There are many transactional processes across systems boundaries at the interface involving the transfer of energy, materials, people, money, and information.

NOTES

27. James G. Miller, "Living Systems: Basic Concepts," *Behavioral Science,* July, 1965, p. 195.

28. Walter Buckley, "Society as a Complex Adaptive System," in Buckley [Walter Buckley, ed., *Modern Systems Research for the Behavioral Scientist,* Chicago: Aldine, 1968], pp. 490–491.

29. Rice [A. K. Rice, *The Enterprise and Its Environment,* London: Tavistock, 1963], p. 182.

30. Katz and Kahn [Daniel Katz and Robert L. Kahn, *The Social Psychology of Organizations,* New York: Wiley, 1966], p. 33.

31. *Ibid.,* pp. 60–61.

32. This point is made by Rensis Likert in *New Patterns of Management,* McGraw-Hill Book Company, New York, 1961. In his interaction-influence system, he recommends the overlapping-group form of organization in which a "linking-pin function" is performed to integrate activities of the various subsystems in the organization.

4 "EVERYTHING ELSE": SCANNING THE ENVIRONMENT

The concept I use to shrink limitless environments to manageable size derives from one of the shortest and most influential books in organization behavior, by James D. Thompson. This excerpt illustrates Thompson's notions of "domains" and "task environments" and how these affect input and output.

DOMAINS OF ORGANIZED ACTION

James D. Thompson

In accounting for the produced automobile, we ultimately must take into consideration the mining of ore and the production of steel, the extraction and refining of petroleum, and the production of rubber or synthetic rubber, all of which are essential (within current technology) if an automobile is to roll from a factory. Along the way the firm may also receive contributions from others who make fabricating machinery and conveyor belts, or build factories, and still others who generate and distribute power and credit. Some automobile manufacturers include within their boundaries a larger proportion or different array of these essential activities than other such firms, but none is self-sufficient.

Consider the technology of treating medical ills. A fairly routine hospital case may now rely on a series of complex organizations which perform research, make pharmaceuticals, ship, store, and prepare medications. It involves use of the products of medical schools and nursing schools (which may be incorporated within the hospital), and of factories which construct x-ray apparatus or weave cloth to make sheets. Hospitals vary in

From *Organizations in Action* by James D. Thompson. Copyright © 1967 by McGraw-Hill Book Company. Used by permission of McGraw-Hill Book Company.

the extent to which they include or exclude certain essential activities, but none is self-sufficient.

The overall technology of producing steel products involves the discovery and extraction of ore, its transportation to points where furnaces and power are concentrated, and the processing of ores into steel. Ultimately it includes the fabrication of steel into items for final consumption. An organization within the steel industry must establish some niche and some boundaries around that part of the total effort for which the organization takes initiative. For reasons to be discussed later, firms involved in extraction, ore transport, and the basic processing of steel seldom undertake the ultimate conversion of steel into products for final use. In any event, the steel firm is dependent on others along the way.

The essential point is that all organizations must establish what Levine and White (1961) have termed a "domain." In their study of relationships among health agencies in a community, domain consists of "claims which an organization stakes out for itself in terms of (1) diseases covered, (2) population served, and (3) services rendered." With appropriate modifications in the specifics of the definition—for example, substituting "range of products" for "diseases covered"—the concept of domain appears useful for the analysis of all types of complex organizations. Thus universities are universities, but their domains may range considerably; some offer astronomy courses, others do not; some serve local populations, others are international; some offer student housing and graduate education, others do not. No two firms in the oil industry are identical in terms of domain. Some refine petroleum, and market gasoline and other derivatives; others buy and market gasoline and oil. Some operate in a regional territory; others are national or international. Some provide credit cards; others are cash and carry. Prisons may be prisons at one level of analysis, but the concept of domain may prevent us from making inappropriate comparisons of prisons with very different domains.

Domain, Dependence, and Environment

In the final analysis the results of organizational action rest not on a single technology but upon a technological matrix. A complicated technology incorporates the products or results of still other technologies. Although a particular organization may operate several core technologies, its domain always falls short of the total matrix. Hence the organization's domain identifies the points at which the organization is dependent on inputs from the environment. The composition of that environment, the location within it of capacities, in turn determines upon whom the organization is dependent.

The organization may find that there is only one possible source for a particular kind of support needed, whereas for another there may be many alternatives; the capacity of the environment to provide the needed support may be dispersed or concentrated. Similarly, demand for that capacity may be concentrated or dispersed; there may or may not be competition for it. If the organization's need is unique or nearly so, we can say that demand for the input is concentrated; if many

others have similar needs, we can say that the demand is dispersed.

Similar distinctions can be made on the output side of the organization. Its environment may contain one or many potential customers or clients, and the organization may be alone in serving them or it may be one of many competitors approaching the client or clients.

The extent to which the sources of input and output support coincide may also be important to the organization. The general hospital in a major metropolitan area may draw its financial support from one sector of the environment, its personnel inputs from another, and its clientele from still a different one; and there may be no interaction among these elements except via the hospital. The general hospital in a small community, however, may find that the necessary parties are functionally interdependent and interact regularly with respect to religious, economic, recreational, and governmental matters.

The public school usually finds its clientele and financial supporters concentrated, and the two interconnected. The municipal university may be in a similar situation, whereas the private university may collect financial inputs, students, faculty, and research data from quite varied and separated sources.

Task Environments

But the notion of environment turns out to be a residual one; it refers to "everything else." To simplify our analysis, we can adopt the concept of *task environment* used by Dill (1958) to denote those parts of the environment which are "relevant or potentially relevant to goal setting and goal attainment." Dill found the task environments of two Norwegian firms to be composed of four major sectors: (1) customers (both distributors and users); (2) suppliers of materials, labor, capital, equipment, and work space; (3) competitors for both markets and resources; and (4) regulatory groups, including governmental agencies, unions, and interfirm associations. With appropriate modifications of the specific referents—for example, substituting "clients" for "customers" in some cases—we have a useful concept to work with, and one much more delimited in scope than environment. We are now working with those organizations in the environment which make a difference to the organization in question; Evan (1966) employs the term "organization set" for this purpose.

[The remaining environment can be set aside for a while, but we cannot discard it for two reasons: (1) patterns of culture can and do influence organizations in important ways, and (2) the environment beyond the task environment may constitute a field into which an organization may enter at some point in the future. We will consider both of these aspects later.]

Just as no two domains are identical, no two task environments are identical. Which individuals, which other organizations, which aggregates constitute the task environment for a particular organization is determined by the requirements of the technology, the boundaries of the domain, and the composition of the larger environment.

Task Environments and Domain Consensus

The establishment of domain cannot be an arbitrary, unilateral action. Only if the organization's claims to domain are recognized by those who can provide the necessary support, by the task environment, can a domain be operational. The relationship between an organization and its task environment is essentially one of exchange, and unless the organization is judged by those in contact with it as offering something desirable, it will not receive the inputs necessary for survival. The elements typically exchanged by the health organizations studied by Levine and White fall into three main categories: (1) referral of cases, clients, or patients; (2) giving or receiving of labor services encom-

passing the use of volunteers, lent personnel, and offering of instruction to personnel of other organizations; and (3) sending or receiving of resources other than labor services, including funds, equipment, case and technical information. The specific categories of exchange vary from one type of organization to another, but in each case, as they note, exchange agreements rest upon *prior consensus regarding domain*.

The concept of domain consensus has some special advantages for our analysis of organizations in action, for it enables us to deal with operational goals (Perrow, 1961a) without inputing to the organization the human quality of motivation and without assuming a "group mind," two grounds on which the notion of organizational goals has been challenged.

Domain consensus defines a set of expectations both for members of an organization and for others with whom they interact, about what the organization will and will not do. It provides, although imperfectly, an image of the organization's role in a larger system, which in turn serves as a guide for the ordering of action in certain directions and not in others. Using the concept of domain consensus, we need not assume that the formal statement of goals found in charters, articles of incorporation, or institutional advertising is in fact the criterion upon which rationality is judged and choices of action alternatives are made. Nor need we accept such ideologies as that which insists that profit is the goal of the firm. The concept of domain consensus can be clearly separated from individual goals or motives. Regardless of these, members of hospitals somehow conceive of their organizations as oriented around medical care, and this conception is reinforced by those with whom the members interact. Members of regulatory agencies likewise conceive of a jurisdiction for their organizations, and members of automobile manufacturing firms conceive of production and distribution of certain kinds of vehicles as the organization's excuse for existence.

MANAGEMENT OF INTERDEPENDENCE

Task environments of complex organizations turn out to be multifaceted or pluralistic, composed of several or many distinguishable others potentially relevant in establishing domain consensus. This appears to be true even of organizations embedded in totalitarian politico-economic systems, since for any specific organization there appears to be alternative sources of some inputs; the several kinds of inputs required come under the jurisdictions of different state agencies; and there are alternative forms of output or places for disposal of output (Berliner, 1957; Granick, 1959; Richman, 1963). The evidence is inescapable that elaborate state planning and decrees do not fully settle for specific industrial organizations in the Soviet Union the questions of domain and domain consensus.

This pluralism of task environments is significant for complex organizations because it means that an organization must exchange with not one but several elements, each of which is itself involved in a network of interdependence, with its own domain and task environment. In the process of working out solutions to its problems, an element of the task environment may find it necessary or desirable to discontinue support to an organization. Thus task environments pose contingencies for organizations.

Task environments also impose constraints. The capacities of supporting organizations and the absence of feasible alternatives may fix absolute limits to the support which may be available to an organization at a given time. The most dramatic example of constraints, perhaps, arises in the case of governmental organizations which are captives of a particular population. The public school system treated badly by its mandatory population may lose some of its members, but the organization as such cannot move to another community; it must stay home and fight the "in-law" battle. The foreign office of a world power cannot elect to negotiate in another, rosier world. The captive organization exists in the business world, as well, in the form of the satellite or subsidiary firm, or the firm which produces for a single buyer, as in the missile business during the 1950s. Carlson (1964) notes that some organizations have no control over selection of clientele, and that the clientele likewise lacks an option. He refers to these as "domesticated" because they are not compelled to attend to all of their needs, society guaranteeing their existence.

Since the dependence of an organization on its task environment introduces not only constraints but also contingencies, both of which interfere with the attainment of rationality, we would expect organizations subject to norms of rationality to attempt to manage dependency.

BIBLIOGRAPHY

Berliner, Joseph S.: *Factory and Manager in the USSR,* Cambridge, Mass.: Harvard University Press, 1957.

Carlson, Richard O.: "Environmental Constraints and Organizational Consequences: The Public School and Its Clients," in *Behavioral Science and Educational Administration, 1964,* Chicago: National Society for the Study of Education, 1964.

Dill, William R.: "Environment as an Influence on Managerial Autonomy," *Administrative Science Quarterly,* vol. 2, March, 1958, pp. 409–443.

Evan, William M.: "The Organization-Set: Toward a Theory of Interorganizational Relations," in James D. Thompson (ed.), *Approaches to Organizational Design*, Pittsburgh, Pa.: The University of Pittsburgh Press, 1966.

Granick, David: *Management of the Industrial Firm in the USSR,* New York: Columbia University Press, 1959.

Levine, Sol, and Paul E. White: "Exchange as a Conceptual Framework for the Study of Interorganizational Relationships," *Administrative Science Quarterly,* vol. 5, March, 1961, pp. 583–601.

Perrow, Charles: "The Analysis of Goals in Complex Organizations," *American Sociological Review,* vol. 26, December, 1961a, pp. 854–866.

Richman, Barry M.: "Managerial Motivation in Soviet and Czechoslovak Industries: A Comparison," *Academy of Management Journal,* vol. 6, June, 1963, pp. 107–128.

5 FORMAL VERSUS INFORMAL SYSTEMS

In the excerpt below, Neale Clapp gives an example of differences between formal and informal systems in an airline maintenance department. Building on this example, he suggests ways to diagnose an informal system, using the concept of "work-group norms."

DIAGNOSING AN INFORMAL SYSTEM

Neale Clapp

Efforts to increase organizational effectiveness generally begin with an analysis of the *formal* organizational structure. This leads to an attempt to determine what changes in roles, responsibilities and authority will bring about improved performance. Even as changes are carried out, there is often a lurking suspicion that "nothing really changes around here."

Consider the examples below:

On-ground aircraft damage for a large airline was a major source of frustration and cost. Every year, despite training, cost campaigns and management exhortation, aircraft damage remained a stubborn, unyielding problem. Efforts to improve "accountability" resulted in a rash of complicated forms and statistical outpourings, and, to no one's surprise, a high degree of unit defensiveness as each suspected group (engineering, fleet service, ramp service, maintenance, etc.) attempted to "cover" itself. Behavior was increasingly directed to "blame avoidance" rather than decreased damage.

High on management priority was the standard of "on-time departure." Rewards and punishments within the formal system reflected this paramount concern. Discipline was stern

Neale W. Clapp, *Workgroup Norms: Leverage for Organizational Change,* Part I—Theory. Block Petrella Associates, 1974. Excerpted by permission.

when this criteria was not met. Each of the responsible groups pressed to meet this criteria, to the point that incidents of aircraft damage, or conditions that would precipitate damage were ignored or suppressed by the responsible units. In several cases, mechanics left replaced nuts and bolts on the runway, later to be ingested by jet engines. Other times, fuselage damage was caused by the mechanic's haste to meet the on-time standard.

Management's efforts to minimize the extent of aircraft damage never recognized or acknowledged the conflicting priorities. A staff member assigned to investigate the incidence and sources of aircraft damage reported the conflict in management decrees and priorities. At last report, the damage continued unabated and new campaigns, consisting of "visual reminders" were contemplated.

Formal System Decisions

1. "On-time departures" standard given operational and organizational priority.

2. Safety requirements necessitate a high degree of functional accountability.

3. Organization determines that negative sanctions are necessary to assure standard performance.

Informal System Outcomes
(Unforeseen Consequences)

1. Other necessary preflight functions neglected. Conflict with other concerns (aircraft damage and cleaning).

2. Units expend energy on "blame avoidance" and defensive behavior. Integration of functions lacking.

3. Units and individuals perceive little reward or positive sanctioning for competence.

. . . The informal system is composed of those unwritten (and often unspoken) rules which govern the behavior of work group members. These unwritten rules are called group norms.

THE GROUP NORM CONCEPT

Group norms are defined as the standards of behavior a group expects of its members. Unfortunately, the term "group norm" can be easily confused with the more common usage indicating a statistical average. The critical word in this definition is "expect." The concept does not mean the average behavior of a group member, but, more accurately, the group's expectation of any member. The group norm is, in this context, an informal standard (often implicit) which enables the group to evaluate and control member behavior. "There is no basis for *organized* interaction until group members reach some agreement about each of these kinds of expectations"[3] (norms and goals).

Before pursuing the concept further, it might be helpful to give one or two examples of typical work group norms and the influence they exert on the individual. For example, what constitutes the length of time of a coffee break in a given work group? Policy may dictate 10 minutes, twice a day, but in actual practice, the length of the break is, to a large extent, determined by the group. They may "stretch" it to 12 or 15 minutes and resist mightily management efforts to demand compliance. If the group is "forced" to adhere to the 10-minute policy, it is likely that a new norm will emerge (with the support of the group) that encourages two to five minutes extra at lunch time.

To a large extent, norms are within the control of the group. The work group will reinterpret or manipulate management actions or intentions in order to keep intact whatever function the norm serves. In this case, the coffee break norm may exist for a variety of reasons. Perhaps the workers need the opportunity for informal social exchange, or to support needs for "belonging" and inclusion. It may be that the "stretched" coffee break is, in fact, a form of resistance to other policies regarding use of work time, which the group sees as unjust. Perhaps their jobs are routine or monotonous and the break enables them to be more productive. Whatever the underlying sources of this particular norm, it can be assumed that at some level, it serves members needs. In some cases, norms may have served needs from an earlier time, remaining intact, despite changes which have eliminated the original rationale.

This is not to be construed as indicating that group norms are merely a subversive activity by which members of organizations express their will or defiance of formal procedure. Group norms also operate to enhance productivity. For example, in one company, the norm for managers is to "skip" vacations if a crisis arises. In a random sampling, it was found that 90% of the managers had, in fact, done just that, even though company policy was quite explicit in stating the necessity and desirability of vacations.

RECOGNIZING GROUP NORMS

One way to visualize norms is to imagine a continuum of possible behaviors, and determine where the expectations and actions of the group reside. As an example, all organizations state, in one fashion or another, the precept "thou shall not steal." In practice, however, most organizations would acknowledge that some degree of theft occurs. This "theft" might range from using the telephone for personal use, to minor items of stationery and stamps, to cheating on expense accounts, taking sick days for personal vacation, to, at the other extreme, embezzlement or major theft of property.

Chart #1 shows a hypothetical continuum, with the curve representing the beliefs of individual organization members concerning the extent of theft acceptable in the total organization.

It is clear that members believe that some theft does occur. Notice, too, that there is no consensus, but a tendency toward grouping somewhere around stationery theft and expense account cheating. If, in fact, this is the group norm, then those members who exceed it (steal more) will be disapproved of by their peers. Individuals who exceed the norm by stealing more will feel the wrath of their peers, i.e., "You'll blow it for all of us." Of equal importance, those at the other end, who would not even make a personal phone call, will also feel the pressure of disapproval, in a variety of ways, i.e., "You'll blow it for the rest of us," or "little goody two-shoes."

Thus, the group norm tends to act as a control upon member behavior, with protential for both positive and negative consequences. As Schein says: "A norm may be defined as a set of assumptions or expectations held by the members of a group or organization concerning what kind of behavior is right or wrong, good or bad, appropriate or inappropriate, allowed or not allowed."[4]

Typical statements that indicate the presence of group norms might include, "that's the way we do it around here," or "listen, in this place everybody. . . ." A statement such as "We, in Organization X, believe deeply in the . . .," since it sounds suspiciously like what *ought to be* or what the organization wants the external world to believe, rather than what *actually* is, is probably not a statement of group norms, unless supported by observed behaviors. . . .

THE SOURCE AND NATURE OF NORMS

Norms usually evolve over a relatively long period of time without explicit statement of their existence by those who adhere to them.

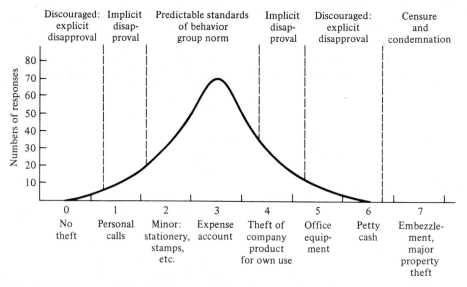

Chart #1. As Member's Behavior Moves Further from the Expectation, the Degree of Disapproval Becomes More Explicit.

Certain elements of group norms can be identified:

Norms exist for "good" reasons. Norms come into being to meet some existing need of a group. They are not random, although they may become anachronistic and endure long after their original purpose is no longer relevant. Norms may also arise from an "accidental" discovery of some behavior which benefits the group. For example, production workers might discover a short-cut process which enables them to do their work with more ease. Incidentally, another norm in this situation might be not to tell management, as that might result in more work provided, or lower rates, etc.

Different norms have different degrees of intensity dependent upon the need of the group and the demands of the job. For example, norms around dress may be more casually violated than norms around "acceptable" productivity. All norms do not carry the same degree of importance. Thus, few members adhere strictly to the multitude of norms operating within their group. It is likely that the individual has a high threshold of awareness regarding those norms critical to the group's survival as an intact unit. He may be less aware of peripheral norms, and violators of expectations will meet with much less disapproval.

Norms operate with different degrees of intensity dependent upon the needs of the in-dividual. Some individual group members will conform more closely to the norms than others. Some will more frequently act as "norm busters." The degree of the individual con formity to groups norms varies widely among members. Oftentimes those individuals who are most instrumental and influential with the group have the capability and authority to break existing norms or create new norms.

Norms are persistent, and resistant to change as long as they have the support of the group. Norms serve the function of ordering and providing predictability for group members. They inhibit chaos, and enable members to find "anchors." In newly formed groups it is not difficult to observe the amount of energy expended in determining group life guidelines. Individuals are highly alert to signals of acceptance or rejection, and by seeking to clarify expectations, increase their comfort with one another. A new member joining an existing group learns as quickly as possible "what goes and doesn't go around here," or "how the wind blows."

Norms serve to keep a group cohesive and minimize external threats. In large organizations, individuals feel the need to attach to a group which provides them with intimacy, security and a sense of familiarity. The potential anonymity in a large organization is precluded by the individual's reliance upon a smaller group. The group may also increase its sense of personal security by "we-they" dynamics. Norms also evolve from modeling behavior by prestigious members of the group, or even from repeated acts which cause other members to believe, "if he does it, so can I."

IMPLICATIONS FOR MANAGEMENT ACTION

Most managers will recognize instances in their own experience which confirm the power of work group norms. Unfortunately, this power is rarely harnessed to support organizational goals. The intention of the foregoing section was to provide a suitable frame of reference by eliminating the chaos of interpreting and comprehending seemingly random individual behavior.

NOTES

3. A. Paul Hare, *Handbook of Small Group Research,* New York: Free Press 1962, p. 47.

4. Edgar Schein, *Process Consultation: Its Role in Organizational Development*, Reading, Mass.: Addison-Wesley, 1969, p. 59.

6 PURPOSES—WHO IS THE CUSTOMER?

I find it difficult to excerpt Peter Drucker. His work is so tightly organized, packed with examples, closely reasoned, and full of insights, I cannot imagine how to trim it. This excerpt is a substantial piece of a chapter entitled ''Business Purpose and Business Mission'' and is the most illuminating statement of the subject I've seen. The book from which it's taken contains 60 more chapters of equal cogency.

BUSINESS PURPOSE AND BUSINESS MISSION

Peter F. Drucker

Every one of the great business builders we know of—from the Medici and the founders of the Bank of England down to IBM's Thomas Watson in our day—had a definite idea, had, indeed, a clear theory of the business which informed his actions and decisions. A clear, simple, and penetrating theory of the business rather than intuition characterizes the truly successful entrepreneur, the man who not just amasses a large fortune but builds an organization that can endure and grow long after he is gone. . . .

Today's theory of the business always becomes obsolete—and usually pretty fast. Unless the basic concepts on which a business has been built are, therefore, visible, clearly understood, and explicitly expressed, the business enterprise is at the mercy of events. Not understanding what it is, what it represents, and what its basic concepts, values, policies, and beliefs are, it cannot rationally change itself. How rapidly even the most brilliant entrepreneurial idea can obsolesce the history

of Henry Ford shows—with only fifteen years between an entrepreneurial idea that literally transformed economy and society and its obsolescence. (See Chapter 29, ''Why Managers?'')

Only a clear definition of the mission and purpose of the business makes possible clear and realistic business objectives. It is the foundation for priorities, strategies, plans, and work assignments. It is the starting point for the design of managerial jobs and, above all, for the design of managerial structures. Structure follows strategy. Strategy determines what the key activities are in a given business. And strategy requires knowing ''what our business is and what it should be.''

THE FALLACY OF THE *UNTERNEHMER*

Insofar as the literature of management and economics has paid attention to the theory of the business, it has dealt with it as a need of the man at the top—or at most of a small top-management group.

The German tradition is most explcit on this point. The *Unternehmer,* that is, the top man and especially the owner-manager, alone

---

''Business Purpose and Business Mission,'' in *Management: Tasks—Responsibilities—Practices* by Peter F. Drucker. Copyright © 1973, 1974 by Peter F. Drucker. Reprinted by permission of Harper & Row, Publishers, Inc.

knows what the business is all about and alone makes entrepreneurial decisions. Everybody else is essentially a technician who carries out prescribed tasks. No one but the *Unternehmer* needs to understand the mission and purpose of the business. Indeed, no one really should know and understand; *Unternehmertum*—entrepreneurship—is a mystique that better be kept hidden from the uninitiated, i.e., ordinary managers and professionals. . . .

In sharp contrast to the organizations of the past, today's business enterprise (but also today's hospital or government agency) brings together a great many men of high knowledge and skill, at practically every level of the organization. But high knowledge and skill also mean decision-impact on how the work is to be done and on what work is actually being tackled. They make, by necessity, risk-taking decisions, that is, business decisions, whatever the official form of organization. And the computer does not alter this fact. In fact, it makes the decisions of top management even more dependent on the decision input from lower levels —which is what then becomes the data of the computer.

When the computer first came in, in the early fifties, we heard a good deal about the imminent disappearance of the middle manager. Instead, the fifties and sixties brought in all developed countries a tremendous growth of middle managers. And, unlike traditional middle managers, the new middle people are largely decision-makers rather than executors of decisions made on high. (On this see Chapter 35, "From Middle Management to Knowledge Organization.")

As a result, decisions affecting the entire business and its capacity to perform are made at all levels of the organization, even fairly low ones. Risk-taking decisions—what to do and what not to do; what to continue work on and what to abandon; what products, markets, or technologies to pursue with energy and what markets, products and technologies to ignore—are in the reality of today's business enterprise (especially the large one)

made every day by a host of people of subordinate rank, very often by people without traditional managerial title or position, e.g., research scientists, design engineers, product planners, and tax accountants.

Every one of these men bases his decisions on some, if only vague, theory of the business. Every one makes assumptions regarding reality, both inside and outside the business. Every one assumes that certain kinds of results are wanted and that other kinds are not particularly desirable. Every one knows, e.g., that "lowering the price of our product does not create new demand," or that "we do this" but "do not do that." Every one, in other words, has his answer to the question " What is our business and what should it be?" Unless, therefore, the business itself—and that means its top management—has thought through the question and formulated the answer—or answers—to it, the decision-makers in the business, all the way up and down, will decide and act on the basis of different, incompatible, and conflicting theories of the business. They will pull in different directions without even being aware of their divergences. But they will also decide and act on the basis of wrong and misdirecting theories of the business.

Common vision, common understanding, and unity of direction and effort of the entire organization require definition of "what our business is and what it should be."

"WHAT IS OUR BUSINESS?" —NEVER OBVIOUS

Nothing may seem simpler or more obvious than to know what a company's business is. A steel mill makes steel, a railroad runs trains to carry freight and passengers, an insurance company underwrites fire risks, a bank lends money. Actually, "What is our business?" is almost always a difficult question and the right answer is usually anything but obvious.

One of the earliest and most successful answers was worked out by Theodore N. Vail (1845–1920) for the American Telephone and Telegraph Company (also known as the Bell System) almost seventy years ago: "Our business is service." This sounds obvious once it has been said. But first there had to be the realization that a telephone system, being a natural monopoly, was susceptible to nationalization and that a privately owned telephone service in a developed and industrialized country was exceptional and needed community support for its survival. Second, there had to be the realization that community support could not be obtained by propaganda campaigns or by attacking critics as "un-American" or "socialistic." It could be obtained only by creating customer satisfaction. This realization meant radical innovations in business policy. It meant constant indoctrination in dedication to service for all employees, and public relations which stressed service. It meant emphasis on research and technological leadership, and it required financial policy which assumed that the company had to give service wherever there was a demand, and that it was management's job to find the necessary capital and to earn a return on it. The United States would hardly have gone through the New Deal period without a serious attempt at telephone nationalization but for the careful analysis of its own business that the Telephone Company made between 1905 and 1915.

Vail's definition served his company for two-thirds of a century, up into the late 1960s; it may have been the longest-lived answer to the question "What is our business?" That the American railroads never thought their way through to any definition of their business is surely a major reason for the perpetual crisis in which they have floundered since World War I, and for the almost complete lack of community support that is their greatest weakness. . . .

The answer to the question "What is our business?" is the first responsibility of top management. Indeed, one sure way to tell whether a particular job is top management or not is to ask whether its holder is expected to be concerned with, and responsible for, answering this question. Only top management can make sure that this question receives the attention it deserves and that the answer makes sense and enables the business to plot its course and set its objectives.

That business purpose and business mission are so rarely given adequate thought is perhaps the most important single cause of business frustration and business failure. Conversely, in outstanding businesses such as the Telephone Company or Sears, success always rests to a large extent on raising the question "What is our business?" clearly and deliberately, and on answering it thoughtfully and thoroughly.

But there are reasons why managements shy back from asking the question; the first is that the question causes controversy, argument, and disagreement.

To raise the question always reveals cleavages and differences within the top-management group itself. People who have worked side by side for many years and who think that they know each other's thoughts suddenly realize with a shock that they are in fundamental disagreement.

THE NEED FOR DISSENT

Most managements shrink back from these disagreements as divisive and painful. But deciding "What is our business?" is a genuine decision; and a genuine decision *must* be based on divergent views to have a chance to be a right and an effective decision. (See Chapter 37, "The Effective Decision.") The answer to the question "What is our business?" is always a choice between alternatives, each of which rests on different assumptions regarding the reality of the business and its environment. It is always a high-risk decision. It always leads to changes in objectives, strategies, organization, and behavior.

This is far too important a decision to be made by acclamation. In the end there must, of course, be a decision. But it must be a decision based on conscious choice of alternatives rather than on suppression of different and dissenting opinions and points of view.

Indeed, to bring these dissents out into the open is in itself salutary. It is a big step toward management effectiveness. It enables the top-management group to work together precisely because each member is cognizant of fundamental differences within the group, and, therefore, far more likely to understand what motivates his colleagues and what explains their behavior. Conversely, hidden or half-understood disagreements on the definition of one's business underlie many of the personality problems, communication problems, and irritations that tend to divide a top-management group.

The main reason why it is important to bring out dissents within the top-management group on the question "What is our business?" is that there is *never one right answer*. The answer never emerges as a logical conclusion from postulates or from "facts." It requires judgment and considerable courage. The answer rarely follows what "everybody knows." It should never be made on plausibility alone, never be made fast, never be made painlessly.

METHOD RATHER THAN OPINIONS

Another reason why managements fail to ask "What is our business?" is their reluctance to listen to opinions. And everyone has an opinion on "what our business is." Managements, however, quite rightly dislike debating societies and bull sessions.

There is need for a method for defining "what our business is." Opinions are, of course, needed—and anyhow are unavoidable. But they need to be focused on a specific, central issue to become productive.

With respect to the definition of business purpose and business mission, there is only one such focus, one starting point. It is the customer. The customer defines the business.

A business is not defined by the company's name, statutes, or articles of incorporation. It is defined by the want the customer satisfies when he buys a product or a service. To satisfy the customer is the mission and purpose of every business. The question "What is our business?" can, therefore, be answered only by looking at the business from the outside, from the point of view of customer and market. What the customer sees, thinks, believes, and wants, at any given time, must be accepted by management as an objective fact and must be taken as seriously as the reports of the salesman, the tests of the engineer, or the figures of the accountant. And management must make a conscious effort to get answers from the customer himself rather than attempt to read his mind.

Management always, and understandably, considers its product or its service to be important. If it did not, it could not do a good job. Yet to the customer, no product or service, and certainly no company, is of much importance. The executives of a company always tend to believe that the customer spends hours discussing their products. But how many housewives, for instance, ever talk to each other about the whiteness of their laundry? If there is something badly wrong with one brand of detergent they switch to another. The customer only wants to know what the product or service will do for him tomorrow. All he is interested in are his own values, his own wants, his own reality. For this reason alone, any serious attempt to state "what our business is" must start with the customer, his realities, his situation, his behavior, his expectations, and his values.

WHO IS THE CUSTOMER?

"Who is the customer?" is the first and the crucial question in defining business purpose and business mission. It is not an easy, let alone an obvious question. How it is being answered determines, in large measure, how the business defines itself.

The consumer, that is, the ultimate user of a product or a service, is always a customer. But he is never *the* customer; there are usually at least two—sometimes more. Each customer defines a different business, has different expectations and values, buys something different. Yet, all customers have to be satisfied in the answer to the question "What is our business?"

The power of the question "Who is the customer?" and the impact of a thoughtful answer to it are shown by the experience of the carpet industry in the United States since World War II.

The carpet industry is an old one, with little glamour and little sophisticated technology. Yet it was a conspicuous marketing success in the American economy of the post-World War II period. For thirty years, until well into the early fifties, the industry had been in a steady, long-term, and apparently irreversible decline. Then, within a few years, the industry completely reversed the trend. Even "good" houses built before the fifties had, as a rule, no more than a cheap rug in the living room. Today, even low-cost homes—including most mobile homes—have wall-to-wall carpeting of fair quality in all rooms, kitchen and bathrooms included. And the home buyer is spending an increasing share of his housing dollar on carpeting.

Floor covering is one of the very few means to alter the appearance and comfort of a home, especially of a cheap and small one. This message had been broadcast by the rug and carpet manufacturers for decades, without the slightest effect of actual customer behavior. The rug and carpet industry achieved its success only when it stopped persuasion and hard selling, and instead thought through the questions "Who is our customer and who should he be?"

Traditionally the rug and carpet manufacturer had defined his customer as the homeowner, and especially as the family buy-

ing its first home. But at that stage, the young couple has no money left over for luxuries. They postpone buying rugs—and this means they are not likely to buy them at all. The industry realized, as a result of asking "Who is our customer, and who should he be?" that it must succeed in making the mass builder its customer. It therefore had to make it profitable for the mass builder to incorporate rugs and carpets into the new home at the time of building. This meant switching from selling individual rugs and carpets to selling wall-to-wall carpeting. In the traditional home the builder had to lay expensive and fully finished floors. Wall-to-wall carpeting can be put over cheap and unfinished flooring—resulting in a better house at lower cost to the builder.

The industry further realized that it must enable the new homeowner to pay for floor covering as part of the monthly payment on the mortgage, rather than expecting him to pay a substantial sum at a time when he is already short of cash. It therefore worked hard at getting the lending agencies, and especially the government agencies insuring home mortgages (such as the Federal Housing Administration), to accept floor covering as part of the capital investment in the house and thus as part of the mortgage value. Finally, the industry redesigned its product to enable the building contractor to act as the informed buyer for his customer, the homeowner. Today home buyers are offered a great variety of patterns and colors, but essentially only three qualities: "good," "better," and "best." The difference among them amounts to very little in the monthly mortgage payment, with the result that most homeowners order at least the "better" carpeting.

As this story shows, the right answer to the question "Who is the customer?" is usually that there are several customers.

Most businesses have at least two. The rug and carpet industry has both the contractor and the homeowner for its customers.

Both have to buy if there is to be a sale. The manufacturers of branded consumer goods always have two customers at the very least: the housewife and the grocer. It does not do much good to have the housewife eager to buy if the grocer does not stock the brand. Conversely, it does not do much good to have the grocer display merchandise advantageously and give it shelf space if the housewife does not buy.

Some businesses have two customers unconnected with each other. The business of an insurance company can be defined as selling insurance. But an insurance company is also an investor. In fact, it can well be defined as a channel that conducts the savings of the community into productive investments. An insurance company needs two definitions of its business, as it has to satisfy two separate customers. Similarly, a commercial bank needs both depositors and borrowers. It cannot be in business without either. Both, even if they are the same person or the same business, have different expectations and define the business of the bank completely differently. To satisfy only one of these customers without satisfying the other means that there is no performance.

One of the great strengths of Vail's definition of Bell Telephone's business was the acceptance in it of two separate customers: the telephone subscriber and the regulating agencies of the various state governments. Both had to be given service. Both had to be satisfied. Yet, they had widely different concepts of value, wanted and needed different things, and behaved quite differently. . . .

It is also important to ask "Where is the customer?" One of the secrets of Sear's success in the 1920s was the discovery that its old customer was now in a different place: the farmer had become mobile and was beginning to buy in town. This made Sears realize early—almost two decades before most other American retailers—that store location is a major business decision and a major element in answering the question "What is our business?"

American leadership in international banking in the last twenty years is not primarily the result of superior resources. It is largely the result of asking, "Where is the customer?" As soon as the question was asked, it became clear that the old customers, the American corporations, were gong multinational and had to be served from a multitude of locations all over the world rather than from New York or San Francisco headquarters. The resources for serving the new multinational customers did not come from the United States but from the international market itself, and, above all, from Europe and the Eurodollar market.

The next question is, "What does the customer buy?"

The Cadillac people say that they make an automobile, and their business is called the Cadillac Motor Division of General Motors. But does the man who spends $7,000 on a new Cadillac buy transportation, or does he buy primarily prestige? Does the Cadillac compete with Chevrolet, Ford, and Volkswagen? Nicholas Dreystadt, the German-born service mechanic who took over Cadillac in the Depression years of the thirties, answered: "Cadillac competes with diamonds and mink coats. The Cadillac customer does not buy 'transportation' but 'status.' " This answer saved Cadillac, which was about to go under. Within two years or so, it made it into a major growth business despite the Depression.

WHAT IS VALUE TO THE CUSTOMER?

The final question needed to come to grips with business purpose and business mission is: "What is value to the customer?" It may be the most important question. Yet it is the one least often asked.

One reason is that managers are quite sure that they know the answer. Value is what they, in their business, define as quality. But this is almost always the wrong definition.

For the teenage girl, for instance, value in a shoe is high fashion. It has to be "in." Price is a secondary consideration and durability is not value at all. For the same girl as a young mother, a few years later, high fashion becomes a restraint. She will not buy something that is quite unfashionable. But what she looks for is durability, price, comfort and fit, and so on. The same shoe that represents the best buy for the teenager is a very poor value for her slightly older sister.

Manufacturers tend to consider this as irrational behavior. But the first rule is that there are no irrational customers. Customers almost without exception behave rationally in terms of their own realities and their own situation. High fashion is rationality for the teenage girl; her other needs—food and housing—are, after all, still taken care of by her parents, as a rule. High fashion is a restraint for the young housewife who has to budget, who is on her feet a great deal, who has "her man," and who no longer goes out every weekend.

The customer never buys a product. By definition the customer buys the satisfaction of a want. He buys value. Yet the manufacturer, by definition, cannot produce a value. He can only make and sell a product. What the manufacturer considers quality may, therefore, be irrelevant and nothing but waste and useless expense.

Another reason why the question "What is value to the customer?" is rarely asked is that the economists think they know the answer: value is price. This is misleading, if not actually the wrong answer.

Price is anything but a simple concept, to begin with. Then there are other value concepts which may determine what price really means. In many cases, finally, price is secondary and a limiting factor rather than the essence of value.

Here are some examples to illustrate what price might mean to different customers:

Electrical equipment such as fuse boxes or circuit breakers are paid for by the homeowners but selected and bought by the electrical contractor. What is price to the electrical contractor is not the manufacturer's price for the product. It is the price of the manufacturer plus the cost of installation—for that, of course, is price to his customer, the homeowner. Contractors are notoriously price-conscious. Yet, a high-priced make of fuse boxes and circuit breakers is the market leader in the U.S. To the contractor this line is actually low-priced because it is engineered to be installed fast and by relatively unskilled labor.

Xerox owes its success, to a large extent, to defining price as what the customer pays for a copy rather than what he pays for the machine. Xerox, accordingly, has priced its machines in terms of the copies used. In other words, the customer pays for the copy rather than for the machine—and, of course, what the customer wants are copies rather than a machine.

In the American automobile industry, where most new cars are sold in trade against a used car, price is actually a constantly shifting configuration of differentials between the manufacturer's price for a new car and prices for a second-hand and third-hand used car, a third-hand and fourth-hand used car, and so on. And the whole is further complicated on the one hand by constantly changing differentials between the amount a dealer will allow on a used car and the price he will ask for it, and on the other hand by the differences in running costs between various makes and sizes. Only advanced mathematics can calculate the real automobile price.

For products and services, price can be determined—as distinct from undifferentiated commodities such as copper of a certain purity—only by understanding what is value to the customer. As the Xerox example shows, it is up to the manufacturer or supplier to design the pricing structure which fits the customer's value concept.

But price is also only a part of value. There is a whole range of quality considerations which are not expressed in price: durability, freedom from breakdown, the maker's standing, service, etc. High price itself may actually be value—as in expensive perfumes, expensive furs, or exclusive gowns.

Here are two examples:

In the early days of the Common Market, two young European engineers opened a small office with a few hundred dollars, a telephone, and a shelf full of manufactures' catalogs of electronic components. Within ten years they had built a large and highly profitable wholesale business. Their customers are the industrial users of electronic equipment such as relays and machine controls. The young engineers manufacture nothing. The components which they supply can be obtained, often at a lower price, directly from the manufacturer. But these young engineers relieve the customer of the tedious chore of finding the right component part. They need only be told the kind of equipment, the manufacturer, the model number, and the part that needs replacement—a condenser, for instance, or a micro-switch. They then immediately identify the specific part needed. They also know what parts made by other manufacturers can be used for a job. They therefore can tell a customer what he needs, give him immediate service, often on the same day, and yet keep their inventory low. Expertise and speedy service is value to the customer for which he is perfectly willing to pay a substantial premium. "Our business is not electronic parts," said one of the young men, "it is information." . . .

What about such concepts of value on the part of the customer as the service he receives? There is little doubt, for instance, that the American housewife today buys appliances largely on the basis of the service experience she or her friends and neighbors have had with other appliances sold under the same brand name. The speed with which she can obtain service if something goes wrong, the quality of the service, and its cost have become major determinants in the buyer's decision.

What a company's different customers consider value is so complicated that it can be answered only by the customers themselves. Management should not even try to guess at the answers—it should always go to the customer in a systematic quest for them.

The marketing approach outlined here will not, by itself, result in a definition of the purpose and mission of a business. For many businesses the approach will raise more questions than it answers. This is true of the business which has as its basic core of unity a common technology rather than a common market. (See Chapter 57, "Building Unity Out of Diversity.") Examples are chemical companies but also commercial banks. Similarly, process businesses—e.g., steel companies or aluminum refiners—need much more than one market definition to define their business. Of necessity, their products go into an infinity of markets, serve a multitude of customers, and have to satisfy a great variety of value concepts and value expectations.

Yet even such businesses should start their attempt to ask "What is our business?" by first asking, "Who are our customers? Where are they? What do they consider value?" A business—and for that matter, any institution—is determined by its contribution; everything else is effort rather than result. What the customer pays is revenue; everything else is cost. The approach from the outside, that is, from the market, is only one step. But it is the step that comes before all others. It alone can give understanding and thereby replace opinions as the foundation for the most fundamental decision that faces every management.

WHEN TO ASK "WHAT IS OUR BUSINESS?"

Most managements, if they ask the question at all, ask "What is our business?" when the company is in trouble. Of course, then it *must* be asked. And then asking the question may, indeed, have spectacular results and may even reverse what appears irreversible decline—as shown by the example of Vail's work at Bell Telephone and of the reversal of the carpet industry's long-term downward trend.

The success of General Motors also resulted from asking "What is our business?" when the company was floundering. When Alfred P. Sloan, Jr., became president in 1920, GM was in deep trouble and barely viable. Sloan's definition of the purpose and mission of GM, and his development of both strategy and structure from this definition, gave GM leadership and outstanding profitability within three years or less.*

To wait until a business—or an industry— is in trouble is playing Russian roulette. It is irresponsible management. The question should be asked at the inception of a business—and particularly for a business that has ambitions to grow. Such a business better start with a clear entrepreneurial concept.

One successful example is the Wall Street firm which in the sixties rose to leadership in the American securities market. Donaldson, Lufkin, and Jenrette (DLJ) was founded by three young men right out of business school. They had little except an idea. Yet the firm rose within five or six years to seventh place among Wall Street houses. DLJ then became the first Wall Street firm to sell its shares to the public and started the long-overdue change of the New York Stock Exchange from a private club to a service institution. It was the first firm to do something about Wall Street's need to broaden its capital base, which thoughtful people had seen for thirty years. "Our business," the founders of DLJ said, "is to provide financial services, financial advice, and financial management to the new 'capitalists,' the institutional investors such as pension funds and mutual funds." In retrospect, this definition was obvious: right answers always are. By 1960 it had become quite clear that these new institutional

*On Sloan's work, see his book, *My Years with General Motors* (Doubleday, 1964), and my book, *Managing for Results* (1964).

investors were rapidly becoming the dominant force in the American capital market and the main channel through which individuals were directing their savings into the capital market. Yet at the time at which this answer was given, it went counter to everything the rest of Wall Street knew.

The man who decides to become his own boss may not have to ask, "What is my business?" If he, for instance, mixes up a new cleaning compound in his garage and starts peddling it from door to door, he needs to know only that his mixture does a superior job in removing stains. But when the product catches on; when he has to hire people to mix it and to sell it; when he has to decide whether to keep on selling directly or through retail stores—department stores, supermarkets, hardware stores, or all three; what additional products he needs for a full line—then he has to ask and to answer the question "What is my business?" Otherwise, even with the best of products, he will soon be back wearing out his own shoe leather peddling from door to door.

The most important time to ask seriously "What is our business?" is when a company has been successful. To understand this has been the great strength of Sears, Roebuck. It is also one of the secrets of the success of Marks & Spencer in Great Britain. (See the next chapter.) And not to have understood this is a major reason for the present crisis of American schools and American universities.

Success always obsoletes the very behavior that achieved it. It always creates new realities. It always creates, above all, its own and different problems. Only the fairy story ends "They lived happily ever after."

It is not easy for the management of a successful company to ask, "What is our business?" Everybody in the company then thinks that the answer is so obvious as not to deserve discussion. It is never popular to argue with success, never popular to rock the boat.

The ancient Greeks knew that the penalty for the hubris of success is severe. The management that does not ask "What is our business?" when the company is successful is, in effect, smug, lazy, and arrogant. It will not be long before success will turn into failure.

The two most successful American industries of the 1920s were anthracite coal mines and railroads. Both believed that God had given them an unshakable monopoly forever. Both believed that the definition of their business was so obvious as to eliminate all need for thought, let alone for action. Neither need have tumbled from its leadership position—the anthracite industry into total oblivion—had their managements not taken success for granted.

Above all: when a management attains the company's objectives, it should always ask seriously, "What is our business?" This requires self-discipline and responsibility. The alternative is decline.

"WHAT WILL OUR BUSINESS BE?"

Sooner or later even the most successful answer to the question "What is our business?" becomes obsolete.

Theodore Vail's answer was good for almost two-thirds of a century. But by the late 1960s it became apparent that it was no longer adequate; the telephone system was no longer, as in Vail's days, a natural monopoly. Alternative ways of telecommunication were rapidly becoming possible. By the late sixties it had also become apparent that the traditional definition of the telephone as an instrument to transmit voice messages had become inadequate, both because of the rapid growth in data transmission over telephone wires and because of the increasing possibility of transmitting visual images together with the voice. Vail's simple and elegant definition of the business of the Bell Telephone System was in need of reexamination.

The brilliant answer which Alfred P. Sloan, as the new president of General Motors, gave in the early 1920s to the question "What is GM's business?" also held

good for an amazingly long time, right through World War II and the postwar recovery. But by 1960 or so, while Sloan, though retired, was himself still alive, the answer had become inadequate and inappropriate. That GM has not raised the question again and apparently has not seen the need to think it through again surely has a lot to do with the evident vulnerability of the company to consumer dissatisfaction, public pressures, and political attack, and with its inability to attain leadership position in the world automobile market.

Very few definitions of the purpose and mission of a business have anything like a life expectancy of thirty, let alone fifty, years. To be good for ten years is probably all one can normally expect.

In asking "What is our business?" management therefore also needs to add, "And what *will* it be? What changes in the environment are already discernible that are likely to have high impact on the characteristics, mission, and purpose of our business?" and "How do we *now* build these anticipations into our theory of the business, into its objectives, strategies, and work assignments?"

The method and approach needed to tackle this question—and the next question—"What *should* our business be?"—will be discussed in Chapter 10, "Strategic Planning." But what basic questions to ask belongs here.

Again the market, its potential and its trends, is the starting point. How large a market can we project for our business in five or ten years—assuming no basic changes in customers, in market structure, or in technology? And, what factors could validate or disprove these projections?

The most important of these trends is one to which few businesses pay much attention: changes in population structure and population dynamics. Traditionally businessmen, following the economists, have assumed that demographics are a constant. Historically this has been a sound assumption. Populations used to change very slowly except as a result of catastrophic events, such as major war or famine. This is no longer true, however. Populations nowadays can and do change drastically, in developed as well as in developing countries.

Every developed country (with the single exception of Great Britain perhaps) had at least a small baby boom in the decade following World War II. Young married women had many more babies than before, and had them in closer sequence. Ten years later this was followed by an equally spectacular "baby bust," in which the number of live births went down very sharply. In the developing countries the birth rate did not increase, but the number of babies who survived infancy increased spectacularly, and is still increasing. In other words, in a short twenty-five years, the whole population structure changed drastically. In the United States, for instance, the largest single age group in 1950 was the thirty-eight- to forty-year-olds. Ten years later the largest age group was the seventeen-year-olds. But by 1980 the largest single age group in America will be the twenty-five-year-olds. Since 1945, also, there has been an educational explosion in every developed country. In the developing countries there has been rapid urbanization, as a result of which Latin America, for instance, has ceased to be rural in its population structure and has become predominantly urban.

The importance of demographics does not lie only in the impact population structure has on buying power and buying habits, and on the size and structure of the work force. Population shifts are the only events regarding the future for which true prediction is possible. People do not enter the labor force till they are at least in their teens—and in the developed countries, increasingly, not until they are twenty. They do not form households until then either, nor become primary customers in their own right. In other words, major trends in markets, buying power and buying behavior, customer needs, and employment can be predicted with near-certainty by analyzing what has already happened in population dynamics and population structure.

Any attempt to anticipate tomorrow—and this is, of course, what we are trying to do by asking "What will our business be?"—has to start with demographic analysis as the sturdiest and most reliable foundation.

The massive impact of even fairly minor demographic changes is illustrated by the sharp shift in the American magazine industry.

As late as 1950 the mass-circulation magazine was America's most successful and most profitable communications medium, and seemed impregnable. But the leaders of those days—*Collier's, The Saturday Evening Post, Look,* and *Life*—have disappeared. The survivors are fighting for their lives. The development is often blamed on television. But magazines as a whole have not suffered from television—just as they did not earlier suffer from radio. On the contrary, total magazine circulation as well as magazine advertising have gone up faster since television appeared than they did before, and they are still going up fast. What has happened is that population has changed—partly because of the change in age structure, but primarily because of the change in educational levels. The undifferentiated mass audience is gone. Its place has been taken by a large number of specialty mass markets, that is, groups of substantial but still limited size, of much higher education and purchasing power, and of sharply defined and specialized interests. These groups read magazines even more than the earlier generation—for the simple reason that they read more. They are a better market for magazine advertisers—for the simple reason that they buy more. Each of these better-educated and affluent audience segments is, in itself, a mass audience—but a specialized one. . . .

Management needs to anticipate changes in market structure resulting from changes in the economy; from changes in fashion or taste; from moves by competition. And competition must always be defined according to the customer's concept of what product or service he buys and thus must include indirect as well as direct competition.

THE UNSATISFIED
WANTS OF THE CUSTOMER

Finally, management has to ask which of the consumer's wants are not adequately satisfied by the products or services offered him today. The ability to ask this question and to answer it correctly usually makes the difference between a growth company and one that depends for its development on the rising tide of the economy or of the industry. But whoever contents himself to rise with the tide will also fall with it.

One example of a successful analysis of the customer's unsatisfied wants is Sears, Roebuck, of course. But the topic is so important as to warrant further illustration.

Sony asked the question "What are the customer's unsatisfied wants?" when it first decided to move into the American consumer market in the mid-fifties. Sony had been founded right after the end of World War II as a manufacturer of tape recorders and had achieved modest success with its products in its own domestic market. It had entered the U.S. as a small but reliable supplier of high-priced professional tape-recording equipment for broadcasting studios. Yet the product with which it first established itself in the American mass-consumer market was a product it had never made before—portable transistor radios. Young people, Sony's analysis of the market showed, were taking the existing heavy, clumsy, and expensive equipment—phonographs weighing many pounds, or battery-powered radios with audio tubes—on picnics, camping trips, and other excursions. Surely here was an unsatisfied want for a light, cheap, and yet dependable instrument. Sony did not develop the transistor—Bell Laboratories had done that, in America. The Bell Laboratories people, how-

ever, as well as all electronic manufacturers in America, had decided that the customer was not yet ready for transistorized equipment. They looked at the wants of the customer that were satisfied by the existing equipment, wants for equipment that was meant to be kept in one place. Sony, by asking "What are the *un*satisfied wants?" identified a new growth market—and within an incredibly short period established itself worldwide as the leader and the pacesetter.

Of the world's leading businesses, Unilever has probably done the most work on "What *will* our business be?" The method Unilever has developed and the models it has built for each of its major product lines and each of its major national markets take into account a large number of factors, from national income to changes in retail distribution, and from eating habits to taxation. But the foundation and starting point are population figures and population trends. These one does not have to forecast; one can build on what has already happened.

"WHAT SHOULD OUR BUSINESS BE?"

"What *will* our business be?" aims at adaptation to anticipated changes. It aims at modifying, extending, developing the existing, ongoing business.

But there is need also to ask "What *should* our business be?" What opportunities are opening up or can be created to fulfill the purpose and mission of the business by making it into a *different* business?

IBM had long defined its business as data processing. Prior to 1950, this meant punch cards and equipment for sorting them. When the computer came, and with it a new technology in which IBM had not the slightest expertise, IBM, asking, "What *should* our business be?" realized that data processing henceforth would have to mean computers rather than punch cards.

Businesses that fail to ask this question are likely to miss their major opportunity.

The American life insurance industry has long defined its business as providing basic investment and financial security to the American family. Right through World War II, the life insurance policy was indeed the best way to discharge this purpose and mission. Since World War II, however, the majority of the American people has attained incomes that enable it to accumulate savings beyond what is needed to buy adequate life insurance protection. At the same time, the whole population has become acutely conscious of inflation, that is, of the erosion of the value of the traditionally conservative and safe investments of fixed money value. The life insurance companies have the access to the market and the selling organization. In their own list of policyholders they have the largest inventory of financial customers in the country. Yet very few of them have asked the question "What *should* our business be?" As a result, life insurance has steadily been losing market standing. Before World War II life insurance was, next to the family's home, the leading investment of the middle class. It has now slipped to third or fourth place and is still going down. The new savings increasingly have not been going into life insurance but into mutual funds and pension funds.

What the life insurance companies lacked was not innovation. The needed financial instruments had all been developed much earlier. What they lacked was the willingness to ask "What *should* our business be?" and to take the question seriously.

Next to changes in society, economy, and market as factors demanding consideration in answering "What should our business be?" comes, of course, innovation, one's own and that of others.

Changes in the nature of the business arising out of innovation are too well known to require much documentation. All major enterprises in the engineering and chemical fields have largely grown by converting innovation into new business. The Eurodollar which these last ten years has financed a good deal of world trade was (as said earlier) not invented by the large American commercial banks. But they immediately saw its significance, and their success in making the Eurodollar into an international currency explains, in large measure, their rapid growth in multinational banking.

Finally—a special but important reason for changing what "our business is" to "what it should be"—then is the business of "the wrong size." (See Chapter 55, "On Being the Wrong Size.")

THE NEED FOR PLANNED ABANDONMENT

Just as important as the decision on what new and different things to do is planned, systematic abandonment of the old that no longer fits the purpose and mission of the business, no longer conveys satisfaction to the customer or customers, no longer makes a superior contribution.

An essential step in deciding what our business is, what it will be, and what it should be is, therefore, systematic analysis of all existing products, services, processes, markets, end uses, and distribution channels. Are they still viable? And are they likely to remain viable? Do they still give value to the customer? And are they likely to do so tomorrow? Do they still fit the realities of population and markets, of technology and economy? And if not, how can we best abandon them—or at least stop pouring in further resources and efforts? Unless these questions are being asked seriously and systematically, and unless managements are willing to act on the answers to them, the best definition of "What our business is, will be, and should be" will remain a pious platitude. Energy will be used up in defending yesterday. No one will have the time, resources, or will to work on exploiting today, let alone to work on making tomorrow.

Planned abandonment was first discussed and advocated in my book *Managing for*

Results. It first was adopted as a systematic policy a few years later by the General Electric Company. Most long-range planning in large companies, like Unilever, focuses on the question "What *will* our business be?" GE's strategic business planning developed in the late sixties is an exception. Its aim is to answer "What *should* our business be?" Yet GE's planning does not start out with the question "What *new* things should we go into?" It starts out with "What existing product lines and businesses should we abandon?" and "Which ones should we cut back and deemphasize?"

Defining the purpose and mission of the business is difficult, painful, and risky. But it alone enables a business to set objectives, to develop strategies, to concentrate its resources and to go to work. It alone enables a business to be managed for performance.

7 STRUCTURE—MATRIX REVISITED

As matrix organizations become more commonplace, people find themselves involved in very ambiguous managerial roles—more so than in product or functional organizations. In this excerpt, Lawrence, Kalodny, and Davis point out some of the *behavior* required for effective matrix management.

Their strategy is to analyze the matrix from three perspectives—"top leadership," "the matrix manager," and the "two-boss manager." Each is in a *different* relationship to the others, requiring its own special orientations and behavior for good results. The authors use Fig. 1 to illustrate the relationship among the perspectives.

THE HUMAN SIDE OF THE MATRIX

Paul R. Lawrence, Harvey F. Kolodny, and Stanley M. Davis

Matrix management and organization have become increasingly common in recent years. If we were pressed to pick one word that characterizes the potential of the matrix organization, it would have to be flexibility. The matrix structure offers the potential of achieving the flexibility that is so often missing in conventional, single-line-of-command organizations and of reconciling this flexibility with the coordination and economies of scale that are the historic strengths of large organizations.

Now that the use of the matrix structure is so widespread, it has become apparent that it calls for different kinds of managerial behavior than are typical in conventional line

This excerpt comes from an adaptation of material from *Matrix,* by Stanley M. Davis and Paul R. Lawrence, Reading, Mass.: Addison-Wesley, 1977. The original adaptation appeared in *Organizational Dynamics* **6**, 1 (Summer 1977): 43–61. Excerpted by permission of the publisher from *Organizational Dynamics,* Summer 1977, © 1977 by AMACOM, a division of American Management Associations.

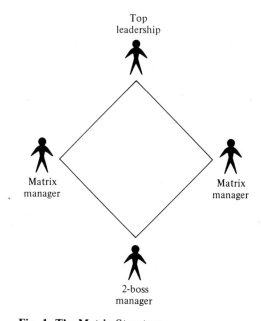

Fig. 1. The Matrix Structure.

organizations. This article will identify the key management roles in a matrix organization and describe the essential aspects called for in each of them. . . .

The top leadership is literally atop, or outside of, the matrix organization (Fig. 2). This is not generally appreciated. Even in totally matrix organizations, the top executives are not *in* the matrix. Despite this, however, they are of it: It is the top leaders who oversee and sustain the balance of power.

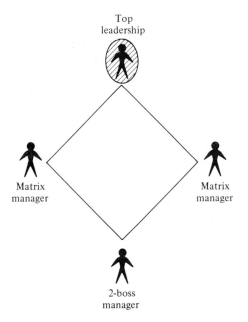

Fig. 2. Top Leadership

In a corporationwide matrix, the top leaders are the chief executive and a few other key individuals; in a product group or a division matrix, the top leader is the senior manager. This individual does not share power with others and there is no unequal separation of authority and responsibility. Formally, the role itself is the same as in any traditional organization. What distinguishes it from the traditional top slot is the leadership process as it is applied to the people in the next levels down.

The top leader is the one who must "buy" the matrix approach. He must be convinced of its merits to the point that he believes it is the best (although not necessarily the ideal) of all alternative designs. He must also "sell" it; he must be very vocal and arti-

culate in developing the concept and arousing enthusiasm for it among the ranks.

One of the several paradoxes of the matrix approach, then, is that it requires a strong, unified command at the top, to ensure a balance of power at the next level down. In some senses this is the benevolent dictator: "You will enjoy democracy (shared power), and I will enjoy autocracy (ultimate power)"; or "I'm OK, you're OK; but I'm still the boss."

Balancing power as a top leader therefore calls for a blend of autocratic and participative leadership styles. . . .

POWER BALANCING

The power balancing element of the general executive's role is, in our experience, vital to mature matrix organization performance. Any general manager must of course pay attention to this process, but it is uniquely critical in matrix organizations. If we contrast the pyramid diagram of a conventional hierarchy and the matrix diamond diagram, we have a clue as to why this is true. The diamond diagram, unlike the pyramid, is inherently unstable. For the structure to remain in place despite environmental pushing and pulling that lead to changed administrative and technical requirements, its emphasis and activities must be constantly rebalanced by hands-on top leadership. The analogy is crude but relevant. Managers in a leadership role are usually quite explicit about this requirement of their job. The "tuning" of a matrix organization needs continuing attention.

The basic methods that general executives use to establish a power balance are both obvious and important. The two arms of a matrix organization are, first of all, usually described in the formal documents that establish the structure as being of equal power and importance. The top executive uses every possible occasion to reinforce this message, and one way that is often used is by establishing dual budgeting systems and dual evaluation systems.

Most mature matrix organizations adopt dual budgeting systems, in which a complete budget is generated within each arm of the matrix. As with a double-entry accounting system, the dual budgets count everything twice—each time in a different way and for a different purpose. Functional budgets are primarily cost budgets—unless the functions sell their services outside. The budgets begin with product- and business-area estimates of work required from each functional area, usually expressed in manhours and materials requirements. Functional groups then add indirect and overhead costs to these direct hours and come up with an hourly rate for services to the product or business managers.

Product or business units accept these rates or challenge them, sometimes by threatening to buy from the outside. This is the time when the difference in outlook is most striking. Business units, for example, have little sympathy for functional desires to hold people in an overhead category for contingencies or for the development of longterm competence. A business unit is hard pressed to see the need to develop competence that may be required three years hence, or for another business when its own central concern is with short-term profit and loss. When the rates are approved for all the different functions, the product or business units develop their own profit and loss budgets for each of their product lines.

The parallel accounting systems provide independent controls that are consistent with the characteristic of the work in each type of unit and that recognize the partial autonomy of each organizational subunit. Each unit has the means to evaluate its own performance and to be evaluated independent of others. The CEO of one organization described the dual control systems in his organization as follows:

"The accounting system matches the organization precisely; so that's an aspect the product manager and I don't have to talk about. He can see how he's doing himself. When resources seem to be a problem, then I must get involved.

Both product managers and functional managers get accounting evaluations. The functional shops have budgets but little spending money. They have a cost budget, but in theory it's all released into the projects. From the functional side, the accounting system locates and isolates unused capacity. As soon as the task requirement disappears the excess capacity turns up. The functional shop then has a "social" problem. The key thing is that the excess turns up immediately. There is no place to hide. Matrix is a free organization, but it's a tough organization."

. . . Dual personnel evaluation systems go hand in hand with dual budgeting to help sustain a power balance. If a person's work is to be directed by two superiors, in all logic both should take part in that person's evaluation. Occasionally, the duality is nothing more than a product or business group sign-off of an evaluation form prepared by the functional boss. At other times, the initiative comes from the other side, primarily because the individual involved may have been physically situated within the product or business unit and had limited contact with the functional unit during the period covered by the evaluation.

Regardless of the particular system design, the person with two bosses must know that both have been a part of the evaluation if that person is to feel committed to consider both orientations in his activities. For this reason many matrix organizations insist that both superiors sit in on the evaluation feedback with the employee and that both advise the employee of salary changes so that rewards will not be construed as having been secured from only one side of the matix.

These basic formal arrangements for setting up a reasonable balance of power are essential in a mature matrix, but they are seldom sufficient. Too many events can upset the balance, and a loss of balance needs to be caught by the general manager or it can degenerate into a major power struggle and even an ill-advised move away from the matrix organization. The matrix can be thrown off balance in many ways, but a common cause of a loss of balance is a temporary crisis on the side of the matrix structure that is used as an excuse for mobilizing resources in that direction. Up to a point such a reaction to a true crisis is certainly appropriate, but it can be the start of a lasting imbalance unless it is corrected by the general manager. . . .

Given the inherent power instability of the matrix, the general managers of mature matrix organizations use a wide variety of supplemental ways to maintain the balance of the matrix. These methods are not new, but they are worth remembering as especially relevant for use in a matrix. Here are five such means:

1. Pay levels, as an important symbol of power, can be marginally higher on one side of the matrix, thus acting as a countervailing force.

2. Job titles can be adjusted between the two sides as a balancing item.

3. Access to the general manager at meetings and informal occasions is a source of power that can be controlled as a balancing factor.

4. Situation of offices is a related factor that carries a status or power message.

5. Reporting level is a frequently used power-balancing method. For instance, product managers can report up through a second-in-command while functional managers report directly to the general manager.

We have talked about the unbalancing potential possessed by profit center managers. But this imbalance of potential fluctuates from situation to situation. In many cases, the organization traditionally gave top priority to the functional side. Here the general manager employs his stratagems to shore up the prestige and position of the business-area or product managers and to make them in fact as well as in name the equals of the functional managers.

MANAGING THE DECISION CONTEXT

There is no substitute in a matrix organization for the sensitive management of the decision context by the top leadership. The existence of a matrix structure is an acknowledgment that the executive leaders cannot make all the key decisions in a timely way. There is too much relevant information to be digested, and too many points of view must be taken into account. But the general manager must set the stage for this decision making by others. He must see that it happens.

We have already seen that dual environmental pressures and complexity make conflict inevitable. To cope with this situation, the top manager must sponsor and act as a model of a three-stage decision process:

1. The conflicts must be brought into the open. This is fostered in the matrix structure, with its dual arms; but beyond this, the given manager must reward those who bring the tough topics to the surface for open discussion.

2. The conflicting positions must be debated in a spirited and reasoned manner. Relevant lines of argument and appropriate evidence must be presented. The executive manager's personal behavior has to encourage this in others.

3. The issue must be resolved and a commitment made in a timely fashion. The leader cannot tolerate stalling by others or passing the buck up the line.

All these decision processes call for a high order of interpersonal skills and a willingness to take risks. They also call for a minimum of status differentials from the top to the bottom ranks. Top leaders can favorably influence these factors by their own openness to dissent and willingness to listen and debate. One of the noticeable features of most leaders of matrix organizations is the simplicity of their offices and the relative informality of their manner and dress. The key point here is that this behavior must start at the top as part of setting the decision context.

STANDARD SETTING

The leadership of matrix organizations is where high performance standards start. We earlier identified environmental pressures for high performance as a necessary condition for matrix organizations. But it is all too easy for organizational members to insulate themselves from these outside pressures. The general executive in a mature matrix organization internalizes the outside pressures and articulates them in the form of performance standards. Each subsystem on both sides of the matrix structure will of course be making its own projections and setting specific targets for higher review. But the overall level of aspiration in the organization begins with the general executive. This is a duty, as we said before, that he cannot afford to delegate.

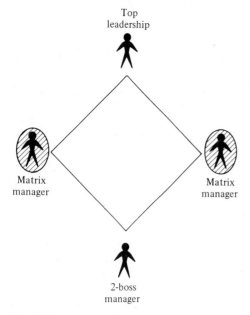

Top
leadership

Matrix
manager

Matrix
manager

2-boss
manager

Fig. 3. The Matrix Boss.

The matrix organization boss shares subordinates in common with another boss (Fig. 3). As matrices evolve, this means that the matrix structure boss will find himself positioned on one of the dimensions in the power balance. Whether the dimension is the one that is given or the one that is grown can make a significant difference for the perspective that evolves. Since one of the most typical evolutions is from a functional structure through a project overlay to a business-function balance, let us examine the matrix-boss role for each of these two dimensions in detail. The same lessons, however, apply to matrix structure bosses who are in charge of areas, markets, services, or clients.

THE FUNCTIONAL MANAGER

One of the greatest surprises of the matrix organization form comes in the changing role of functional managers. In a functional organization, managers have authority over the objectives of their function, the selection of individuals, the priorities assigned to different tasks, the assignment of subordinates to different tasks and projects, and evaluation of progress on projects, the evaluation of subordinates' performance, and decisions on subordinate pay and promotions. They consult or take direction only from their boss in these matters, but much of the function is self-contained.

In a matrix organization, by contrast, none of these responsibilities is the sole responsibility of the functional manager. He must share many of the decisions with program or business managers or other functional managers at his level. Many matrix structures require dual sign-offs on performance evaluations and on pay and promotion decisions. Even when this is not so, consultation on these matters with others is essential for the effective functioning of the matrix and the power balance discussed previously. Tasks, assignments, and priority decisions have to be shared with business managers and indeed often come about as the result of decisions made by project or business teams. Even a function's objectives are partially determined by the resource demands of projects and businesses. The functional manager in his matrix role is responding in areas in which he has traditionally been the initiator. A manufacturing manager, for example, struggled against and for several years resisted the notion that many of the plant managers who reported to him had to set their goals in response to a business team's needs and that review of goal accomplishment, from a time point of view, was the business manager's and team's responsibility. He had difficulty in understanding that his responsibility was to review goal accomplishment from the point of view of a functional specialty.

Thus, for the functional manager, a matrix organization is often experienced as involving a loss of status, authority, and control. He becomes less central and less powerful as parts of his previous role as initiator move from the function to the business manager. The ultimate example of this is the increased confrontation of functional managers by their functional subordinates, who are now also members of a business team that provides the legitimate need and social support for such upward initiation and confrontation. For managers who have been in relative control of their domain, this is a rude awakening that can create initial hostility and a quite predictable resistance to a matrix form of management.

As a matrix organization matures, however, functional managers adapt to these changes, and they find the role not only tolerable but highly challenging. Even though in matrix organizations it is the business managers who tend to control the money that buys human resources, functional managers must engage in very complex people planning.

They must balance the needs of the different product lines and/or businesses in the organization, they must anticipate training needs, and they must handle union negotiations if layoffs or promotions are involved.

They must also administer support staff (supervisors, managers, secretaries, clerks) and accompanying resources (equipment, facilities, space, maintenance), many of which must be shared with the business units. . . .

THE BUSINESS MANAGER

As we have pointed out, in a matrix organization various functional specialists are brought together in temporary (project) or permanent (business or product) groupings. These groups are led by product or business managers who have the responsibility for ensuring that the efforts of functional members of the team are integrated in the interest of the project or business. In this regard they have the same responsibilities as a general executive; their objective is project accomplishment or the long-term profitability of a business.

However, in a matrix organization these business managers do not have the same undivided authority as does the general executive. People on the team do not report to them exclusively since many also report to a functional manager. Thus, as many such managers have complained, "We have all the responsibility and little of the required authority."

Top leaders in traditional organizations have the benefit of instant legitimacy because people understand that reporting to them means being responsive to their needs. This is because their boss not only has formal title and status, but influences their performance evaluation, their pay, their advancement, and, in the long run, their careers. In a matrix organization these sources of authority are shared with functional managers, thus lessening, in the eyes of team members, the power of the project or business manager. He does not unilaterally decide. He manages the decision process so that differences are aired and tradeoffs made in the interest of the whole. Thus he is left with the arduous task of influencing with limited formal authority. He must use his knowledge, competence, relationships, force of personality, and skills in group management to get people to do what is necessary to the success of the project or business.

This role of the matrix organization (business) boss creates both real and imagined demands for new behaviors that can be particularly anxiety producing for individuals who face the job for the first time. The matrix (business) manager must rely more heavily on his personal qualities, on his ability to persuade through knowledge about a program, business, or function. He must use communication and relationships to influence and move things along. His skills in managing meetings, in bringing out divergent points of view and, it is to be hoped, working through to a consensus are taxed more than the skills of general managers in conventional organizations.

Thus, for individuals who face these demands for the first time, the world is quite different. They can easily experience frustration, doubt, and loss of confidence as they begin to rely on new behaviors to get their job done. They begin to question their competence as they experience what in their eyes is a discrepancy between final and complete responsibility for a program and less certain means of gaining compliance from others. Some individuals learn the required new behaviors; others never do.

Not only does the actual and required change in behavior create a problem for new matrix organization business managers, but so does their own attitude toward the change. In our experience, individuals assigned to this role must first break through their perception of the job as impossible. Individuals who have spent all their time in traditional organizations have firmly implanted in their minds the notion of hierarchy and formal authority as the source of influence and power. They are convinced that the job cannot be done because they have never had to think through how power and influence, in reality, are wielded in the traditional organization. They cling to the myth that the formal power a boss has is what gives him influence.

This myth remains even after they themselves have developed and used other means of gaining influence. The myth about power and influence is often the first barrier that must be broken before the individual can be motivated to address the real demands for new behavior.

In his relations with his peers in both arms of the matrix organization, a business manager needs to assume a posture that blends reason and advocacy; bluster and threats are out. It is through these relations that he obtains the human resources needed to accomplish his goals. He has to expect that a number of these resources will be in short supply and that competing claims will have to be resolved.

In these dialogues the business manager must stand up for his requirements without developing a fatal reputation of overstating them. He must search with his peers for imaginative ways to share scarce resources. He must reveal any developing problems quickly while there is still time for remedial action. These actions do not come easily to managers conditioned in more traditional structures.

Last, in his relations with the various functional specialists represented on his team, the matrix organization business manager must establish a balanced or intermediate orientation. He cannot be seen as biased toward one function. He cannot have an overly long or short time horizon. His capacity to obtain a high-quality decision is dependent on an approach that seeks to integrate the views and orientations of all the various functions. If he shows a bias, team members will begin to distrust his objectivity and his capacity to be a fair arbiter of differences. This distrust can be the seed of a team's destruction.

For many individuals, this is a difficult task. A career spent in one side of the matrix structure creates a bias imperceptible to the individual but quite obvious to others. The need to wear multiple hats believably and equally well creates heavy attitudinal and behavioral demands.

It requires of an individual the capacity to have empathy with people in a number of functional areas and to identify with them while at the same time maintaining a strong personal concept and orientation that guides his own behavior and role performance. . . .

The rule for success in this role is to accept that while it can place contradictory demands on people, it is the best solution to accommodate simultaneous competing demands. Assume that there is no one best way to organize; each alternative has equally important claims, and the correct choice is both—in varying proportions.

The most obvious challenge built into this matrix organization role is the sometimes conflicting demands of two bosses (Fig. 4). For example, a representative from a manufacturing plant on a business team may know that his plant is having profitability problems and that the last thing the plant manager wants is to disrupt ongoing production activities with developmental work such as making samples or experimenting with a new process. Yet, as a business-team member, the plant's representative may see the importance of doing these things immediately to achieve project success.

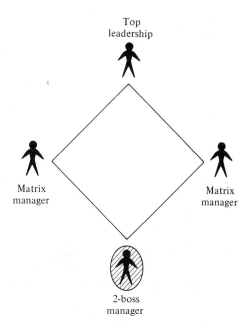

Top leadership

Matrix manager

Matrix manager

2-boss manager

Fig. 4. 2-Boss Managers.

In this situation the individual in a 2-boss position experiences a great deal of anxiety and stress. These come from the difficulties of weighing the conflicting interests of his function and his project team. Both have legitimate viewpoints. But which is the more important viewpoint from the perspective of the whole organization? This is not an easy question to answer or an easy conflict to resolve. But added to this are the questions of identification and loyalty to the individual's function or business team and the consequences of rejection or even punishment from the side of the matrix organization that perceives it has lost in a given conflict. To compound the problem, even if the plant representative on a project team decides that he needs to go against what he knows is in the interest of his plant, how does he communicate this back to his organization members and convince them of the merits of his views? The same problem would exist if he were to favor his functional orientation and have to persuade the team that sample runs will have to be delayed. . . .

One operating manual for this role, developed after about a year's experience in a matrix organization, included the following points in a section titled "Practices for Managing Matrix Relationships":

- Lobby actively with relevant 2-boss counterparts and with your matrix bosses to win support before the event.
- Understand the other side's position in order to determine where tradeoffs can be negotiated; understand where your objectives overlap.
- Avoid absolutes.
- Negotiate to win support on key issues that are critical to accomplishing your goals; try to yield only to the less critical points.
- Maintain frequent contact with top leadership to avoid surprises.
- Assume an active leadership role in all committees and use this to educate other matrix players; share information/help interpret.

- Prepare more thoroughly before entering any key negotiation than you would in nonmatrix situations; and use third-party experts more than normally.
- Strike bilateral agreements prior to meetings to disarm potential opponents.
- Emphasize and play on the supportive role that each of your matrix bosses can provide for the other.
- If all else fails:
  a. You can consider escalation (going up another level to the boss-in-common).
  b. You can threaten escalation.
  c. You can escalate.

Before traveling this road, however, consider your timing. How much testing and negotiating should be done before calling for senior support? Does the top leadership want to be involved? When will they support and encourage your approach? Does escalation represent failure?

This kind of advice relies on managerial behavior, not on organization structure, for success. It sees personal style and influence as more important than power derived from either position or specialized knowledge. Success flows from facilitating decisions more than it does from making them. To remain flexible in this managerial role, it suggests, the manager must minimize the formal elements; move from fixture to actor, from bureaucracy to process.

The role problems of the 2-boss manager can of course become manageable in a mature matrix organization. This happens primarily because for the most part the functional and business managers learn to avoid making irreconcilable demands of their shared subordinates. This will still happen on occasion, however, even in a smoothly functioning matrix organization. In a familiar instance, the 2-boss manager may be directed to be in two places at the same time.

In addition to a balanced structure and shared roles, a matrix organization should have mechanisms for processing information along overlapping dimensions simultaneously. In a product-area matrix organization, a way of dealing with such situations is to establish the norm that the 2-boss individual is expected, and even directed, to convene a meeting between his two bosses to resolve any such conflict. The 2-boss manager is reprimanded only if he suffers such a conflict in silence.

Beyond handling such occasional problems, the 2-boss manager learns in a mature matrix organization that his role gives him a degree of influence not usually experienced at his level in a conventional organization. He not infrequently finds himself striking a balance in a discussion with his two bosses over some point of conflict. If he knows his facts and expresses his judgment on the merits of the particular issue, he often finds it is taken very seriously. This is the heart of training for general management . . . .

THE FUTURE OF THE MATURE MATRIX

A matrix organization includes matrix behavior, matrix systems, and a matrix culture, as well as a matrix structure. After years of working with a matrix, some organizations find that they no longer need the contradictory architecture of the matrix structure to accomplish their goals. Instead, they revert to the simpler pyramid for their structural form, while at the same time retaining the dual or multiple perspective in their managerial behavior, in their information processing, and in the culture of their firms.

This interpretation suggests that the matrix organization is not likely to become the dominant feature in the *structure* of American organizations. Its utility is more likely to be in helping organizations become more flexible in their responses to environmental pressures. Structures are intended to channel people's behavior in desired ways. Like laws, they are strongest when they are not invoked or tested. To the extent that managers behave effectively, they have little need to bump up against formal structures and reporting walls. In traditional pyramids, managers were always bumping against something—either the structure was centralized, and there wasn't enough freedom, or it was decentralized, and there wasn't enough control.

Organizations with mature matrix structures therefore appear to follow one of two paths, and the extent to which the structural framework survives depends on the path an organization takes. One is to maintain dual command, shared use of human resources, and an enriched information processing capacity. The other is to maintain matrix behavior, matrix systems, and a matrix style or culture, but without using the matrix's structural form. Some organizations tear down the matrix entirely and revert to the traditional forms, practices, and managerial behavior of the pyramid.

The distinction between a pathological breakdown and an evolutionary rotation, where the matrix is a transitional form, is a matter of interpretation. As we observe the change in these organizations we may ask, was the matrix thrown out or did the firm grow beyond it? The distinction is more than academic. As long as the environmental pressures that initially propelled an organization into a matrix structure remain, the original inadequacies of the pyramid form will reappear if the matrix structure is actually abandoned. Our observations suggest that this would be fairly evident in three to six months and painfully obvious within one to one and a half years.

Because the structural element of the matrix is so fiendishly difficult to many, we observe organizations trying to shed the form while maintaining the substance. Our diagnosis is that it can be done successfully only where appropriate matrix behavior is so internalized by all significant members that no one notices the structural shift. Even then, however, we anticipate that through the years the structural imbalances will increase.

Where We Stand on the Learning Curve

Not too many years ago few managers in our classrooms had heard of matrix organization,

and today nearly half of them raise their hands when asked whether they work in a matrix organization. Objectively, this self-reporting is inaccurate. What is relevant, however, is the perception itself. Like Molière's gentleman who was surprised to learn that he had been speaking prose all his life, many managers find that they have been "matrixing" all along. The word is jargon, but the grammar connotes people's behavior more than the form of their organization. The unrealistically high self-reporting also demonstrates an increasing comfort and familiarity with the idea among a very large body of executives.

Our major purposes have been to broaden traditional treatments of the matrix structure by demonstrating its applicability in diverse settings and by suggesting ways to change a seemingly radical conception into a familiar and legitimate design. The matrix structure seems to have spread despite itself. It is complex and difficult; it requires human flexibility in order to provide organizational flexibility. But the reverse is also true. For these reasons, we believe, many managers shied away. The academic literature, until now, has limited the utility of the matrix structure to high-technology project organizations. We have shown how both in organization theory and in application, the matrix structure has a much broader applicability. Behavioral descriptions were replete with words like "tension," "conflict," and "confusion." For many it was not pleasant, but it seemed to improve performance. Success gave it legitimacy, and as the concept spread, familiarity seemed to reduce the resistance.

Matrix structure gained acceptance in the space age of the late 1960s. In fact, for a while in the early 1970s it almost seemed to be a fad. Organizations that should never have used it experimented with the form. It was in danger of becoming another hot item from the behavioral science grab bag for business. When this occurred, the results were usually disastrous, thus fueling the sense that if an organization played with the matrix structure it might easily get burned. Despite many misadventures, however, the matrix structure gained respectability. What was necessary was made desirable.

More organizations are feeling the pressure to respond to two or more critical aspects of their businesses simultaneously—that is, to consider and organize by function *and* by product, by service *and* by market area at the same time. There is also increasing pressure to improve information processing capacity, and recent technological advances make multiple matrix systems feasible. Last, it is clear that there is an increased sense of the scarcity of all resources and hence pressures for achieving economies of scale. As we described, these were the necessary and sufficient conditions for the emergence of matrix organizations in the first place. Because these conditions are increasingly prevalent, we feel that more organizations will be forced to consider the matrix organizational form.

Each organization that turns to the matrix structure has a larger and more varied number of predecessors that have charted the way. Despite our belief that matrix structures must be grown from within, the examples of wider applicability must nevertheless suggest that we are dealing less and less with an experiment and more and more with a mature formulation in organization design. Familiarity, here, reduces fear. As more organizations travel up the matrix structure learning curve, the curve itself becomes an easier one to climb. Similarly, as more managers gain experience operating in matrix organizations they are bound to spread this experience as some of them move into other organizations on their career journeys.

When pioneers experiment with new forms of organization, the costs are high and there are usually many casualties. In the case of the matrix structure, this has been true for both organizations and individuals. As the matrix has become a more familiar alternative, however, the costs and pressures have been reduced. Today, we believe that the concept is no longer a radical one, the understanding of the design is widespread, and the economic and social benefits have increased.

This is the summary article from a unique and, I think, important work. Are new structures necessary? The authors say yes and explain why in terms anyone can understand. Are new structures possible? What would a "self-designing organization" look like? These are frontier issues. I find this piece frustrating and stimulating, and I believe that it raises issues anybody interested in understanding organizations cannot avoid.

DESIGNING ORGANIZATIONS TO MATCH TOMORROW

Bo L. T. Hedberg, Paul C. Nystrom, and William H. Starbuck

Organizations might be matched to tomorrow's world on the basis of accurate forecasts. But who knows which forecasts, if any, will turn out to have been accurate? Some forecasts have said that energy shortages, famines, and ecological decay will occur unless limits are placed on resource consumption [6, 17, 25]; these limits would require that nonindustrialized societies consume more resources while industrialized societies consume less. Other forecasts have stated that different societies will grow at different rates, with the important constraints on consumption arising from social and political decisions rather than from ecology [18]. Still other forecasts have asserted that consumption can rise indefinitely because vast potentials remain for using solar energy, new agricultural methods, pollution controls, and innovations that are still to be discovered [4, 13]. The diverse forecasts even outnumber the forecasters.

Bo L. T. Hedberg, Paul C. Nystrom, and William H. Starbuck, "Designing Organizations to Match Tomorrow," *Prescriptive Models of Organizations,* pp. 171–181. (Amsterdam: North Holland Publishing Company, TIMS Studies in the Management Sciences, Vol. 5, 1977). Reprinted by permission.

However, the most effective designs for tomorrow's organizations vary little from forecast to forecast, because all of the forecasts imply that there will be rapid social and technological change. Equilibrium in resource consumption would not eliminate change. Quite the contrary. A fixed resource pool means some activities must be deleted whenever new activities are undertaken, and hence means an increased proportion of activities that are in decline. Since most forms of social and technological change are insuppressible, equilibrium in resource consumption would bring more rapid change between and within societies. Moreover, if organizations continue to behave inertially, consumption in the industrialized societies would exceed the long-run equilibrium levels; cutting back consumption would cause distress that might be avoided through gradual transitions.

Organizational inertia also impedes the creation and use of technological innovations. If technological innovations escalate consumption per capita while allowing populations to multiply, the world's saturating ecology would likely impose more and more constraints. Ecologically destructive or inefficient methods would have to be nonbenevolently forced out of use as soon as better methods appear. Either organizations would have to be made less inertial or traditionally inertial organizations would have to be replaced more frequently.

Because social and technological change appear likely to accelerate, social institutions ought to be designed to accommodate rapid change and to extract the benefits from it. Today's institutions find rapid change stressful largely because of networks of private and public organizations that lack adaptiveness. This article discusses ways to increase organizations' adaptiveness so that societies can respond creatively to ecological constraints and technological innovations. The next section explains how organizations in benevolent environments accumulate inertia and become less capable of handling transitions into new, perhaps non-benevolent, environments. Then follows a statement of the basic alternatives open to policy makers who want to steer populations of organizations. It is advocated that top managers and policy makers stimulate the evolution of self-designing organizations—organizations that continuously diagnose their important problems, explore their future options, and invent new solutions as they develop. Some key properties of self-designing organizations are spelled out in the final sections: participatory information systems that transmit diverse messages, strategic experiments that disrupt complacency and stimulate curiosity, and jobs and careers that provide satisfying lives despite rapidly changing work environments.

GROWING INFLEXIBLE BECAUSE OF BENEVOLENCE

The mental characteristics of people are important determinants of how organizations act. Human brains can analyze the implications of only a few simultaneous influences, and they bog down in the difficulties of weighing numerous future uncertainties. Therefore, organizations have to keep activities simple—by breaking big tasks down into small ones,

by ignoring contingencies and potential options, by grouping stimuli and responding to them with standardized routines. For example, accountants and internal revenue agents compare tax returns with various rules of thumb: careful investigations are not wasted on returns that conform to ordinary patterns.

Whether standardized routines produce good solutions depends on an environment's constancy and benevolence. Environments that change slowly provide time in which to create new methods and to refine old ones. However, organizations are unlikely to try to improve methods that appear to work, and familiar results are usually assumed to be nearly optimal. Benevolent environments rarely make enough threats to keep organizations alert: lost opportunities are less visible than are customers' complaints, law suits, or financial losses.

Decades of almost continuous economic growth have encouraged the organizations in industrialized societies to depend on standardized routines. Signals that routines are failing are rare; resource margins are adequate to absorb the errors from slightly inappropriate responses to slightly misperceived stimuli; responses can be invented gradually. Organizational failures are typically attributed to managerial inexperience and to deviations from conventional practices rather than to stresses originating in environments.

Furthermore, standardized routines have been tailored to gradually expanding economies. Budgets are thought of as minimum aspirations rather than as upper limits to expansion; financial plans focus on maximizing growth while retaining small buffers against temporary setbacks. Long-term commitments, such as purchase contracts, assume that productivities will rise through learning and through returns to scale as well as through technological innovations. Forecasts of demands for products or services reflect managers' ambitions more than external realities [5, 26, 27].

Consistently benevolent environments undermine organizations' readiness to act and their sensitivity to environmental events. Fewer resources are expended monitoring environmental happenings. Plans replace messages as the media for intraorganizational coordination. Redundancies and irrationalities are shifted out of job assignments and authority domains. Organizational ideologies grow up about standardized routines, and conformity to tradition becomes a primary criterion for accomplishment [3, 10, 20, 24].

STEERING THE POPULATION OF ORGANIZATIONS

If the future is going to expose organizations to rapid change and possibly to less benevolent environments, policy makers will have two basic options. Substantial increases in organizational death rates can be accepted, with resources being transferred from dying to newly born organizations. Alternatively, organizations can be made more adaptive so that they can survive to explore and to develop in altered environments.

These two options are not mutually exclusive, and policy makers are likely to use both. However, improving organizations' adaptiveness wastes fewer resources and promises more benefits than does stimulating higher turnovers in the population of organizations. Small, incremental changes cause less difficulties for organizations and their members than do abrupt, revolutionary shifts. Organizational death nearly always causes psychological stress and consumes human and material resources. Policies to increase organizations' deaths and births require effective systems for transferring resources from dying to newborn organizations. At present, efficient transfer systems exist mainly for financial resources: transfers of people, knowledge, and equipment are handled poorly. Unless the new organizations are more congruent with long-term environmental constraints than were the former organizations, replacing one organization with another brings only the temporary benefits of

change as such. It is doubtful that anyone knows enough about the future to say reliably which organizations are the most appropriate ones to die or what kinds of organizations ought to be created.

Traditional strategies for designing organizations start with forecasts of what stresses tomorrow's organizations will face, and then attempt to design organizations that meet the envisioned needs. Although these forecast-oriented designs are common, both their realism and effectiveness must be questioned.

Some liabilities of forecast-oriented designs derive from the difficulty of taking the future into account. To the extent that the future can be predicted, it is easier to specify some of its constraints than to imagine opportunities that might be realized within these constraints. Consequently, forecast-oriented designs tend to be conservative solutions that fail to reap full advantage from their environments.

Forecast-oriented designs readily become self-fulfilling prophesies: they can create the situations they were designed to meet. For example, if forecasts predict considerable technological innovation, organizations will incorporate large research departments that generate technological innovations. Similarly, if public agencies expect aggressive animosity from their clients, they will use physical barriers and rigid rules to protect employees from clients and will use esoteric jargon and impersonal procedures to keep clients at a disadvantage; frustration and bewilderment then breed ill will and noncompliance. In many instances, the major contribution of forecasts is to foster social change in one direction instead of another.

If policy makers are going to facilitate particular kinds of social change, they certainly ought to acknowledge the value premises underlying their social policies, and they should choose their social policies overtly after comparing alternative futures. But it is far from clear that top managers and policy makers ought to control social change directly.

The alternative way to design organizations to match the future is to adopt a meta-strategy in which the top managers and policy makers define their role as similar to that of arithmetic teachers, whose effectiveness is measured by their students' ability to solve arithmetic problems rather than by their own ability to solve such problems. Within this meta-strategy, the goal shifts from solutions invented by policy makers to combinations of hardware, software and people which continually invent, revise, adapt, generate and modify their own solutions [11].

Self-designing organizations are more promising vehicles for approaching the uncertain future than are organizations that rely on forecasts. Self-designing organizations would evaluate their own defects and strong points; they would develop opportunities instead of defending past actions; they would adapt to surprises; and they would resist the accumulating of inertia.

The main prerequisite for self-designing organizations is probably an ideological commitment to impermanence. Organizations should be seen as means, not ends. Members should avoid basing their personal satisfactions on the roles and methods that characterize the present, and they should seek satisfactions in the activities and skills that are creating the future. Current methods and policies should be questioned continuously, and strategies should be chains of experiments; even apparently adequate methods should be discarded in order to make way for new trials [15, 31, 32].

Self-designing organizations will encounter at least three groups of technical problems. Firstly, self-designing organizations need timely information about changes in their environments and their performances, so that they will have enough time to invent appropriate methods. Secondly, means are needed to counteract organizational inertia and to keep organizations exploring alternative futures. Thirdly, self-designing organizations have implications for their members' jobs and reward systems; they are likely to require new attitudes toward work and new job systems. The ensuing sections of this article discuss these problem areas in sequence and point out actions that policy makers and managers can take in order to foster self-designing organizations.

TRANSMITTING CHANGE SIGNALS

Self-designing organizations depend on efficient information systems that can trigger timely adjustments to changing internal and external conditions. The important characteristics of information systems include input signals from diverse sources and rapid perceptions of change. For example, one study found that hospitals with information systems that highlight both expenses and medical performances can better achieve high-quality treatments at low cost and better match their internal structures to environmental requirements than can hospitals with information systems that focus primarily on monetary measures [8]. Another study found that the more profitable business firms are those that use diverse criteria to evaluate themselves [9].

Although new computer technologies can improve information processing, crucial improvements are needed in the information being processed. Most organizations currently rely on accounting systems and formal reports to measure their performances, but these measures are at best partial. Organizations that suddenly find themselves in trouble evidently are ones that have relied on routine, formal reports too heavily [24]. Because accounting systems mainly reflect material and financial resources—neglecting such resources as skilled personnel, know-how, or investments in future markets—organizations can accumulate hidden resources and dissipate them without recognizing these trends or measuring most of the trends' effects [12].

When there are no generally accepted performance measures, organizations can respond to observed deficiencies by shifting to new performance measures that portray their activities favorably [22]. Even when performance measures are generally accepted ones, evaluation and adaptation suffer from insufficient upward communication; messages are often distorted or blocked while traveling from lower organizational levels toward decision centers.

Participation in organizational governance can improve organizational self-evaluations by bringing in outside expertise and by making better use of inside expertise. Representatives of workers, customers, clients, suppliers, patients, governments, interest groups, and citizens can supply additional information about opportunities and threats in organizations' environments or expose obscure difficulties within organizations, thereby improving organizations' reaction times and their decision bases. Participation in organizational governance may also reinforce members' loyalty and increase organizations' cohesion in the face of rapid change. Organizations with informal, nonhierarchical communication links react faster and more easily to changes in their environments.

Widespread participation in organizational governance will require information systems that keep each participant adequately informed. Although, so far, electronic information technology has been used mainly to increase control by top-level personnel, it could help to decentralize decisions and to distribute decision aids and accurate information to lower-level personnel, customers, clients, or community members [21, 28].

How should managers and policy makers improve performance measurements? Rather than allocating resources to elaborate performance evaluations, policy makers should foster informal communications and should encourage managers to elicit brief performance appraisals from diverse groups. Policy makers and managers also should combat reliance on formal accounting systems, and they should reject misleading precision in statements about past performances and future expectations. Top managers ought to monitor environments more and internal methods less. Time and effort ought to be invested searching for new measures of organizational success that include ecological consequences.

STIMULATING ORGANIZATIONAL CURIOSITY

Management theories have long prescribed skill specialization, systematic coordination, clear objectives, and unambiguous authority structures. These widely accepted prescriptions say an organization should be internally differentiated and yet harmonious, should use explicit communication channels and explicit decision criteria, and should act decisively and consistently. Such properties can enhance the performances of organizations that inhabit slowly changing environments: ad hoc analyses can be replaced by standardized routines; routines can be multiplied, reduced to their essential elements, and then preserved in capital equipment and training programs; communications can be compressed with efficient codes; and responsibilities can be delineated precisely [7, 14, 30]. Because they are designed for benevolent and relatively slowly changing environments, today's organizations avoid debates and conflicts, and they impose rationality on activities.

Rapid change will require increased risk-taking and experimentation by organizations that seek to survive. Competition in a stabilized population of organizations or pressures from technological innovations will favor organizations that can seize opportunities and create unique niches of competence. Increased risk-taking will raise organizational death rates, but will also improve the adaptiveness of the surviving organizations.

Self-designing organizations will need planning systems that expect the unexpected and that stimulate curiosity; such systems will differ from the systems currently advocated for long-range planning. In fact, a study of British firms found no evidence that consensus about objectives, clearly defined roles, or formal planning correlated positively with financial performance or innovativeness. Instead, financial performance correlated positively with reliance on informal, unofficial communication channels and with the number of different kinds of information used during reviews of company policies. Organizations with elaborate long-range planning systems seemed less able to explore their futures than organizations with less programmatic ways of forming strategies [9].

Organizations' searches for new modes of behavior are motivated by dissatisfaction and triggered by signs of failure, and intervals of doubt and reappraisal precede genuine efforts to reorient strategies. Reappraisals are not fostered by the organizational practices that clarify goals and that allocate tasks logically and unambiguously. Consequently, self-designing organizations ought to use logical contradictions, ambiguities, and overlaps to counteract complacency and to stimulate innovations.

The essence of all efforts to reduce organizational inertia is to induce organizations to act as if optimal is an impossible state. Links between current methods and current goals should be seen as transient. Behaviors should be planned as sequences of experiments to test the stability of environmental phenomena and to discover better ways of behaving in the future, and the experiments should continue even after optimal behaviors appear to have been found. Because shifting environments and uncertain futures give organizations the task of optimizing unknown criteria, continuous experimenting along a trial-and-error trajectory makes better sense than does attempting once-and-for-all solutions to problems that will change [1, 2, 16, 29].

Experiments can be stimulated by making organizations pursue different goals at different times, by letting separate departments pursue incompatible goals simultaneously, and by undertaking iterative improvements instead of attempting to find overall optima immediately [32]. All of these strategies remind organizations' members that goals and criteria are erroneous approximations that can be corrected and improved.

The key design challenge is to balance the levels of discretionary, uncommitted resources. Discretionary resources must be available if organizations are to try experiments, to develop new capabilities, to take risks, and to survive transitions to new environments. But when discretionary resources grow too large, there are not enough warnings of change, and so adaptive capabilities wither.

If policy makers and managers want to encourage adaptiveness, they should think thrice before punishing entrepreneurial ventures. Promotions and incentives ought to reward people who deviate from familiar methods, who take risks, and who ask imaginative questions. Occasional failure ought to be every manager's right, and policies and educational programs ought to foster ideological commitments to exploring unknowns rather than to mastering the known. Instead of criticizing organizational subunits for having unclear and contradictory goals or for duplicating the activities of other subunits, policy makers and top managers should interpret conflict and ambiguity as generators of healthy changes. Investment policies and tax incentives ought to favor flexible assets that convert to diverse uses and ought to nurture efforts to recycle existing assets. Hiring criteria should place high values on people's versatility and their preparedness to learn, and organizations ought to set up programs to help their personnel unlearn outdated traditions and standardized routines. Contracts and commitments should shirk the long term and focus on the short term.

LIVING IN SELF-DESIGNING ORGANIZATIONS

An orientation toward flexibility will mean that most interpersonal relationships are temporary ones, that job assignments will change frequently, and that hierarchical statuses and prerogatives will shift. There may be high job turnover as people depart who dislike newly adopted task arrangements, and as people arrive who possess needed abilities. Departments, work groups, and individuals require latitude in which to evaluate and to reorient themselves, and this in turn means latitude in which to err and to harm themselves.

There are real reasons for wondering how satisfying such jobs can be. How much pride can people take in rapidly vanishing accomplishments and in solutions which are automatically assumed to be faulty? Can the people who prefer clear, stable assignments learn to be happy with endless sequences of experiments and reorientations? Will inconsistencies and ambiguities induce apathy and alienation in people, as they did in Pavlov's dogs? Little is known about such issues. Unstable, experimental situations may make today's people uncomfortable mainly because today's organizations promote stability, consistency, and permanence. Perhaps people can draw as much satisfaction from the activities that keep organizations viable as they now draw from repeated routines and familiar structures [32]. Perhaps people can take pride in creating new methods rather than in reusing elegant methods, and people can enjoy partially answering important questions instead of precisely answering inaccurate questions [19]. Perhaps careers that aggregate similar jobs in different organizations can be more satisfying than careers that aggregate different jobs in the same organizations [23].

What actions should policy makers and managers take to improve jobs and employment systems? People should be encouraged to try out alternative jobs, and transfer systems should be developed that reduce the difficulties and expenses of discovering new employment opportunities, of moving into new organizations, or of changing occupations. A person's long-term financial security should not depend on continued employment with the same organization. Information about job openings and available people should be widely disseminated, perhaps through publicly supported information systems. Educational curricula ought to deemphasize narrow specialization, and educational policies ought to treat learning as a lifetime activity. Opportunities should be created for people to distribute through time

the costs of mid-career reorientations. There should be as much freedom for individual people—to innovate, to experiment, and to adapt—as there is for the organizations people can and will create.

STARTING TO BEGIN

Because no one can accurately forecast the future, no one can design organizations that match tomorrow's challenges. However, self-designing organizations would reduce the costs of forecast errors by rapidly adapting to what really occurs. Self-designing organizations redesign themselves to match tomorrow.

Individual organizations can strive to become self-designing and to remain so, and some organizations may succeed. But today's social environments seriously impede the redesign efforts of isolated, individual organizations, and self-designing organizations will not grow prevalent unless they receive support from compatible social institutions and appreciative ideologies. People will have to face up to the deficiencies in systematic methods, rational analyses, and consistent behaviors; and people will have to acknowledge the virtues of impermanence, dissension, bare adequacy, uncertainty, and ambiguity. Societies will have to follow new policies and put new social technologies into operation—technologies that encourage flows of people and of information, and policies that foster continuous experiments and strategic versatility by people and by organizations. Policy makers and managers as well as everyone else will have to honor the complementarities among actions by individuals, by organizations, and by societies, because the social institutions needed to support self-designing organizations must themselves be supported from below.

It is far from obvious what steps can take the world from where it is to where it ought to be. Yet this ignorance is itself an informative guide to action: it implies that steps will have to be discovered progressively through incremental experiments in pursuit of ambiguous, shifting goals. Ignorance of what steps to take is also reassuring, for it means that experiments still lie ahead. The excitement and fun come from designing, not from having designed.

REFERENCES

[1] Box, George E. P. and Draper, Norman R., Evolutionary Operation, Wiley, New York, N.Y., 1969.

[2] Campbell, Donald T., "Reforms as Experiments," American Psychologist, Vol. 24 (April 1969), pp. 409–429.

[3] Clark, Burton R., "The Organizational Saga in Higher Education," Administrative Science Quarterly, Vol. 17 (June 1972), pp. 178–184.

[4] Cole, H. S. D., Freeman, Christopher, Jahoda, Marie, and Pavitt, K. L. R., (eds.), Models of Doom: A Critique of The Limits to Growth, Universe, New York, N.Y., 1973.

[5] Crecine, John P., Governmental Problem Solving, Rand McNally, Chicago, Ill., 1969.

[6] Forrester, Jay W., World Dynamics, Wright-Allen, Cambridge, Mass., 1971.

[7] Galbraith, Jay R., Designing Complex Organizations, Addison-Wesley, Reading, Mass., 1973.

[8] Gordon, Gerald, Tanon, Christian, and Morse, Edward V., Hospital Structure, Costs, and Innovation, Cornell University, Ithaca, N.Y. (working paper), 1974.

[9] Grinyer, Peter H. and Norburn, David, "Planning for Existing Markets: Perceptions of Executives and Financial Performance," Journal of the Royal Statistical Society, (Series A), Vol. 138 (Part 1, 1975), pp. 70–97.

[10] Hedberg, Bo L.T., Organizational Stagnation and Choice of Strategy, International Institute of Management, Berlin, Germany (working paper), 1973.

[11] Hedberg, Bo L.T., Nystrom, Paul C., and Starbuck, William H., "Camping on Seesaws: Prescriptions for a Self-Designing Organization," Administrative Science Quarterly, Vol. 21 (March 1976), pp. 41–65.

[12] Hopwood, Anthony G., "Problems with Using Accounting Information in Performance Evaluation," Management International Review, Vol. 13 (2-3, 1973), pp. 83–98.

[13] Kahn, Herman, Brown, William, and Martel, Leon, The Next 200 Years: A Scenario for America and the World, Morrow, New York, N.Y., 1976.

[14] Khandwalla, Pradip N., "Mass Output Orientation of Operations Technology and Organizational Structure," Administrative Science Quarterly, Vol. 19 (March 1974), pp. 74–97.

[15] Landau, Martin, "On the Concept of a Self-correcting Organization," Public Administration Review, Vol. 33 (November-December 1973), pp. 533–542.

[16] Lindblom, Charles E., "The Science of Muddling Through," Public Administration Review, Vol. 19 (Spring 1959), 79–88.

[17] Meadows, Donella H., Meadows, Dennis L., Randers, Jørgen, and Behrens, William W., III, The Limits to Growth: A Report for The Club of Rome's Project on the Predicament of Mankind, Universe, New York, N.Y., 1972.

[18] Mesarovic, Mihajlo and Pestel, Eduard, Mankind at the Turning Point: The Second Report of The Club of Rome, Dutton, New York, N.Y., 1974.

[19] Mitroff, Ian I. and Featheringham, Tom R., "On Systematic Problem Solving and the Error of the Third Kind," Behavioral Science, Vol. 19 (November 1974), pp. 383–393.

[20] Mitroff, Ian I. and Kilmann, Ralph H., "On Organization Stories: An Approach to the Design and Analysis of Organizations Through Myths and Stories," in The Management of Organization Design: Volume I, Strategies and Implementation, Ralph H. Kilmann, Louis R. Pondy and Dennis P. Slevin (eds.), Elsevier North-Holland, New York, N.Y., 1976, pp. 189–207.

[21] Mumford, Enid and Sackman, Harold, (eds.), Human Choice and Computers, North-Holland, Amsterdam, The Netherlands, 1975.

[22] Nystrom, Paul C., "Input-Output Processes of the Federal Trade Commission," Administrative Science Quarterly, Vol. 20 (March 1975), pp. 104–113.

[23] Nystrom, Paul C., "Designing Jobs and Personnel Assignments," in Handbook of Organizational Design, Paul C. Nystrom and William H. Starbuck (eds.), Elsevier North-Holland, New York, N.Y., forthcoming.

[24] Nystrom, Paul C., Hedberg, Bo L. T., and Starbuck, William H., "Interacting Processes as Organization Designs," in The Management

of Organization Design: Volume I, Strategies and Implementation, Ralph H. Kilmann, Louis R. Pondy, and Dennis P. Slevin (eds.), Elsevier North-Holland, New York, N.Y., 1976, pp. 209-230.

[25] Oltmans, Willem L., On Growth, Putnam's, New York, N.Y., 1974.

[26] Pondy, Louis R., "Effects of Size, Complexity, and Ownership on Administrative Intensity," Administrative Science Quarterly, Vol. 14 (March 1969), pp. 47-60.

[27] Schumacher, Ernst Friedrich, Small Is Beautiful: A Study of Economics as if People Mattered, Blond and Briggs, London, England, 1973.

[28] Simon, Herbert A., "Applying Information Technology to Organizational Design," Public Administration Review, Vol. 33 (May-June 1973), pp. 268-278.

[29] Starbuck, William H., "Systems Optimization with Unknown Criteria," Proceedings of the 1974 International Conference on Systems, Man and Cybernetics, Institute of Electrical and Electronics Engineers, New York, N.Y., 1974, pp. 67-76.

[30] Starbuck, William H. and Dutton, John M., "Designing Adaptive Organizations," Journal of Business Policy, Vol. 3 (Summer 1973), pp. 21-28.

[31] White, Orion F., Jr., "The Dialectical Organization—An Alternative to Bureaucracy," Public Administration Review, Vol. 29 (January-February 1969), pp. 32-42.

[32] Wildavsky, Aaron B., "The Self-Evaluating Organization," Public Administration Review, Vol. 32 (September-October 1972), pp. 509-520.

9 RELATIONSHIPS: DIAGNOSING CONFLICT BETWEEN INDIVIDUALS

This succinct statement breaks down the analysis of interpersonal conflict into three categories:

1. *The nature of the difference.* Are the parties fighting over *facts, goals, methods,* or *values*?

2. *Underlying factors.* Do the parties have access to the same information? Do they see the same information differently? How much is each influenced by his or her role?

3. *Stage of evolution.* Are the parties at the point of *anticipating* a fight, in open conflict, or somewhere between? The authors identify five possible stages that can be diagnosed.*

MANAGEMENT OF DIFFERENCES

—How to Diagnose An Issue and Its Causes.

—How to Decide on The Best Course of Action.

Warren H. Schmidt and Robert Tannenbaum

The manager often experiences his most uncomfortable moments when he has to deal with differences among people. Because of these differences, he must often face disagreements, arguments, and even open conflict. To add to his discomfort, he frequently finds himself torn by two opposing desires. On the one hand, he wants to unleash the individuality of his subordinates in order to tap their full potential and to achieve novel and creative approaches to problems. On the other hand, he is eager to develop a harmonious, smooth-working team to carry out his organization's objectives. The manager's lot is further troubled by the fact that when differences do occur, strong feelings are frequently aroused, objectivity flies out the window, egos are threatened, and personal relationships are placed in jeopardy.

TOWARD EFFECTIVE MANAGEMENT

Because the presence of differences can complicate the manager's job in so many ways, it is of utmost importance that he understand them fully and that he learn to handle them effectively. It is the purpose of this article to assist the manager to manage more effectively by increasing his understanding of differences among the people he works with, and by improving his ability to deal with others.

*Warren H. Schmidt and Robert Tannenbaum, "Management of Differences," Section III: "Managing Conflict," in John Adams, ed., *New Technology in Organization Development,* NTL Institute, 1973. See this section and article for intervention ideas.
Reprinted from W. Warner Burke and Harvey A. Hornstein, *The Social Technology of Organization Development,* La Jolla, Calif.: University Associates, © 1972. Reissued by University Associates, 1976. Used with permission.

A large part of what follows will focus, for simplicity of exposition, on the differences which occur among a manager's individual subordinates. However, we would like to suggest that the principles, concepts, methods, and dynamics which we discuss throughout much of the article apply to intergroup, to interorganizational, and to international differences as well.

Our basic thesis is that a manager's ability to deal effectively with differences depends on:

- His ability to diagnose and to understand differences.
- His awareness of, and ability to select appropriately from, a variety of behaviors.[1]
- His awareness of, and ability to deal with, his own feelings—particularly those which might reduce his social sensitivity (diagnostic insight) and his action flexibility (ability to act appropriately).[2]

There are two basic assumptions underlying our approach to this problem. Let us examine them before going any further:

1. *Differences among people should not be regarded as inherently "good" or "bad."* Sometimes differences result in important benefits to the organization; and sometimes they are disruptive, reducing the overall effectiveness of individuals and organizations.

2. *There is no "right" way to deal with differences.* Under varying circumstances, it may be most beneficial to avoid differences, to repress them, to sharpen them into clearly defined conflict, or to utilize them for enriched problem solving. The manager who consistently "pours oil on troubled water" may not be the most effective manager. Nor is the manager necessarily successful who emphasizes individuality and differences so strongly that cooperation and teamwork are simply afterthoughts. We feel, rather, that the effective manager is one who is able to use a *variety* of approaches to differ-

ences and who chooses any specific approach on the basis of an insightful diagnosis and understanding of the factors with which he is faced at that time.

DIAGNOSING DISAGREEMENTS

When a manager's subordinates become involved in a heated disagreement, they do not tend to proceed in a systematic manner to resolve their difference. The issues often remain unclear to them, and they may talk *at* rather than *to* one another. If a manager is to be helpful in such a situation, he should ask three important diagnostic questions:

1. What is the nature of the difference among the persons?
2. What factors may underlie this difference?
3. To what stage has the interpersonal difference evolved?

Nature of the Difference

Now, looking at the first of these three important questions, the nature of the difference will vary depending on the kind of issue on which people disagree. And there are four basic kinds of issues to look for:

- *Facts.* Sometimes the disagreement occurs because individuals have different definitions of a problem, are aware of different pieces of relevant information, accept or reject different information as factual, or have differing impressions of their respective power and authority.

- *Goals.* Sometimes the disagreement is about what should be accomplished—the desirable objectives of a department, division, section, or of a specific position within the organization.

- *Methods.* Sometimes individuals differ about the procedures, strategies, or tactics which would most likely achieve a mutually desired goal.

- *Values.* Sometimes the disagreement is over ethics—the way power should be exercised, or moral considerations, or assumptions about justice, fairness, and so on. Such differences may affect the choice of either goals or methods.

Arguments are prolonged and confusion is increased when the contending parties are not sure of the nature of the issue over which they disagree. By discovering the source of the disagreement, the manager will be in a better position to determine how he can utilize and direct the dispute for both the short- and long-range good of the organization. As we will indicate later, there are certain steps which are appropriate when the differences are about facts, other steps which are appropriate when the differences are over goals, and still other steps which are applicable when differences are over methods or values.

Underlying Factors

When people are faced with a difference, it is not enough that their manager be concerned with what the difference is about. The second major diagnostic question he should ask is *why* the difference exists. As we try to discover useful answers to this, it is helpful to think in terms of:

- Whether the disputants had access to the same information.
- Whether the disputants perceive the common information differently.
- Whether each disputant is significantly influenced by his role in the organization.

These questions involve informational, perceptual, and role factors. Thus:

Informational factors exert their influence when the various points of view have developed on the basis of different sets of facts. The ancient legend of the blind men and the elephant dramatizes this point as vividly as any modern illustration. Because each of the men had contact with a different part of the elephant, each disagreed violently about the nature of the animal. In the same way, when two persons receive limited information about a complex problem, they may well disagree as to the nature of that problem when they come together to solve it.

Perceptual factors exert their influence when the persons have different images of the same stimulus. Each will attend to, and select from the information available, those items which he deems important. Each will interpret the information in a somewhat different manner. Each brings to the data a different set of life experiences which cause him to view the information through a highly personal kind of filter. The picture which he gets, therefore, is unique to him. Thus it is not surprising that the same basic "facts" may produce distinctive perceptual pictures in the minds of different individuals.

Role factors exert their influence because each of the individuals occupies a certain position and status in society or in the organization. The fact that he occupies such a position or status may put certain constraints on him if the discussion is related to his role.

The concepts we have been discussing can be best illustrated by a concrete case. Such a case is presented in detail in EXHIBIT I.

Stage of Evolution

Important conflicts among people ordinarily do not erupt suddenly. They pass through various stages, and the way in which the energy of the disputing parties can be effectively directed by the manager depends to some extent on the stage of the dispute when he enters the picture.

One way of diagnosing a dispute—the third major question—is to identify it as being at one of these five stages in its development:

Exhibit I. Hypothetical Situation Illustrating a Difference

The Facts

There is a disagreement over whether a company should introduce automated record keeping to replace its present manual system. The company's expert on office methods favors immediate introduction of such a system. The head of accounting is opposed to it. Some of the bases of disagreement and possible reasons for this disagreement are represented below.

Nature of the Difference

	Over facts	Over methods	Over goals	Over values
Expert on office methods	"Automation will save the company money."	"The new system should be installed fully and at once."	"We want a system that gives us accurate data rapidly—whenever we want it."	"We must be modern and efficient."
Head of accounting department	"The new system will be more expensive to install and operate."	"Let us move slower—one step at a time."	"We need most a flexible accounting system to meet our changing needs—managed by accountants who can solve unexpected and complex problems."	"We must consider the welfare of workers who have served the company so loyally for many years."

Reasons for the Difference

	Explanation of position of methods expert	Explanation of position of head accountant
Informational (Exposure to different information	He has studied articles about seemingly comparable companies describing the savings brought about by automation. Representatives of machine companies have presented him with estimates of savings over a 10-year period.	He has heard about the "hidden costs" in automation. He has priced the kind of equipment he believes will be necessary and has estimated its depreciation. This estimated cost is much higher than the salaries of possible replaced workers.
Perceptual (Different interpretation of the same data because of differing backgrounds, experience, and so forth)	He regards the representatives of the machine company as being alert, businesslike, and knowledgeable about the best accounting procedures. He feels that their analysis of the company's needs is dependable and to be trusted.	He sees the representatives of the machine company as salesmen. Their goal is to sell machines, and their report and analysis must be read with great caution and suspicion.
Role (Pressure to take a certain stand because of status or position)	He believes that the company looks to him as the expert responsible for keeping its systems up-to-date and maximally efficient.	He feels responsible for the morale and security of his team in the accounting office. He must defend their loyalty and efficiency if it is ever doubted.

Stage #1—the phase of anticipation. A manager learns that his company is about to install new, automated equipment which will reduce the number and change the nature of jobs in a given department. He can anticipate that when this information is released, there will be differences of opinion as to the desirability of this change, the way in which it should be introduced, and the way in which the consequences of its introduction should be handled.

Stage #2—the phase of conscious, but unexpressed, difference. Word leaks out about the proposed new equipment. Small clusters of people who trust one another begin discussing it. They have no definite basis for the information, but tensions begin to build up within the organization. There is a feeling of impending dispute and trouble.

Stage #3—the phase of discussion. Information is presented about the plans to install new equipment. Questions are asked to secure more information, to inquire about the intentions of management, to test the firmness of the decision that has been made. During the discussion, the differing opinions of individuals begin to emerge openly. They are implied by the questions which are asked, and by the language which is used.

Stage #4—the phase of open dispute. The union steward meets with the foreman to present arguments for a change in plans. The foreman counters these arguments by presenting the reasons that led management to decide to install the equipment. The differences which have heretofore been expressed only indirectly and tentatively now sharpen into more clearly defined points of view.

Stage #5—the phase of open conflict. Individuals have firmly committed themselves to a particular position on the issue; the dispute has become clearly defined. The outcome can only be described in terms of win, lose, or compromise. Each disputant attempts not only to increase the effectiveness of his argument and his power in the situation, but also to undermine the influence of those who oppose him.

The power of the manager to intervene successfully will differ at each of these stages.

He is likely to have the most influence if he enters the picture at stage #1; the least influence if he enters at stage #5. This range of possible behavior and action changes as the conflict passes through the various stages. For this reason, it is important for the manager not only to assess the nature of the given dispute and the forces affecting the individuals involved, but also to assess the stage to which the dispute has evolved.

SELECTING AN APPROACH

After the manager has diagnosed a given dispute (or a potential one) between subordinates, he is next confronted by the problem of taking action. And here there are two additional questions that it will be helpful to him to consider:

1. What courses of action are available?

2. What must be kept in mind in selecting the best one?

Assuming, first, a situation in which the manager has time to anticipate and plan for an impending dispute, we suggest that the general approaches typically available to him are (a) avoidance, (b) repression, (c) sharpening into conflict, and (d) transformation into problem solving. In deciding which to use, the manager's primary concern should be to select the alternative that will yield optimum benefits to the organization.

Avoidance of Differences

It is possible for a manager to avoid the occurrence of many differences among his subordinates. He can, for example, staff his organization with people who are in substantial agreement. Some organizations select and promote individuals whose experiences are similar, who have had similar training, and who come from a similar level of society. Because of such common backgrounds, these individuals tend to see things similarly, to have common interests and objectives, and to approach problems in much the same way. A staff thus developed tends to be a very secure one: the reactions of one's fellows are both readily predictable and congenial to one's own way of thinking and doing.

The manager may also avoid differences among his subordinates by controlling certain of their interpersonal contacts. He can, for example, assign two potentially explosive individuals to different groups or physical locations, or he can choose not to raise a particularly divisive issue because it is "too hot to handle." But let us take a closer look:

When is this alternative appropriate? Some organizations depend heavily on certain kinds of conformity and agreement among their employees in order to get the work done. Political parties and religious denominational groups are perhaps extreme examples of this. If an individual holds a different point of view on a rather fundamental issue, he may become a destructive force within the organization. This approach may be especially important if he is dealing with somewhat fragile and insecure individuals. Some persons are so threatened by conflict that their ability to function effectively suffers when they operate in a climate of differences.

What are the difficulties and dangers in this approach? The manager who uses this approach consistently runs the risk of reducing the total creativity of his staff. Someone has said, "When everyone in the room thinks the same thing, no one is thinking very much." In an atmosphere in which differences are avoided, new ideas not only appear less frequently, but old ideas also are likely to go unexamined and untested. There is genuine danger of the organization's slipping unknowingly into a rut of complacency.

Repression of Differences

Sometimes a manager is aware that certain differences exist among members of his staff, but he feels that the open expression of these differences would create unproductive dissension and reduce the total creativity of the group. He

may, therefore, decide to keep these differences under cover. He may do this by continually emphasizing loyalty, cooperation, teamwork, and other similar values within the group. In such a climate, it is unlikely that subordinates will express disagreements and risk conflict.

The manager may also try to make sure that the potentially conflicting parties come together only under circumstances which are highly controlled—circumstances in which open discussion of latent differences is clearly inappropriate. Or he may develop an atmosphere of repression by consistently rewarding agreement and cooperation and by punishing (in one way or another) those who disrupt the harmony of the organization by expressing nonconformist ideas. But once again:

When is this alternative appropriate? It is most useful when the latent differences are not relevant to the organization's task. It is to be expected that individuals will differ on many things—religion, politics, their loyalty to cities or states, baseball teams, and so forth. There may be no need to reach agreement on some of these differences in order to work together effectively on the job. It may also be appropriate to repress conflict when adequate time is not available to resolve the potential differences among the individuals involved. This might be particularly true if the manager's concern is to achieve a short-run objective and the potential disagreement is over a long-run issue. The wounds of disagreement should not be opened up if there is insufficient time to bind them.

What are the difficulties and dangers in this approach? Repression almost always costs something. If, indeed, the differences are important to the persons involved, their feelings may come to be expressed indirectly, in ways that could reduce productivity. Every manager has witnessed situations in which ideas are resisted, not on the basis of their merit, but on the basis of who advocated them. Or he has seen strong criticism arising over mistakes made by a particularly disliked individual.

Much has been said and written about "hidden agenda." People may discuss one subject, but the *way* they discuss it and the positions they take with respect to it may actually be determined by factors lying beneath the surface of the discussion. Hidden agenda are likely to abound in an atmosphere of repression.

When strong feelings are involved in unexpressed differences, the blocking of these feelings creates frustration and hostility which may be misdirected toward "safe" targets. Differences, and the feelings generated by them, do not ordinarily disappear by being ignored. They fester beneath the surface and emerge at inopportune moments to create problems for the manager and his organization.

Differences Into Conflicts

When this approach is used, the manager not only recognizes the fact that differences exist, but attempts to create an arena in which the conflicting parties can "fight it out." However, like the promoter of an athletic contest, he will want to be sure that the differing persons understand the issue over which they differ, the rules and procedures by which they can discuss their differences, and the kinds of roles and responsibilities which each is expected to bear in mind during the struggle. Again:

When is this alternative appropriate? A simple answer is: "when it is clarifying and educational." Many an individual will not pause to examine the assumptions he holds or the positions he advocates until he is called on to clarify and support them by someone who holds contrary views. In the same way, the power realities within an organization can come into sharper focus and be more commonly recognized through conflict.

For example, the manager of production and the manager of engineering may develop quite different impressions of how the board of directors feels about the relative importance of their respective units. Each is sure that the board is most impressed with the caliber of the staff, output, and operational efficiency of his department. When a dispute arises over which group is to get priority space in a new building, top management may permit both departments

to exert all the influence they can on the board. During the struggle, the two managers may each gain a more realistic assessment of, and respect for, the power of the other.

Another valuable thing learned is the cost of conflict itself. Almost invariably at the end of a long dispute, there is a strong resolve that "this shall not happen again," as the individuals reflect on the financial costs, tensions, embarrassments, uneasiness, and wasted time and energy it caused.

What are the difficulties and dangers in this approach? Conflict can be very costly. It not only saps the energy of those involved, but also may irreparably destroy their future effectiveness. In the heat of conflict, words are sometimes spoken which leave lifelong scars on people or forever cloud their relationship.

Because the risks involved in conflict are so great and the potential costs so high, the manager will want to consider carefully the following questions before he uses this approach:

1. What does he hope to accomplish?
2. What are the possible outcomes of the conflict?
3. What steps should be taken to keep the conflict within organizational bounds and in perspective?
4. What can be done after the conflict to strengthen the bonds between disputants, so that the conflict will be of minimum destructiveness to them and to their ongoing relationship?

Making Differences Creative

"Two heads are better than one" because the two heads often represent a richer set of experiences and because they can bring to bear on the problem a greater variety of insights. If the differences are seen as enriching, rather than as in opposition to each other, the "two heads" will indeed be likely to come up with a better solution than either one alone. For example, had the six blind men who came into contact with different parts of the same elephant pooled their information, they would have arrived at a more accurate description of the animal. In the same way, many problems can be seen clearly, wholly, and in perspective only if the individuals who see different aspects can come together and pool their information. Here, too, let us take a more specific look:

When is this alternative appropriate? When it comes to choosing courses of action for a given problem, differences among the individuals in an organization can help to increase the range and variety of alternatives suggested.

The channeling of differences into a problem-solving context may also help to deal with some of the feelings which often accompany disagreement—frustration, resentment, and hostility. By providing an open and accepted approach, the manager helps to prevent undercurrents of feelings which could break out at inopportune moments. He also helps to channel the energy generated by feelings into creative, rather than into destructive, activities. Whereas conflict tends to cause individuals to seek ways of weakening and undermining those who differ with them, the problem-solving approach leads individuals to welcome differences as being potentially enriching to one's own goals, ideas, and methods.

What are the difficulties and dangers in this approach? To utilize differences requires time. Often it is easier for a single individual (rather than two or more persons) to make a decision. Also, when a rapid decision is required, it may be easier and more practical to ignore one side of an argument in order to move into action. Finally, unless a problem-solving situation is planned with some care, there is always the risk of generating conflict which will be frustrating to all parties concerned.

ENRICHED PROBLEM SOLVING

Let us assume that the course of action decided on is the one just discussed—turning the difference into creative problem solving. Let us

further assume, now, that the manager enters the picture when his subordinates are already involved in conflict. What are the things he can do if he wishes to transform this conflict into a problem-solving situation?

- *He can welcome the existence of differences within the organization.*
  The manager can indicate that from the discussion of differences can come a greater variety of solutions to problems and a more adequate testing of proposed methods. By making clear his view that all parties contribute to the solution of problems by sharing their differences, he reduces the implication that there will be an ultimate "winner" and "loser."

- *He can listen with understanding rather than evaluation.*
  There is abundant evidence that conflicts tend to be prolonged and to become increasingly frustrating because the conflicting parties do not really listen to one another. Each attempts to impose his own views and to "tune out" or distort what the other person has to say.

  The manager may expect that when he enters the picture, the individuals will try to persuade him to take a stand on the issue involved. While each adversary is presenting his "case" to the manager, he will be watching for cues which indicate where the manager stands on the issue. It is therefore important that the manager make every effort to understand both positions as fully as possible, recognizing and supporting the seriousness of purpose of each where appropriate, and to withhold judgment until all available facts are in.

  In the process of listening for understanding, the manager will also set a good example for the conflicting parties. By adopting such a listening-understanding attitude himself, and by helping the disputants to understand each other more fully, he can make a most useful contribution toward transforming potential conflict into creative problem solving.

- *He can clarify the nature of the conflict.*

  In the heat of an argument, each participant may primarily focus on either facts, specific methods, goals, or values. Frustration and anger can occur when one individual talks about facts while another is eager to discuss methods. The manager, having carefully listened to the discussion, can clarify the nature of the issues so that the discussion can become more productive.

- *He can recognize and accept the feelings of the individuals involved.*

  Irrational feelings are generated in a controversy, even though the participants do not always recognize this fact. Each wants to believe that he is examining the problem "objectively." The manager, recognizing and accepting feelings such as fear, jealousy, anger, or anxiety, may make it possible for the participants squarely to face their true feelings. The effective manager does not take a critical attitude toward these feelings by, in effect, saying, "You have no right to feel angry!" Rather, he tries sincerely to communicate his sympathetic feelings.

  Ordinarily, we do no real service to people by encouraging a repression of their feelings or by criticizing them for experiencing fear, anger, and so forth. Such criticism—whether implied or expressed openly—may block the search for new ways out of the controversy. There is considerable evidence that when a person feels threatened or under attack, he tends to become more rigid and therefore more defensive about positions to which he has committed himself.

- *He can indicate who will make the decision being discussed.*

  Sometimes heated disputes go on with respect to issues over which one or more of the persons involved has no control. When people have differing notions about the formal authority available to each, a clarification by the manager of the authority relationships can go far toward placing the discussion in clearer perspective.

- *He can suggest procedures and ground rules for resolving the differences.*

  If the disagreement is over *facts,* the manager may assist the disputants in validating existing data and in seeking additional data which will more clearly illuminate the issues under dispute.

  If the disagreement is over *methods,* the manager may first want to remind the parties that they have common objectives, and that their disagreement is over means rather than ends. He may suggest that before examining in detail each of their proposed methods for achieving the goals, they might together establish a set of criteria to be used in evaluating whatever procedures are proposed. He may also want to suggest that some time be spent in trying to generate additional alternatives reflecting new approaches. Then after these alternatives have been worked out, he may encourage the parties to evaluate them with the aid of the criteria which these persons have developed together.

  If the disagreement is over *goals* or *goal priorities,* he may suggest that the parties take time to describe as clearly as possible the conflicting goals which are being sought. Sometimes arguments persist simply because the parties have not taken the trouble to clarify for themselves and for each other exactly what they do desire. Once these goals are clearly stated, the issues can be dealt with more realistically.

  If the disagreement is over *values,* the manager may suggest that these values be described in operational terms. Discussions of abstractions often tend to be fruitless because the same words and concepts mean different things to different people. To help individuals become more fully aware of the limitations to which their actions are subject, the question, "What do you think you can do about this situation?" usually leads to a more productive discussion than the question, "What do you believe in?" Because value systems are so closely related to a person's self concept, the manager may want to give particular attention to protecting the egos involved. He may make clear that an individual's entire ethical system is not being scrutinized, but only those values which are pertinent to the particular instance.

- *He can give primary attention to maintaining relationships between the disputing parties.*

Sometimes, during the course of a heated dispute, so much attention is paid to the issue under discussion that nothing is done to maintain and strengthen the relationship between the disputing parties. It is not surprising, therefore, that disputes tend to disrupt ongoing relationships. Through oversight or deliberate action, important functions are neglected which sustain or further develop human relationships—for example, the functions of encouraging, supporting, reducing tension, and expressing common feelings. If a conflict is to be transformed into a problem-solving situation, these functions need to be performed by someone—either by the manager or, through his continuing encouragement, by the parties themselves.

- *He can create appropriate vehicles for communicating among the disputing parties.*

One of the ways to bring differences into a problem-solving context is to ensure that the disputants can come together easily. If they can discuss their differences *before* their positions become crystalized, the chances of their learning from each other and arriving at mutually agreeable positions are increased. Having easy access to one another is also a way of reducing the likelihood that each will develop unreal stereotypes of the other.

Misunderstanding mounts as communication becomes more difficult. One of the values of regular staff meetings, there-fore, is that such meetings, properly conducted, can provide a continuing opportunity for persons to exchange ideas and feelings.

If the manager wishes his subordinates to deal with their differences in a problem-solving framework, he will want to ask himself, "In what kind of setting will the parties to this dispute be best able to discuss their differences with a minimum of interference and threat?" He will exclude from such a setting any individuals whose presence will embarrass the disputants if the latter "back down" from previously held points of view. It will be a setting which reflects as much informality and psychological comfort as possible.

- *He can suggest procedures which facilitate problem solving.*

One of the key needs in a dispute is to separate an idea from the person who first proposes it. This increases the chance of examining the idea critically and objectively without implying criticism of the person. Techniques like brainstorming, for example, are designed to free people from the necessity to defend their ideas during an exploration period. Another facilitating action is outlining an orderly set of procedures (e.g., examining objectives, obtaining relevant data) for the disputants to follow as they seek a constructive resolution of their difference.

MANAGERIAL OBJECTIVITY

Thus far we have tended to make the unrealistic assumption that the manager is able to maintain his own objectivity in the face of a difference among his subordinates. Obviously, this does not easily happen because his feelings also tend to become involved. It is, in fact, not unusual for people to react to differences more on the basis of their own feelings than on the basis of some rational approach to the problem at hand.

A manager may be deeply concerned about the disruptive effects of a disagreement. He may be troubled about how the persistence of a dispute will affect him personally or his position in the organization. He may worry about the danger of coming under personal attack, or of incurring the anger and hostility of important subordinates or a superior. He may become anxious as another person expresses deep feelings, without really understanding why.

While sometimes personal feelings of this kind are at the conscious level, often they are unrecognized by the manager himself because they lie in the area of the unconscious. This, then, highlights the importance of the manager's own self-awareness. While we do not intend to deal with this topic here, it might be well to note some *"alerting signals"* to which the manager might pay attention when he confronts a difference.

Certain kinds of behavior may indicate that the manager's handling of differences is strongly influenced by his personal needs and feelings rather than by the objective interests of the organization—as, for example:

- A persistent tendency to surround himself with yes men.

- Emphasizing loyalty and cooperation in a way that makes disagreement seem equivalent to disloyalty and rebellion.

- A persistent tendency to "pour oil on troubled waters" whenever differences arise.

- Glossing over serious differences in order to maintain an appearance of harmony and teamwork.

- Accepting ambiguous resolutions of differences which permit conflicting parties to arrive at dissimilar interpretations.

- Exploiting differences to strengthen his personal position of influence through the weakening of the position of others.

Any of these kinds of behavior could, as we have already suggested, be appropriate in certain situations and actually serve the general interest of the organization. If, however, they represent rather consistent patterns on the part of the manager, then it may be worth his while

to examine more closely the reasons for his actions.

There are times in the lives of most of us when our personal needs are the strongest determinants of our behavior. Fortunately, most organizations can tolerate a limited amount of such self-oriented behavior on the part of their managers. The danger occurs if an individual believes that his actions are solely motivated by the "good of the organization" when, in fact, he is operating on the basis of other kinds of personal motivation without being aware of it.

The manager who is more fully aware of his own feelings and inclinations *is in a better position to diagnose a situation accurately* and to choose rationally the kind of behavior which is in the best interests of the organization.

CONCLUSION

This article began with the assumption that many managers are uncertain and uneasy when differences arise. Because their own emotions and the feelings of others quickly become involved, they often deal with differences in a haphazard or inappropriate manner. We have attempted to suggest some more systematic ways to view differences and to deal with them. We believe that if a manager can approach a difference with less fear and with greater awareness of the potential richness that lies in it, he will better understand the basic nature and causes of the difference. And having done this, he will be in a better position to discover and implement more realistic alternatives for dealing with it.

"Conflict . . . is a theme that has occupied the thinking of man more than any other, save only God and love. In the vast output of discourse on the subject, conflict has been treated in every conceivable way. It has been treated descriptively, as in history and fiction; it has been treated in an aura of moral approval, as in epos; with implicit resignation, as in tragedy; with moral disapproval, as in pacifistic religions. There is a body of knowledge called military science, presumably concerned with strategies of armed conflict. There are innumerable handbooks, which teach how to play specific games of strategy. Psychoanalysts are investigating the genesis of "fight-like" situations within the individual, and social psychologists are doing the same on the level of groups and social classes. . . .

I suspect that the most important result of a systematic and manysided study of conflict would be the changes which such a study could effect in ourselves, the conscious and unconscious, the willing and unwilling participants in conflicts. Thus, the rewards to be realistically hoped for are the indirect ones, as was the case with the sons who were told to dig for buried treasure in the vineyard. They found no treasure, but they improved the soil.''*

---

*Anatol Rapoport, *Fights, Games, and Debates,* Ann Arbor, The University of Michigan Press, 1960, pp. II, 360.

NOTES

1. For insightful treatments of the causes and consequences of conflict, and the alternative means of dealing with it—as well as with other expressions of difference—see Lewis A. Coser, *The Function of Social Conflict* (London, Routledge and Kegan Paul, Ltd., 1956); and Raymond W. Mack and Richard C. Snyder, "The Analysis of Social Conflict—Toward an Overview and Synthesis," *Conflict Resolution,* June 1957, pp. 212-248.

2. For definitions and discussions of social sensitivity and action flexibility see Robert Tannenbaum and Fred Massarik, "Leadership: A Frame of Reference,"*Management Science,* Vol. 4, No. 1, October 1957; and Robert Tannenbaum and Warren H. Schmidt, "How to Choose a Leadership Pattern," HBR March–April 1958, p. 95.

10 RELATIONSHIPS: DIAGNOSING CONFLICT BETWEEN UNITS

In the following excerpt Petrella and Block outline a theory of interunit conflict based on the work of Lawrence and Lorsch. They also indicate the kinds of issues and strategies in use when conflict is present.

In addition, they add two insights for the diagnostician whose intent is change. Are the parties in conflict *motivated* to resolve it? Do they have roughly *equal power* over the situation?

DIAGNOSING CONFLICT BETWEEN GROUPS IN ORGANIZATIONS

Tony Petrella and Peter Block

INTRODUCTION

In order to deal with the diversity of complexity of modern industrial processes, most large organizations organize their work force into specialized functional groupings. The act of segmenting an organization into specialized units, however, creates a need to integrate their separate efforts to produce a finished product.

Integration is not easily achieved. We often see units locked in serious combat where someone must win and someone must lose. One way out of the dilemma of win/lose situations is to try to understand the dynamics of conflict in order to determine what can be done to resolve, control or constructively use the conflict. In our experience, everyone seems to be yearning for a little more acceptance of interdependence as a fact of industrial life and to be searching for the means to achieve productive collaboration.

The goal of productive collaboration, along with the challenge of bringing it about, has been the focus of our efforts for some time. This has grown from our interest in conflict and its constructive outcomes along with a certain horror about its destructive consequences.

If you look at any organization chart, you will note that vertical relationships are clearly defined. Vertical relationships mean, primarily, authority relationships. We will not argue against the need for clarity in these vertical relationships. Lateral relationships, however, are not so clearly drawn. The typical organization chart provides few clues concerning the extensive lateral coordination that is required to get work done. This lack of clarity is a little puzzling in view of the growing awareness of top managers that integrating the efforts of specialized units is mandatory for effective operation.

The destructive effects of intergroup conflict are well known. A variety of coping strategies have been used to deal with lateral conflict. A common approach is to transfer one of the combatants to a distant unit. Another approach is to redefine jurisdictional boundaries, or rede-

Tony Petrella and Peter Block, "Managing Conflict in Lateral Interfaces," Block Petrella Associates, 1975. Adapted by permission.

fine work flow procedures to prevent competitive maneuvering. Another approach is to reorganize to decrease conflict producing interactions. A much favored approach is to present the conflict situation to the next higher level in such a way as to get a judgment in favor of one of the combatants. This, in effect, provides the "winner" with the "authority" to suppress the conflict.

We can call all of these approaches *administrative change strategies*. All of them try to rearrange authority relationships or redefine responsibilities toward the goal of eliminating or controlling destructive conflict. In most cases, the surface fighting ceases, but the basic conflict producing factors remain unchanged.

Another approach is the use of *conflict avoidance strategies*. Instead of facing up to obvious conflict, the parties concerned elect to smooth them over. Here we find managers pointing to "communication" problems or unfortunate misunderstandings that should not be allowed to disrupt friendly relations. The problem here is that smoothing over real conflict won't work. Task performance will suffer or the conflict will increase or both.

Another avoidance strategy is the use of compromise. Here the managers involved agree to give a little and take a little. Neither gets what he wants or needs. The conflict goes underground. The total organization pays the price as compromise solutions seldom meet the needs of the organization.

An alternative to administrative or avoidance change strategies is the use of *attitude change strategies*. Here, the central focus is on changing attitudes, perceptions, and working styles; on consciously building lateral relationships that will meet the needs of integration under conditions of conflict.

Under administrative or avoidance change strategies, conflict is seen as unhealthy and all efforts are aimed at suppression, elimination or containment. Under attitude change strategies, conflict is seen as a natural consequence of organizational life. The size and complexity of modern organizations demands segmentation into specialized units. This segmentation has a direct influence on the behavior of organization members. Managers not only develop specialized skills, but more important, they develop different attitudes, different working styles, and are *assigned* to serve divergent goals. Top managers will quickly agree that the sales manager's job is "different" from the production chief's job. The problems and the people they face are different. For each to succeed, the skills, attitudes, predispositions, and working styles must be congruent with the special problems presented by their "different" working environments. If they became the same, neither would succeed. It is in this sense that we say that specialization has a price; it automatically produces the conditions for conflict. In a real sense, the existence of lateral conflict is evidence that specialization is working. The question is not how to eliminate conflict. With specialization of functions, conflict is inevitable, even desirable! The question we need to work is, "How can the specifics of each conflict incident be managed and resolved constructively without expecting conflict to disappear?"

The use of attitude change strategies requires confrontation of real issues. Confronting conflict requires emotional and intellectual energy, reassessment of some deeply rooted attitudes and values and some degree of interpersonal skill. When and how to achieve productive confrontation is the central focus of this paper.

WHEN IS CONFRONTATION IN THE CARDS?

Our experience with lateral relationships under conditions of stress has begun to form a definite pattern.

CRISIS

More often than any other triggering mechanism, the call for help comes to us when conflict between units gets to the crisis stage.

The points at issue are diverse:

1. A project needs to proceed from one unit to another but somehow the baton never gets passed without being dropped for a costly delay.

2. Unit A needs timely and accurate data from Unit B, but somehow the data is never quite accurate enough nor on time.

3. A joint action needs to be taken by two units for an important proposal effort to a new customer; but the joint action doesn't occur.

4. A work pattern that makes life comfortable for Unit A makes life miserable for Unit B.

5. Two units competing for the same resources (usually manpower, budget or equipment) are locked into mutually destructive interchanges that make effective decision making almost impossible for a coordinating executive.

The tune played in time of crises is usually some variation of a destructive blaming cycle which has at its base the theme: "It's their fault (A pointing to B), No! It's their fault (B pointing to A)."

Although there are an infinite number of subtle and not so subtle maneuvers, the blaming game is relatively simple to detect, but not so easy to redirect to productive outcomes.

The blaming cycle leads to unproductive stalemates which literally cry for action. The forces generated become emotional and intense. It is particularly painful to watch the kind of shock, panic and embarrassment that goes along with the experience of losing control. One of our clients said it all when he said, "I have a sickening feeling that I am finding out about all of this when it is too late."

The feeling of losing control leads to a great sense of urgency. Actions taken under conditions of great stress are often inappropriate to the actual situation leading to short-term relief at best. The basic conflicts tend to intensify and resurface in a new form at a later time.

WHAT MAKES FOR EFFECTIVE CONFRONTATION?
Proper Conditions*

There are two ingredients critical to productive confrontation:

1. Mutual positive motivation, and
2. Power parity between combatants

Mutual positive motivation as used here means that both parties want to resolve, better utilize or control the conflict rather than have it continue. If one party feels he stands to gain by letting the conflict continue, the use of confrontation strategies will very likely escalate the conflict.

The logic is simple. If I have all the cards and I know I will win; and I want to win; and I want to win in a way that puts the other guy down; then escalating the conflict becomes a rational approach in this kind of win/lose dynamic.

In this case, the consultant moves with great caution. To proceed with the substantive issues may very well lead to disaster. At this point, the need is to help the "underdog" get a clear picture of the situation as it is and to assist in the development of action plans designed to achieve motivation parity. Without motivation parity, collaboration under conditions of stress is unlikely.

In addition to motivation parity, effective confrontation requires that both parties have roughly equal power over each other and over the situation in which they find themselves. Power can be the right to accept or reject (quality control inspection) or the ability to give or withhold help (manufacturing's support or nonsupport of a sales group). Our experience tells us that if the power relationship is asymmetrical, it becomes mandatory for the underpowered principal to back off and take whatever actions are necessary to develop power parity.

*R. E. Walton, *Interpersonal Peacemaking: Confrontations and Third-Party Consultation.* Reading, Mass.: Addison-Wesley Publishing Co., 1969.

In gross terms, the person in a position of power can ask, "If I don't accede to your requests, what will it cost me?" If the answer is, "Essentially nothing," movement towards resolution is unlikely. When we speak of power and cost, we are using these terms in a very generic sense. For example, cost may simply be the guilt feelings we might experience when he becomes aware that he has been behaving in an exploitative manner. Thus, the costs and payoffs include the very subjective and psychological as well as the economic and organizational.

The Willingness to Confront and Make Sacrifices

To insure a successful confrontation, the principals need to work toward explicit differentiation, that is, they must own up to differences in orientation and style, personal and organizational desires, needs, anxieties about personal or organizational inadequacies, and finally, that which is uniquely individual, their personal feelings. The process is anything but simple. Failure is a real possibility, but the payoff for success is enormous. Another condition for success, and perhaps most difficult of all, is that both parties need to make concessions —even sacrifices. Make no mistake, there are real costs to collaboration. One cost may be diminished control over decisions in one's own bailiwick. Changing from a competitive to a collaborative stand means a sharing of power which is often seen as a loss by both parties. Another cost can be the loss or blurring of credit for success or failure which, for the manager looking toward the next move up, can produce real anxieties.

We will not argue against the logic of delegating authority and responsibility to a specific person or unit. Close collaboration between units, however, can make clear delegation difficult which will cause one or both units to experience dilution of identity or reward.

Finally, collaboration takes time. It takes time to confront and genuinely work through differences and misunderstandings. It takes time, patience, and a firm belief that the payoff, for all concerned, is in favor of collaboration—all of which takes a little doing in a business atmosphere that expects solutions by next Tuesday.

To point to the possible costs of collaboration is not to argue against efforts to achieve it. On the contrary, to bring all real costs clearly into focus is a precondition for success. In a culture that teaches its young men that competition is goodness, working together in a truly collaborative relationship can be somewhat strange. The transition is neither easy nor free. There are costs. The costs must be examined openly and matched against the probable payoffs before any lasting change can be expected.

PHASES IN THE PROCESS OF EFFECTIVE CONFRONTATION

The resolution of conflict, or more important, the constructive utilization of conflict generally goes through three phases:

1. Problem identification/third-party contract
2. Confrontation between persons involved
3. Establishing/bonding a working contract between combatants

We have found that knowledge of the three-phase process is important but not especially helpful. The real test comes in knowing when to move from one phase to the next.

If you move too fast through the problem identification phase, i.e., before you can see motivation/power parity, you will very likely be working the wrong problem. Getting the right answer to the wrong problem gets you nowhere.

If you begin to confront too early, before you have positive problem identification, again, you run the risk of working the wrong problem. Willingness to confront, to own up to differences and anxieties doesn't come easy. There are traps all along the way. Honest, sincere, intelligent managers will point you toward all kinds of problem areas: engineering, methods, systems, organizational problems—all of which may be very real, but curiously, none of them will have people in them. But experience breeds caution; organizations don't have conflict, only people have conflict. Unless the interpersonal issues are on the table, you are surely working the wrong problem.

As there are problems associated with confronting too early, there are also problems with confronting too late. If you wait too long before confronting, you lose some of the energy generated during the problem identification phase. Momentum lost is difficult to recover.

One way to delay confrontation is to engage in extensive studies at the data gathering stage. We will not argue against gathering data. Valid data is crucial. But the data gathering process can be a trap. Weeks can be spent on data gathering and analysis. This tends to make the exchange between parties an intellectual exercise and provides an easy escape from the need to focus on the human interactions that lie at the base of every conflict situation. Overemphasis on data analysis also leads to overinvestment in the historic "why" of the conflict versus the present "how" of dealing with each other within the here and now conflict setting.

There are also risks in moving to bonding and integrating activities before confrontation has been accomplished to the depth required. If there are important differences between the parties that have not been explored, the bonding may not hold.

Another dangerous trap, dangerous because it is so rational and so visibly productive, is to jump from problem identification to problem solution avoiding the confrontation phase altogether. Solutions to problems developed without confrontation can be excellent solutions. But any "solution" that does not include the ability to confront important differences is a short-term solution at best. The inability to confront differences will surely lead to recurring conflict.

Parties should move to the confrontation phase when they can clearly identify:

1. the important substantive issues
2. the existence of mutual positive motivation
3. the existence of a reasonable balance of power
4. psychological readiness to confront differences
5. and a belief, grounded in fact, that they control enough elements of the conflict to make the changes stick.

CONFRONTATION IS ABOUT CONFLICT—DON'T TRY TO SMOOTH IT OVER

We see the primary objective of confrontation sessions as owning up to differences and disagreements. Owning up requires differentiating oneself from the other party to the conflict and squarely facing the fact that the differences are factors in the conflict. Being open and direct about conflict is a difficult and uncomfortable process. All sorts of defenses come into play.

A much favored defense is the achievement of quick verbal agreement among the parties not to surface any interpersonal feelings or attitudes. We call this the "O.K. gang, let's stop all the name calling and get back to work" approach. As no one in the group is prepared to argue for "name calling," the group quickly begins to sort out all the substantive issues without giving vent to their feelings of frustration, disappointment, helplessness, anger, etc. This leads straight to fantasy land, and in fantasy land you *can* resolve conflict by changing the procedure manual.

Another defense is to reach quick agreement that the group cannot resolve the conflict without review by higher levels in the hierarchy. This is called the "we don't have the authority" approach. As long as they can convince themselves that they lack the needed authority, they do indeed lack the needed authority. This defense is perfect. Not only does it avoid dealing with real issues, it permits the parties to the conflict to assume a posture of righteous indignation: "We just can't get the higher levels in this outfit to move off dead center on anything!"

A third defense is classical in its logic and simplicity. After four minutes of confrontation, all parties to the conflict agree that the problem is now solved. This is the "quick cure on sudden flight to health" approach. Without diagnosis or prescription, the prognosis is all bad. It will take a crisis of major proportions before anyone would dare to take another look. Prognosis for another crisis is excellent.

We repeat. To be open and direct about conflict is a difficult and uncomfortable process. We would be completely insensitive to the plight of the parties involved to condemn these defenses as silly or irrational. However, we know from bitter experience that we will be completely ineffective if we go along. As third-party consultants, we really have no choice. Clearly, "resolutions" sired by defense mechanisms are unstable. We must identify and resist these defenses and point all our energies to the goal of bringing the parties to the point of looking at the real issues between real people in the here and now.

BONDING—DEVELOPING A STABLE PEACE

Let's assume that the substantive issues have been identified, that we have achieved motivation and power parity, differentiation has been achieved and differences have been explored. We are now ready for a transition to the bonding phase.

The transition involves a judgment on the part of the third party that it is time to ease out of confrontation and encourage movement toward bonding. Readiness for bonding can be identified in a number of ways:

1. *Group pressure to develop solutions.* As the parties work through the confrontation phase there is a point where the group begins to discuss solutions and press for future plans.

2. *Recognition that critical issues have been explored.* There is recognition that critical issues have been identified, explored to the depth required and that mutual understanding has been achieved.

3. *There is visible symmetry in the parties' perception of:*
   a) the injustice each has endured in the relationship
   b) the motivation/power balance
   c) the competency and the kind of contributions each has to offer
   d) the interdependence or the need each has for the other.

If any of these elements are strongly out of balance, it will undermine the incentive to work toward a negotiated settlement.

INJUSTICE

As long as one party feels it has suffered more than the other, there will be difficulties in working toward a balanced settlement. This may force the consultant to focus on the perceived injustice, help the party to a better bargaining position and work to decrease the "go for total victory" stance of the other combatant.

BALANCE OF POWER

The actual and perceived power balance must be roughly equal for the parties to work towards an effective settlement. If A and B believe that A has all the power, then A may not feel a strong enough need to truly collaborate with B, and B will not trust A to do so. A peaceful settlement involves some sacrifice on both sides. If no sacrifice is required, there would have been no conflict in the first place. It is unrealistic to expect people to give up something they want and feel they need unless they (a) are forced to, or (b) have high trust in the other party. Unbalanced power means unbalanced sacrifice and this leads to unstable agreements. In this case, the consultant must work to build the weapons and the perceived potency of the low power group. When both parties see power parity, effective integration becomes a possibility.

COMPETENCY AND INTERDEPENDENCE

For A and B to generate the energy needed to work through a conflict, give and receive concessions and commit to a collaborative approach, they must feel dependent upon each other.

This requires A and B to value each other's competence and contribution. If A has no respect for B's competence, then A has little incentive to enter an agreement with B. If this is the case, then the consultant has to test A's perception and evaluation of B. This might involve encouraging B to sell his ware more aggressively or it might involve the establishment of measurable standards for A to judge B on over a given time period. If A's evaluation of B does not change, then finding a solution to the conflict is made much more difficult.

During the bonding and working contract stages, the groups (or individuals) tend to take on a different mood and outlook. Typically there is a great release of tension, moves to reconciliation, an improved quality of listening, an increased understanding and acceptance of the other's position and a certain interpersonal closeness. The time orientation shifts from a concentration on past events to a rich mixture of here and now with future expectations.

As the parties complete their bonding and truce making, the focus very rapidly switches to a discussion of future expectations. This is what we have termed the working contract stage and it is the time for the consultant to become very active in testing the degree of resolution or the mutual acceptability of the bargained contract.

If there is a high degree of resolution on both the substantive and emotional issues,

genuine problem solving and collaboration can take place. If this is the case, it will be clear that the principals are operating within a context of shared goals, feelings of trust, respect and confidence in each other's competence. During the beginning of this stage, there will be some increase in the tension level, but this will mostly be connected with uncertainty about the effectiveness of joint decisions. There will be an informality and tentativeness about the plans being laid, but commitment to the plans will be mutually high and there will be strong indications of extensive interchange and joint decision making going into the future.

The essential role of the consultant here is to enjoy the peace and harmony if he is satisfied that there is sufficient and genuine resolution of the emotional and substantive issues. However, the picture just painted is rare indeed and the consultant is more likely to find himself dealing with partially unresolved conflicts and expectations of their recurrence.

When resolution is not complete and/or recurring conflict is expected, the parties will wish to impose considerable control and structure on future relationships and events. Anxiety over violation of understandings and agreements will be the best tipoff on the extent of resolution and satisfaction with the working agreement. There will also be many recurrences of confrontation. These confrontations will sometimes be on previously unsurfaced conflicts or they will be the last rounds of semicompleted fights. The frequency of these conflicts will increase immediately prior to closure on commitment to future actions. The consultant's role here is as it was during the confrontation stage except he is concentrating on helping the clients be explicit and direct about reciprocal demands for future behavior, i.e., "What behavior I want that I'm not getting; what I'm getting that I don't want." He is also helping the participants frame these demands so that they will be very operational, behavioral, and observable. If, because of the extent of conflict left, there is need for considerable control, the consultant can suggest contingency plans to deal with violation of agreements, i.e., if one party does not deliver, the cost to him will be defined in advance.

Finally, under either case, resolution or contracted mutual control, the third party can suggest future meetings designed for decision making, bargaining, conflict resolution, relationship building, etc.

SHOULD THE PRINCIPALS BARGAIN OR PROBLEM SOLVE?

In the lateral interfaces in which we have worked, substantive disagreements have been the first order issue with negative attitudes and feelings emerging as an outcome. The emotions then feed back into the substantive conflict. Emotional issues can become serious blocks to working out lateral interunit conflicts. However, working through emotional issues will not lead to interunit harmony. From our experience, recurring conflict between units is to be expected, for it stems from realistic understandings of differences in goals, roles, and reward structures.*

MIXED-MOTIVE CONSULTATION

Although we have had experiences with a few cases where something close to pure collaborative and integrative behaviors were appropriate and where emotional blockages were the first order problem, the large majority of the cases have actually been "mixed-motive" situations. In these settings the participants are faced with a confusing intermingling of shared and disparate goals, role conflicts and countervailing cues in the reward structure. These are legitimate incentives to compete.

---

*P. R. Lawrence and J. W. Lorsch, *Organization and Environment,* Boston: Harvard University, 1967.

The principals involved in these mixed-motive situations must be particularly skillful. They must have the behavioral flexibility to compete and collaborate with the same people within the same general context. They must develop decision making and "contract setting" processes which correspond with issues which require problem solving in one case and bargaining in another. They must take close and collaborative stances in one case and tough stances in another. It is critical that the principals have a considerable awareness of their attitudes about conflict vs. harmony. Without such awareness, ambiguous and complex situations are likely to lead them to fall back into patterns of behavior based on their historically constructed personal beliefs about the consequences of conflict. In less complex situations, it is easier to isolate emotional and substantive issues. In mixed-motive situations, it is exceedingly difficult to make this distinction.

IMPLICATIONS FOR CONSULTANT INTERVENTIONS

Cases in which there is considerable complexity and mixture of motives require certain attitudes and approaches to action on the part of the consultant. To begin with, the consultant with predispositions toward exclusively competitive or exclusively collaborative behaviors and processes for conflict resolution had better be very cautious in this setting. For example, a tendency to wish to "program" collaboration through his interventions will be particularly dysfunctional in the case described above.

This setting calls for a more protracted diagnosis and a real patience and persistence in developing a full differentiation of positions. One way to accomplish this is to produce a written report which explicates the forces leading to conflict and the countervailing forces leading to collaboration. This might come even before a face-to-face confrontation in such cases.

Another practice that appears useful in this case is extensive separate discussion with key principals to develop a fairly complete cognitive formation of the elements and dynamics of a mixed-motive situation. Training sessions using cases, etc., though more elaborate and usually more time consuming, might also be useful. The idea here is that extensive cognitive understanding will probably be important in coming to an effective processing of ideas. Please notice here the analytic and cognitive stance of the consultant as contrasted to a counseling stance related to more affective issues.

During confrontation sessions in these settings, the consultant has to ask many questions concerning practical outcomes of the various positions taken by the principals and has to be more tentative than usual in making interpretive remarks about the principals' behavior.

Because of the complexity of these situations, it is important that the consultant join in the planning and structuring of meeting formats and information exchange processes. This activity can help set expectations about what the ''game'' is—peace or war—and also can serve to limit the forms of fight tactics employed. These interventions help reduce the extent to which one principal feels betrayed or entrapped by the other and they also tend to mitigate some especially destructive fight spirals.

Even though it might already be exceedingly obvious, we wish to emphasize our belief that the consultant must be able to range effectively between:

1. the cognitive, mediative, and problem solving work it takes to deal effectively with substantive conflict

2. the affective and conciliative work that is required to work through emotional conflicts.

We find that the mixed-motive situation taxes our cognitive consulting skills much more than other interunit difficulties.

INTERGROUP MYTHS CAN BE KILLED

There are cases, usually where the two parties have withdrawn a great emotional distance from one another, where simple stereotype reduction can bring about a great improvement in the working relationship.

In these cases the consultant helps the parties shed outworn legacies and misperceptions. Structural interventions with minor interpersonal work is often sufficient. What is important for the intervention strategy here is that parties get a jolt of significantly increased exposure, that they name the stereotypes, that they get a chance to really listen to each other, and that they get several opportunities to work together to discover the fact that there is differentiation around issues *within* groups, not merely between groups.

Blake's structural intervention is suited to looking at the sequence of interventions needed in these situations.

TWO ASSUMPTIONS ABOUT CONFLICT

We have attempted in this paper to describe some useful frameworks and guidelines for people working on lateral conflicts. Underlying our strategy for intervening are two assumptions about conflict that need to be made explicit.

First, we feel the parties in conflict are almost always acting with integrity and good intentions. It is the pursuit of enlightened self and organizational interest that brings them in conflict. Particularly managers who expose their troubles to a third party act out of great commitment to the organization's success. It is because of this commitment that they are willing to fight so hard for what they need and want.

Second, we assume that responsibility for the conflict rests equally on both parties. It is the action or nonaction of each party which fuels the fight. No matter how it looks on the surface, underneath there exists each party's significant contribution to the conflict. Our intervention is constantly aimed at achieving full expression of both sides' responsibility.

Despite the enormous literature of rewards, we still don't know all the ins and outs of systematically building organizations so that people are motivated toward "right" behavior. Lawler's monograph sums up a great deal about what has been learned from research on how organizations reward people. I have reproduced those charts which give clues to different ways of diagnosing reward systems.

For example, Table 1—Overview—gives four criteria which add to "quality of work life" and four which add to "organizational effectiveness." It provides a useful guide for discovering reward-system gaps in any organization.

Table 1.   Overview of Reward-System Requirements

Quality of Work Life

a. Reward level	A reward level high enough to satisfy the basic needs of individuals
b. External equity	Rewards equal to or greater than those in other organizations
c. Internal equity	A distribution of rewards that is seen as fair by members
d. Individuality	Provision of rewards that fit the needs of individuals

Organizational Effectiveness

a. Performance motivation	Important rewards perceived to be related to performance
b. Membership	High overall satisfaction, external equity, and higher reward level for better performers
c. Absenteeism	Important rewards related to actually coming to work (high job satisfaction)
d. Organization structure	Reward-distribution pattern and decision-making approach that fit the management style and organization structure

Edward E. Lawler, III, "Improving the Quality of Work Life: Reward Systems," from *Improving Life at Work: Behavioral Science Approaches to Organizational Change,* ed. J. Hackman and J. Suttle (p. 172). Copyright © 1977 by Goodyear Publishing Co. Reprinted by permission.

REWARD SYSTEMS—INFORMAL

The following diagram, also from Lawler, indicates how an informal reward system sanctions productive behavior when people mistrust management. It can be used as a diagnostic model of a situation very common in industry and also found in hospitals, schools, and social service and government agencies.

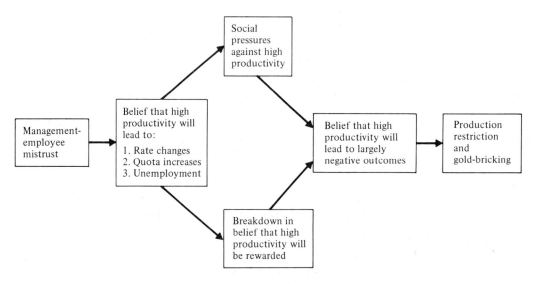

Fig. 2. Model of the Determinants of Production Restriction. (From *Improving Life at Work: Behavioral Science Approaches to Organizational Change,* **by J. Richard Hackman and J. Lloyd Suttle (p. 172), copyright © 1977 by Goodyear Publishing Company. Reprinted by permission.)**

REWARD SYSTEMS—OVERVIEW

Finally, here are Lawler's conclusions. Table 7 expresses his opinions as a result of having studied rewards for many years, about how good various reward practices are for furthering certain important criteria—the ones named in Table 1. The higher the number, the more likely that practice will lead to an *increase* or improvement over what usually happens in organizations. Cafeteria fringe benefits, for instance, will likely have a high impact on individuality and none at all on performance motivation. If cutting down absenteeism is a goal, skill-based evaluation plans seem like the best shot, though they will not have any affect on external equity. And so on.

OVERVIEW: REWARD SYSTEMS

Edward E. Lawler

If there is one message that the readers of the monograph should take away from it, it is that there are reward system practices which can contribute to a high quality of work life. True, there are no ideal practices, no universal "goods," but there are better and worse practices. Admittedly what is good and what is bad depends partially on organizational and environmental conditions, but these can be identified and dealt with. This monograph has provided a great deal of data to refute the two extreme positions with respect to the relationship between extrinsic rewards and quality of work life. On the one hand it seems clear that improving the quality of work life is not simply a matter of more extrinsic rewards as

Edward E. Lawler, III, "Improving the Quality of Work Life: Reward Systems," from *Improving Life at Work: Behavioral Science Approaches to Organizational Change,* ed. J. Hackman and J. Suttle (p. 172). Copyright © 1977 by Goodyear Publishing Co. Reprinted by permission.

some would have us believe. On the other hand it seems clear that reward systems cannot be ignored in efforts to produce a high quality of work life as others would have us believe.

Table 7 summarizes what has been said so far about the effect of various reward system practices and processes. Each of the practices which was discussed is rated on six dimensions. The first three are dimensions that contribute to a high quality of work life, and the next three are dimensions that contribute to organizational effectiveness. Since these are "new" practices, the question that concerns us is whether they represent improvements over traditional practice (e.g., secrecy versus openness). Thus, each practice is rated on five point scales running from 0 to 4. A 0 indicates that the practice leads to a negligible *increase* over what is usually present in organizations. A 4 indicates that the practice produces a large increase over what is usually

Table 7. Evaluation of Reward Practices

Reward Practice	External Equity	Internal Equity	Individuality	Performance Motivation	Membership	Absenteeism
Open promotion and job posting	1	3	0	2	2	1
Participation in promotion decisions	1	4	0	2	2	1
Cafeteria fringe benefits	2	0	4	0	2	1
Skill-based evaluation plans	0	2	3	2	2	2
All salary plans	2	0	1	0	1	0
Lump-sum salary increase plans	0	0	3	1	2	1
Performance pay plans	2	2	3	3	1	1
Scanlon plan	2	0	0	2	2	1
Variable-ratio plans	0	0	0	0	0	0
Open pay	1	2	0	2	0	1
Participation in decisions	1	2	0	2	1	1

present. A note of caution is in order in interpreting these figures. They should be viewed as averages across all situations. They obviously may not be applicable to any particular situation because of the many factors which condition their validity. Further, they represent the opinions of the author and are supported by little research.

The ratings suggest that improvements can be obtained both by changing the process and the mechanics of reward administration. The process changes that move to a more open and participative system are all *rated* favorably. The one practice that seems to offer little is variable ratio reward plans. All the others seem to have something to contribute to both a high quality of work life and organizational effectiveness. Since many of these practices are new it will be interesting to see if this optimistic conclusion will stand up under the research which needs to be done to test its validity.

Much contemporary thinking on this hardy perennial is being published in *Organizational Dynamics*, a quarterly journal, cited below. I've selected three exhibits to supplement the workbook text.

I—FRED FIEDLER

In Fig. 1, Fiedler organizes his extensive research on situations in which "task-motivated" and "relationship-motivated" leaders do best. The "performance" line at the left indicates the *group* or *organization's* performance. The solid and dotted lines indicate the *leader's* performance, based on task or relationship orientation.

   The figure also outlines eight sets of situations—some good for one orientation, some for the other. Relationship-oriented managers (solid line), Fiedler finds, do best when they have good relations with subordinates *and* the task structure and their position power is low. Also—surprisingly—they tend to do well under conditions of high task structure and strong position power *even when* they have poor subordinate relationships.

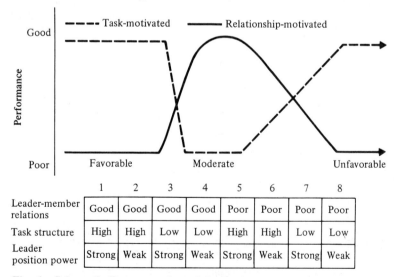

	1	2	3	4	5	6	7	8
Leader-member relations	Good	Good	Good	Good	Poor	Poor	Poor	Poor
Task structure	High	High	Low	Low	High	High	Low	Low
Leader position power	Strong	Weak	Strong	Weak	Strong	Weak	Strong	Weak

Fig. 1. Schematic Representation of the Performance of Relationship- and Task-Motivated Leaders in Different Situational Favorableness Conditions. (Reprinted by permission of the publisher from *Organizational Dynamics* 4, 3 (Winter 1976), © 1976 by AMACOM, a division of American Management Associations.)

By contrast, task-oriented managers (dotted line) do best when all three situation factors (relationships, task structure, position power) are *either* high (situations 1, 2, 3) or low (situation 8).

Fiedler contends, then, that training may *decrease* the effectiveness of a task-oriented leader who performs well under the unfavorable conditions of situation 8, because most training seeks to *increase* a leader's control and influence, which would make things *worse* for a task-oriented leader with poor relationship skills in a low-structure situation. On the other hand, a relationship-oriented leader with the same training might move in a way *more* favorable to his or her abilities and thus increase performance. Though this is contrary to "common sense," Fiedler cites evidence of studies in which the theory has held up.

II—CHRIS ARGYRIS

In his article "Leadership, Learning, and Changing the Status Quo," Argyris poses the issue in terms of two different sets of variables on which leaders base their actions. Model I—which has some of the flavor of Douglas McGregor's Theory X—reflects a closed system, high personal control, low emotionality, high defensiveness, etc. Model II—based on Argyris's key concepts of valid data, free choice, and commitment to act—is a model of open learning, collaboration, expressiveness, etc. Here are summaries of important dimensions in each model.

Model I

Governing Variables for Action	Action Strategies for the Individual and Toward His Environment	Consequences on the Individual and His Environment	Consequences on Learning	Effectiveness
Achieve purposes as the individual perceives them	Design and manage environment so that the individual is in control over the factors relevant to him	Individual is seen as defensive	Self-sealing	Decreased effectiveness
Maximize winning and minimize losing	Own and control task	Defensive interpersonal and group relationships	Single-loop learning	
Minimize eliciting negative feelings	Unilaterally protect self	Defensive norms	Little public testing of theories	
Be rational and minimize emotionality	Unilaterally protect others from being hurt	Low freedom of choice, internal commitment, and risk taking		

Governing Vari-ables for Action	Action Strategies for the Individual and Toward His Environment	Consequences on the Individual and His Environment	Consequences on Learning	Effectiveness
Valid information Free and informed choice Internal commit-ment to the choice and constant monitoring of the implementations	Situations or en-counters are de-signed to enable participants to originate actions and experience high personal causation Task is controlled jointly Protection of self is a joint enter-prise and oriented toward growth Protection of others is bilateral	Individual is ex-perienced as mini-mally defensive Minimally defen-sive interpersonal relations and group dynamics Learning-oriented norms High freedom of choice, internal commitment, and risk taking	Disprovable processes Double-loop learning Frequent public testing of theories	Increased effective-ness

Reprinted by permission of the publisher from *Organizational Dynamics* 2, 3 Winter 1976. © 1976 by AMACOM, a division of American Management Associations.

III—WARREN BENNIS

Bennis, author of many books on organization development and a former management professor at MIT, has been a university president for some time. In the excerpt below from "Leadership: A Beleaguered Species?" he distinguishes between "managing," an administrative concept, and "leading," which implies setting a course, tone, and direction and speaking for particular values.

LEADERSHIP: A BELEAGUERED SPECIES?

Warren Bennis

MANAGING, NOT LEADING

For the most part, the leaders are neither coping nor leading. One reason, I fear, is that many of us misconceive what leadership is all

Reprinted by permission of the publisher from *Organizational Dynamics* 5, 1, Summer 1976, © 1976 by AMACOM, a division of American Management Associations.

about. *Leading* does not mean *managing*: The difference between the two is crucial. I am ac-quainted with many institutions that are very well *managed* and very poorly *led*. They may excel in the ability to handle daily routines and yet never ask whether the particular routines should exist at all. To lead, so the dictionary tells us, is to go in advance of, to show the way, to influence or induce, to guide in direction, course, action, opinion. To manage means to bring about, to accomplish, to have charge of or responsibility for, to conduct. The difference may be summarized as activities of vision and judgment versus activities of efficiency.

In his decision making, the leader today is a multidirectional broker who must deal with four estates—his immediate management team, constituencies within his organization, forces outside his organization, and the media. While his decisions and actions affect the people of these four estates, their decisions and actions, too, affect him. The fact is that the concept of "movers and shakers"—a leadership elite that determines the major decisions—is an outdated notion. Leaders are as much the "shook" as the shakers. Whether the four estates force too many problems on the leader or whether the leader takes on too much in an attempt to prove himself, the result is what I call "Bennis's First Law of Pseudodynamics," which is that routine work will always drive out the innovational.

Securing the certainty of routine can be detected in the following example:

I noticed that frequently my most enthusiastic deputies were unwittingly keeping me from working any fundamental change in our institu-tion. My own moment of truth came toward the end of my first ten months as head of the uni-versity. It was one of those nights in the office. The clock was moving toward three in the morning, and still I was not through with the incredible mass of paper stacked before me. Bone weary and soul weary, I found myself muttering, "Either I can't manage this place or it is unmanageable." I reached for my daily ap-pointments calendar and ran my eye down each hour, each half-hour, each quarter-hour, to see where my time had gone that day, the day be-fore, the month before.

I had become the victim of an amorphous, unintentional conspiracy to prevent me from *doing anything whatever to change the univer-sity's status quo.* Even those of my associates who fully shared my hopes to set new goals and work toward creative change were uncon-sciously doing the most to ensure that I would never find the time to begin. People play the old army game. They do not want to take responsi-bility for or bear the consequences of decisions that they should properly make. Everybody dumps his "wet babies" (as old hands in the State Department call them) on my desk even though I have neither the diapers nor the infor-mation to take care of them.

I've not been able to find books or articles which speak to the issue as broadly as I would wish. The paper below discusses many of the broad implications of the concept. It's in the form of notes made by Peter Vaill as a sort of dialogue with himself and colleagues. It's full of provocative questions about what constitutes a "technology" and the conditions under which people may be helped or hampered by systems, procedures, methods, and so on.

NOTES ON TECHNOLOGY

Peter B. Vaill

1. The first thing to understand about technology is that it is not necessarily machinery; it need not be greasy and it need not clank and whir. A technology, if you think about the way we use the word in everyday language (rather than the way it was used in Erpi Classroom films—remember the Earth turning and the bad fidelity music coming out of the 16-mm Ampex projector at the back of the room?), is usually in reference to some *method* of doing something. And we often modify technology with words like "complex" or "expensive" or "advanced." We usually mean something identifiable, though—some relatively stable set of actions which, taken together, constitute the technology. We probably wouldn't use the word to talk about some brand new, spontaneous method that people did not yet agree on, or that had a highly personal component which prevented the method from ever being reduced to a set of rules and steps and procedures. We tend to call these more variable

Reproduced by special permission from *Social Change*, "Reflections on Technology," by Peter B. Vaill, Vol. 5, No. 4, pp. 3–7. Copyright NTL Institute 1975.

methods "arts" or "crafts." Another closely related word, "technique," is used when we want to emphasize the behavioral component of the method: so we talk about a carpenter's or a violinist's or a therapist's technique.

2. A technology is a standardized method for converting energy in a purposeful way from one form, an "input," to another form, "output." The process of conversion is often called the "transformation." The operation by one or more men of the technology *is* the transformation.

3. The reason a high degree of sensitivity to technology is important is that if you're trying to improve an organization's output, i.e., help it reach existing goals more effectively and efficiently, or help it reach new goals, you have to understand how its present transformation is going and why. And you can't understand the transformation—you may not even be able to *detect* the transformation—if you're not sensitive to technology.

4. I think it pays to keep the ideas of "transformation" and "technology" distinct, even though they're pretty close to the same thing. In the first place, in an organization's overall transformation, it may make use of multiple technologies. Think how many technologies are employed by an oil refinery, or a hospital, or a rock band. Each organization has a main mission and a basic transformation designed to carry out that main mission. I like to reserve the idea of transformation for that collection of activities which constitute the organization's pursuit of its main purposes. "Transformation" is for me a more "active" word than "technology," too. A technology can just exist, whereas "transformation" implies action and things happening. Also, all systems have transformations. Only some systems use technologies.

5. I use the term technology all through these notes. Anytime I talk about a technology, though, you could just as easily locate it in a specific organization pursuing a specific goal and you'd be talking about the transformation process of that organization.

6. Going back to (4) where I mentioned how many different technologies an organization uses, that is a point worth reflecting on a bit more. I suppose at a high level of abstraction one could say a hospital only uses one technology. That would be the collection of methods we have developed to heal disease and repair damage to the body and the psyche. But such a high level of abstraction is hardly ever useful to the person who is consulting to one organization. The nooks and crannies of the operation are more important. It becomes crucial to see that therapeutic technologies are interacting with technologies for producing electric power, with technologies for admitting people, with technologies for managing hospital manpower, with technologies for determining costs, with technologies for allocating space, with technologies for evaluating outcomes, with technologies for planning, and so on through the full range of *activities* one would find in any hospital.

7. If you can't see how the technology of healing, which the hospital is mainly in business

to operate, is being affected—augmented, undercut, modulated, altered—by all these other technologies, you'll never understand why things are going the way they are, and the crucial interventions that need to be made to make the main technology work better will be missed.

8. There's another way to talk about this and that is at the level of the single person's activity. When you're interviewing someone, can you hear the technology they are describing to you? Can you hear it in their comments about "first I do this, and then I do that, and every week I have to check this, and annually I request funds to improve that . . ."? Can you hear this collection of methods as a holistically experienced technology for discharging one's responsibility? Initially, if you're not well acquainted with the organization, these accounts sound like a hodge podge of unrelated things. If one knew nothing of automobiles, a service station attendant describing what he does about gas and oil and windshields and brakes and mufflers, and how on some cars he pays special attention to one thing while on other cars he doesn't—all that would sound like a pretty jumbled list of unrelated actions. You have to have some kind of a Gestalt yourself on the automobile to understand everything he's telling you.

9. But note how you'd be missing a key thing about his job if you assumed that the car was the technology and his behavior toward it was just . . . behavior, not the operation of a "servicing technology." You might mistakenly think that his pure interpersonal relationship with the car owner was the crucial ingredient in organizational success and put him through a program of listening and interpersonal sensitivity, and *never realize* that everything you-the-trainer said to him about behaving effectively was going through a "technology filter" in his mind. He would be asking himself, "Can I use these techniques to operate my servicing technology in the way I know that it should be operated?" Is it any wonder that we trainers and change agents often seem a little irrelevant to the practitioner? We aren't talking to him about the behavior that he experiences as important, a lot of the time at least.

10. Another thing I've found about technology is that it is a royal road into questions of motivation, human potential, perception, attitudes, likes and dislikes, hangups and obsessions. People need something to talk *about*, even if what they're "really, really" feeling is something different. In this culture, people talk about technologies. Violinists talk about violins, which is o.k. Computer guys talk about computers, which is not o.k. because computers, as we all know, are cold and mechanistic and anyone who talks about them all the time is obviously out of touch with himself and his real needs and has retreated into a clean predictable world of neat circuits and equations. If you're trying as hard as you can not to understand a computer guy, such a set of assumptions about computers will guarantee you success. Engineers in general get put down by too many in the helping professions because we can't hear in their talk the feelings of awe, excitement, creativity, aspiration, frustration, and every other variety of human feeling that is there. It's not surprising that in many organizations, the people who are charged with the development of technologies for doing things get defensive. It's not right, somehow, for anyone to be in love with a technology. An accountant who sees his new cost system as a thing of beauty needs counseling badly.

11. And so we misunderstand a lot about people. If you're not interested in sailboats or harpsichords or the technologies that go with running long distances or the technologies that assist creativity, you will miss a lot of important stuff about me. And I'll bet you have your list, too, of things which, as we say, are important to you. Don't you think if I'm going to "help" you I should be reasonably in touch with and accepting of those things?

12. Herzberg comes in here. One way of interpreting what Job Enrichment is all about is to say it is an attempt to put people more in control of the technologies they are supposed to operate. What motivates a person is intrinsic to the operation of one or more sets of technologies.

13. You want to know how a person is feeling? What turns them on? What will get them out of a rut and moving again? Well, pay attention to the technologies that they get a kick out of operating and you'll have a pretty good clue. What do they like to DO?

14. That's o.k. for the inner directed ones, you may say, but what about people who don't seem to get a kick out of doing anything? My first answer to that one is that you may not have looked closely enough at their behavior. The person who doesn't appear to be turned on by anything may be operating a technology that is invisible to you. This culture is full of time managers, for example—people who make a project out of scheduling their time, being on time, allocating pieces of time to various activities. The kicks are not "in" the activity, but rather in performing it right on the button. Watch it, watch it—we've got diagnostic routines that label such people compulsive. Call 'em compulsive if you want to, but if you do you're going to miss what their time management TECHNOLOGIES mean to them. And you might miss an intervention that would help one of these time managers be more valuable to himself and the organization.

15. I only know one thing: the world is full of invisible technologies—routines, techniques, procedures which people have developed for achieving ends that are important to them. My personal hunch is that what we call "resistance to change" could be largely explained if we knew what personal technologies we were inadvertently trampling on as we try to get some person to change his behavior. I know a manager who estimated the level of activity of a day by eyeballing the thickness of a stack of cards on his secretary's desk. He had a personal calibration etched on his retina that told him whether it had been a busy day or a slack day. A new computer technology became available which would do away with the cards and transfer the data reported on those cards to magnetic tape. All the data would still be available. He would have his own terminal with a printout and a cathode ray display. He'd know not just at the end of the day, but all through the day as well, just how things were going. He resisted buying and installing the new systems for two years after the time his boss told him he ought to change over. I'll let you figure out why.

16. In talking this way about technology, I'm not leading up to advocating some comprehensive model or diagnostic strategy by which all the technologies that are operating in an organization can be analyzed together. I think that is too tall an order. The point is somewhat different. You are trying to understand why things are going as they are. You're trying to visualize the ways in which an organization can improve from its present level of operation. You need a way of thinking that helps you with these problems and that forms a foundation for the kinds of interventions in the system you may wish to make. The approach to technology that I am suggesting is a kind of activity analysis I suppose for it asks you to focus on what people are doing. But in saying that you should think of what they are doing as components of technologies that they are operating, I am adding a few more ideas:

a) That the operation of the technology has been learned—an investment has been made in it by the person or group.

b) That operating it has been incorporated into the person's way of thinking about himself, and/or the group's identity.

c) That operating the technology involves the person or group in certain key boundary relations with others in the organization, for no technology is totally autonomous. These relations involve exchanges of information, of materials, of people, of power. They are both feedback relations (I find out the meaning of something I did in the past) and feedforward relations (I find out the meaning of something I will do in the future).

d) That the technology is probably multifunctional: it gets organizational work done, but it gets personal and group work done too. It may do the former much better than the latter, or vice versa.

e) That there is no clearcut boundary between men and methods or men and machines. *There isn't a people system and a technical system.* There is an integrated "something" from the point of view of the people involved in it. A house is not a home—we all know that, but by the same token, any lathe is not the right lathe, any office layout is not the right layout, any car is not your car. This is an important point, and it is worth going into a little more because I think it involves a wholly different way of thinking about what an organization is, and what is involved in changing it.

17. In Organization Development, we tend to focus rather exclusively on human entities: individual persons, groups, intergroups, organizations, teams, temporary systems, transorganizational networks, etc. All of our language for talking about these entities goes heavy on the fact that they are populated by people, and light on the question of what else besides people is part of the system. We would look to the people to explain what is different between the Boston Symphony and the Philadelphia Orchestra, or what is different between the Celtics with Bill Russell and the Celtics without Bill Russell.

18. Is this quibbling . . . to say that part of the difference in the two orchestras derives from the halls they play in, the nature of their instruments, the preferred repertoire of each, the physical positioning of the instrumental sections? Some would even argue for their latitude and longitude. We can talk about those things in considerable detail. Do we not make a mistake if we either ignore them entirely, or treat them as separate and distinct from the behavioral stuff—the leadership of the conductors, the climate in the groups, the motivations and skill levels of the players?

19. Maybe you don't think it is quibbling to introduce such factors, but you do feel it's getting kind of mystical to talk about an organization as an "integrated something" in which the people processes and the technologies are not usefully separated. For that is what I am suggesting: that we have to find a way of talking about entities that does not draw some arbitrary boundary between all the elements of the system which have an internal temperature of 98.6 degrees and those which do not. You can draw that boundary of course, but what I am asserting is that to understand an organization for the purpose of changing it you are advised not to.

20. Take my favorite chair away and ask me to be comfortable. Hand me a new typewriter on which to type these notes and expect them to be the same. Put the Redskins on Astroturf to improve their quickness and cut your costs. Assure me that anyone can adapt to contact lenses. Notice how impoverished is our way of talking about the feelings of connectedness we develop with objects outside ourselves. We are stuck in a morass of subjectivism: "All I know is I've always shaved with a brush."

21. Remember, the technology is not the object. The technology is the method. The method is a behavioral event that integrates the neural/psychological properties of the man with the physical properties of the object. What else can behavior possibly be? I can walk in a way that misuses my shoes to the point where either they will wear out quickly or I will get blisters or both. I don't; I walk in a way that integrates, but I *could* walk in a way that disintegrates.

22. And so query: how often does it happen in an organization that men are forced or inadvertently thrown into disintegrative relations with physical objects, and then asked to operate that technology at a high level of efficiency and effectiveness? Well, it happens very often because our culture lacks a way of talking abut harmonious relations, probably because in the first instance it lacks a way of *valuing* harmonious relationships. As long as there is no valuing and no language to talk about the consequences, we will continue to be in the soup where men are asked to achieve goals that they can't reach with the equipment they have; or just about the time they get in sync with the equipment, someone changes it and provides no real support in the process of changeover.

23. This is probably an overstatement. The Detroit assembly line worker can stand around the pro shop for hours on a weekend fiddling with a new set of irons, trying to decide if they feel right. But he's not allowed to do that on the job. The result is that he's probably a better golfer—gets into a more integrative relationship with those clubs—than he is an assembly line worker. So its an overstatement to say there is no place in the culture where the fiddling and experimentation that is necessary for an integrative relationship is allowed. It's just that we don't permit much of it in formal organizations.

24. Where would one look for harmonious relations? They're all around if you know what you're looking for. That's what (15) is getting at—invisible technologies.

25. Marshall McLuhan has influenced my ideas about technology a great deal. When he says "the medium is the message" it is clear that he sees media as methods, as "extensions of man," which is the subtitle of *Understanding Media*. Pay attention, he is saying, to the ways men extend themselves for that's the key to understanding a culture and to understanding how it is changing and how it differs from other cultures.

26. McLuhan makes a great deal of the cultural transition we are going through from a visual/verbal society to a society which processes data through more channels than the visual and which relies more and more on nonverbal symbols. Whether he is right or wrong is not important to me in these notes. The thing to be learned from McLuhan is how to understand nonvisual media, and that ties into my comments above about invisible technologies.

27. The time management technology I referred to earlier is a relatively nonvisual one because so much of its operation resides in the invisible awareness of the person—his awareness of what time it is, of the passage of time, of whether he is "early" or "late." Sometimes the person's awareness of time and his time management routines become visible in his behavior, but that is usually only the tip of the iceberg. A good pro quarterback has to be a skillful time manager both in terms of the game clock and in the physical coordination we call "timing." The *effects* of his management of time (the output of his technology) are quite visible, but much of his real time management of time is invisible.

28. You have to know how to look at that pro quarterback to see him managing time. That is learned diagnostic behavior. In the organizational world, you rarely have an instant replay capability to go back over the behavior that just occurred to search for a more precise understanding of what happened. Query: what are the analogues to instant replay for an OD consultant?

29. Some years ago I had a theory about these integrative relationships with equipment—these "extensions of man which work well." My theory was that as equipment becomes more sophisticated, the *relation* of men to the equipment is simplified and thus the *technology* is simpler although the equipment component is more complex. A gun, for instance, is a simpler technology than a bow and arrow because the achievement of an effective interactive relation between man and machine is simpler. "Aiming" is simpler; "firing" is simpler; the output of the action (propelling an object toward a target) is simpler in execution and more reliably produced.

30. It seems to me that anywhere one looks in the modern world you can see this process of complication-of-the-object/simplification-of-the-man/object-relation going on. Here is a sample list:

Simpler Object *More Complex Man/* *Object Relation*	*More Complex Object* *Simpler Man/* *Object Relation*
Pencil	→ Manual typewriter
Manual (sic) typewriter	→ Electric typewriter
Electric typewriter	→ Programmable typewriter
Bicycle	→ Motorcycle
Hand beater	→ Mixmaster
Horse-drawn wagon	→ Auto
Spanish guitar	→ Electric guitar
Tepee	→ All-electric townhouse etc.

31. What I mean by the simplification of the relation between man and object in these examples is that the items in the right hand column depend less on the uniqueness of the person operating them than the corresponding items on the left. The right hand items *reduce* (but certainly do not eliminate) the need for the application of personal unique talents.

32. In McLuhan's language, the right hand items are relatively "hotter" media than the corresponding left hand items.

33. I am not sure this theory of mine stands up, but it was a train of thought triggered by the following comment of the philosopher Owen Barfield: "Penetration to the meaning of a thing or a process requires a participation of the knower in the known." Some people think this is pure mystical garbage, but I don't. I think it is directly relevant when we talk about alienation from work. We don't really mean alienation from *work*. We mean alienation from an *empty relation* between the self and the objects one uses to produce outputs.

34. Elsewhere in a paper called "Towards a Behavioral Description of High Performing Systems" I have theorized about "joint optimization," a term Professor Eric Trist uses to talk about harmonious, productive socio-technical systems—systems in which meaningful relations do exist between men and objects such that the output draws on and is expressive of these relations; such that the laws men must conform to and the laws that objects must conform to are not violated. Men are governed by psychobiological laws. Objects are governed by physical and biological laws. In the simplest case, how do you design a job for a man running a lathe that integrates the potentialities of both sets of laws? Good question.

35. I also mentioned in passing in the paper on High Performing Systems that we may be able to write down some "laws of joint optimization"—propositions about the man/object interface which permit us to understand *why* it is working well when it is, and what has gone wrong when the relation isn't working. In the field called Human Engineering we already have many such laws which have been developed as design guides for furniture, visual displays, and many other kinds of equipment. But these laws tend to treat man as only a biological entity rather than as a social-psychobiological entity. The assumption is that if man is put in an environment where he is physically comfortable, he will be psychologically comfortable. He won't; we know that now. One way of talking about OD is to say it attempts to help men get more psychologically comfortable at work by attempting to inject more intrinsic challenge into work and to facilitate social relationships which men find enjoyable and growthful.

36. But we aren't very close yet to the discovery of laws which underlie these efforts. We are still experimenting widely with techniques like team development, MBO, job enrichment, and so forth.

37. Some people think the laws can't ever be developed because there is too much complexity and variability among men, and there are too many different kinds of environments in which they try to function. But I think that's a failure of nerve on our part. Or else it's that we are too ambitious. We look for laws that apply to everything, whereas we might be smarter to look for laws that apply to defined populations of people in relatively defined environments. Why worry for the moment if the laws which govern the development of a winning basketball team seem to differ from the laws which govern excellence for a string quartet. Their technologies are different.

14 INTERVENTIONS

There are as many classification systems for interventions as there are bird guides. Unfortunately, most intervention typologies are too long, too comprehensive, and too controversial to be useful in the field. I have found list making a good way to reduce anxiety, but I am always subject to a kind of vertigo when faced with two- and three-dimensional charts which purport to outline what's available and when to use it.

The problem of most typologies is that they omit the key question: "Which *gap* is this intervention intended to close?" Moreover, although every intervention is good for something, none is good for everything, and some are not good responses to the diagnosis on which they are based. For example, it is an act of faith to enter into Management By Objectives (MBO) exercises, intending to influence how goals are set and measured, if a diagnosis shows considerable controversy over what the organization's major goals should be (one, though not the only, reason that MBO programs have not served government as well as industry).

It's a mistake to go into training workshops hoping to improve interpersonal skills in use between *particular* individuals and/or departments unless all agree to take and use the same training.

The two intervention schemes devised by French and Bell, which follow, have the virtue of simplicity. The first sorts by whether methods are task- or process-oriented and targets individuals or groups. The second classifies specific methodologies in terms of relationships among persons whose performance is to be improved. Keep in mind, however, that "improving effectiveness" is the goal of *every* intervention. In choosing any one, it helps to ask, "In what way will it deal with the most pressing blips on my radar screen? Which issues will, as a result, be postponed?"

OD INTERVENTIONS—AN OVERVIEW

Wendell L. French and Cecil H. Bell, Jr.

SOME CLASSIFICATION SCHEMATA FOR OD INTERVENTIONS

There are many possible ways to classify OD interventions. Several have already been given: the families of interventions represent one approach, and Bennis's types of interventions

Wendell L. French and Cecil H. Bell, Jr., *Organization Development: Behavioral Science Interventions for Organization Improvement,* © 1973, pp. 84–111. Adapted by permission of Prentice-Hall, Inc., Englewood Cliffs, New Jersey.

represent another approach. Our desire is to construct several classificatory schemata showing interventions from several perspectives. In this way, we can better accomplish our objective of examining OD from a kaleidoscopic rather than from a microscopic point of view.

One way to gain a perspective on OD interventions is to form a typology of interventions based on the following questions: (1) Is the intervention directed primarily toward individual learning, insight, and skill building or toward group learning? (2) Does the intervention focus

	Focus on the individual	Focus on the group
Focus on task issues	Role analysis technique Education: technical skills; also decision making, problem solving, goal setting, and planning Career planning Grid OD phase 1 (see also below) Possibly job enrichment and Management by Objectives (MBO)	Technostructural changes Survey feedback (see also below) Confrontation meeting Team-building sessions Intergroup activities Grid OD phases 2, 3 (see also below)
Focus on process issues	Life planning Process consultation with coaching and counseling of individuals Education: group dynamics, planned change Stranger T-groups Third party peacemaking Grid OD phase 1	Survey feedback Team-building sessions Intergroup activities Process consultation Family T-group Grid OD phases 2, 3

Task vs. process dimension

Fig. 9-1. OD Interventions Classified by Two Independent Dimensions: Individual-Group and Task-Process.

on *task* or *process* issues? (Task is what is being done; process is how it is accomplished, including how people are relating to each other and what processes and dynamics are occurring.) A four-quadrant typology constructed by using these two questions is shown in Figure 9–1.

This classification scheme presents one approximation of the categories of various interventions; it is difficult to pinpoint the interventions precisely because a single intervention may have the attributes of more than one of the quadrants. Interventions simply are not mutually exclusive; there is great overlap of emphasis and the activity will frequently focus on, say, task at one time and process at a later time. Generally, however, the interventions may be viewed as belonging predominantly in the quadrant in which they are placed. It is thus possible to see that the interventions do differ from each other in terms of major emphasis.

Another way to view interventions is to see them as *designed to improve the effectiveness of a given organization unit.* Given different organizational targets, what interventions are most commonly used to improve their effectiveness? This is shown in Figure 9–2. The elasticity of different interventions really becomes apparent in this figure, with many interventions being placed in several categories.

Examination of Figures 9–1 and 9–2 reveals redundancy and overlap in that specific interventions and activities appear in several classification categories. This may be confusing to the reader who is new to the area of organization development, but it nevertheless reflects the use to which various interventions are put. Perhaps a positive feature of the redundancy is that it suggests patterns among the interventions that the practitioner knows but that may not be readily apparent to the layman. Some of these patterns become more apparent in Figure 9–3.

Another conceptual scheme for categorizing the OD interventions rests on an attempt to

Target group	Types of interventions
Interventions designed to improve the effectiveness of **Individuals**	Life- and career-planning activities Role analysis technique Coaching and counseling T-group (sensitivity training) Education and training to increase skills, knowledge in the areas of technical task needs, relationship skills, process skills, decision making, problem solving, planning, goal setting skills Grid OD phase 1
Interventions designed to improve the effectiveness of **Dyads/Triads**	Process consultation Third-party peacemaking Grid OD phases 1, 2
Interventions designed to improve the effectiveness of **Teams & groups**	Team building — Task directed 　　　　　　 — Process directed Family T-group Survey feedback Process consultation Role analysis technique "Start-up" team-building activities Education in decision making, problem solving, planning, goal setting in group settings
Interventions designed to improve the effectiveness of **Intergroup relations**	Intergroup activities — Process directed 　　　　　　　　　 — Task directed Organizational mirroring (three or more groups) Technostructural interventions Process consultation Third-party peacemaking at group level Grid OD phase 3 Survey feedback
Interventions designed to improve the effectiveness of the **Total organization**	Technostructural activities Confrontation meetings Strategic planning activities Grid OD phases 4, 5, 6 Survey feedback

Fig. 9-2. Typology of OD Interventions Based on Target Groups.

determine the central, probable underlying causal mechanisms of the intervention, that is, the underlying dynamics of the intervention that probably are the cause of its efficacy. This scheme is more controversial: different authors might hypothesize different causal dynamics. This is due partly to the relative paucity of theory and research on interventions. But the practitioner chooses and categorizes interventions on the basis of assumed underlying dynamics of change and learning, and it might therefore be helpful to present a tentative classification scheme based on these mechanisms.

WHO GETS POWER AND HOW THEY HOLD ON TO IT: A STRATEGIC-CONTINGENCY MODEL OF POWER

Gerald R. Salancik and Jeffrey Pfeffer

There are as many views of organizational power as there are organizations and authors. One useful perspective that squares with my own biases is Salancik and Pfeffer's "contingency model." Power, in their framework, goes to organizations, units, and people who deal with problems important to the organizations's functioning. In the excerpts that follow, the authors sketch out this view, give some examples, and suggest possible diagnostic errors—"mistaking" a critical contingency simply for something you want to do, for example.

The model of power we advance is an elaboration of what has been called strategic-contingency theory, a view that sees power as something that accrues to organizational subunits (individuals, departments) that cope with critical organizational problems. Power is used by subunits, indeed, used by all who have it, to enhance their own survival through control of scarce critical resources, through the placement of allies in key positions, and through the definition of organizational problems and policies. Because of the processes by which power develops and is used, organizations become both more aligned and more misaligned with their environments. This contradiction is the most interesting aspect of organizational power, and one that makes administration one of the most precarious of occupations.

Excerpted by permission of the publisher from *Organizational Dynamics* **5**, 3, Winter 1977, © 1977 by AMACOM, a division of American Management Associations.

WHAT IS ORGANIZATIONAL POWER?

You can walk into most organizations and ask without fear of being misunderstood, "Which are the powerful groups or people in this organization?" Although many organizational informants may be *unwilling* to tell you, it is unlikely they will be *unable* to tell you. Most people do not require explicit definitions to know what power is.

Power is simply the ability to get things done the way one wants them to be done. For a manager who wants an increased budget to launch a project that he thinks is important, his power is measured by his ability to get that budget. For an executive vice-president who wants to be chairman, his power is evidenced by his advancement toward his goal.

People in organizations not only know what you are talking about when you ask who is influential but they are likely to agree with one another to an amazing extent. Recently, we had a chance to observe this in a regional office of an insurance company. The office had 21 department managers; we asked ten of these managers to rank all 21 according to the influence each one had in the organization. Despite the fact that ranking 21 things is a difficult task, the managers sat down and began arranging the names of their colleagues and themselves in a column. Only one person bothered to ask, "What do you mean by influence?" When told "power," he responded, "Oh," and went on. We compared the rankings of all ten managers and found virtually no disagreement among them in the managers ranked among the top five or the bottom five. Differences in the rankings came from department heads claiming more influence for themselves than their colleagues attributed to them.

Such agreement on those who have influence, and those who do not, was not unique to this insurance company. So far we have studied over 20 very different organizations —universities, research firms, factories, banks, retailers, to name a few. In each one we found individuals able to rate themselves and their peers on a scale of influence or power. We have done this both for specific decisions and for general impact on organizational policies. Their agreement was unusually high, which suggests that distributions of influence exist well enough in everyone's mind to be referred to with ease—and we assume with accuracy.

WHERE DOES ORGANIZATIONAL POWER COME FROM?

Earlier we stated that power helps organizations become aligned with their realities. This hopeful prospect follows from what we have dubbed the strategic-contingencies theory of organizational power. Briefly, those subunits most able to cope with the organization's critical problems and uncertainties acquire power. In its simplest form, the strategic-contingencies theory implies that when an organization faces a number of lawsuits that threaten its existence, the legal department will gain power and influence over organizational decisions. Some-

how other organizational interest groups will recognize its critical importance and confer upon it a status and power never before enjoyed. This influence may extend beyond handling legal matters and into decisions about product design, advertising production, and so on. Such extensions undoubtedly would be accompanied by appropriate, or acceptable, verbal justifications. In time, the head of the legal department may become the head of the corporation, just as in times past the vice-president for marketing had become the president when market shares were a worrisome problem and, before him, the chief engineer, who had made the production line run as smooth as silk.

Stated in this way, the strategic-contingencies theory of power paints an appealing picture of power. To the extent that power is determined by the critical uncertainties and problems facing the organization and, in turn, influences decisions in the organization, the organization is aligned with the realities it faces. In short, power facilitates the organization's adaptation to its environment—or its problems.

We can cite many illustrations of how influence derives from a subunits's ability to deal with critical contingencies. Michael Crozier described a French cigarette factory in which the maintenance engineers had a considerable say in the plantwide operation. After some probing he discovered that the group possessed the solution to one of the major problems faced by the company, that of troubleshooting the elaborate, expensive, and irascible automated machines that kept breaking down and dumbfounding everyone else. It was the one problem that the plant manager could in no way control.

The production workers, while troublesome from time to time, created no insurmountable problems; the manager could reasonably predict their absenteeism or replace them when necessary. Production scheduling was something he could deal with since, by watching inventories and sales, the demand for cigarettes was known long in advance. Changes in demand could be accommodated by slowing down or speeding up the line. Supplies of tobacco and paper were also easily dealt with through stockpiles and advance orders.

The one thing that management could neither control nor accommodate to, however, was the seemingly happenstance breakdowns. And the foremen couldn't instruct the workers what to do when emergencies developed since the maintenance department kept its records of problems and solutions locked up in a cabinet or in its members' heads. The breakdowns were, in truth, a critical source of uncertainty for the organization, and the maintenance engineers were the only ones who could cope with the problem.

The engineers' strategic role in coping with breakdowns afforded them a considerable say on plant decisions. Schedules and production quotas were set in consultation with them. And the plant manager, while formally their boss, accepted their decisions about personnel in their operation. His submission was to his credit, for without their cooperation he would have had an even more difficult time in running the plant. . . .

POWER SHARING IN ORGANIZATIONS

Power is shared in organizations; and it is shared out of necessity more than out of concern for principles of organizational development or participatory democracy. Power is shared because no one person controls all the desired activities in the organization. While the factory owner may hire people to operate his noisy machines, once hired they have some control over the use of the machinery. And thus they have power over him in the same way he has power over them. Who has more power over whom is a mooter point than that of recognizing the inherent nature of organizing as a sharing of power.

Let's expand on the concept that power derives from the activities desired in an organization. A major way of managing influence in organizations is through the designation of activities. In a bank we studied, we saw this principle in action. This bank was planning to install a computer system for routine credit evaluation. The bank, rather progressive-minded, was concerned that the change would have adverse effects on employees and therefore surveyed their attitudes.

The principal opposition to the new system came, interestingly, not from the employees who performed the routine credit checks, some of whom would be relocated because of the change, but from the manager of the credit department. His reason was quite simple. The manager's primary function was to give official approval to the applications, catch any employee mistakes before giving approval, and arbitrate any difficulties the clerks had in deciding what to do. As a consequence of his role, others in the organization, including his superiors, subordinates, and colleagues, attributed considerable importance to him. He, in turn, for example, could point to the low proportion of credit approvals, compared with other financial institutions, that resulted in bad debts. Now, to his mind, a wretched machine threatened to transfer his role to a computer programmer, a man who knew nothing of finance and who, in addition, had ten years less seniority. The credit manager eventually quit for a position at a smaller firm with lower pay, but one in which he would have more influence than his redefined job would have left him with.

Because power derives from activities rather than individuals, an individual's or subgroup's power is never absolute and derives ultimately from the context of the situation. The amount of the power an individual has at any one time depends, not only on the activities he or she controls, but also on the existence of other persons or means by which the activities can be achieved and on those who determine what ends are desired and, hence, on what activities are desired and critical for the organization. One's own power always depends on other people for these two reasons. Other people, or groups or organizations, can determine the definition of what is a critical contingency for the organization and can also undercut the uniqueness of the individual's personal contribution to the critical contingencies of the organization. . . .

THE CRITICAL CONTINGENCIES

The critical contingencies facing most organizations derive from the environmental context within which they operate. This determines the available needed resources and thus determines the problems to be dealt with. That power organizes around handling these problems suggests an important mechanism by which organizations keep in tune with their external environments. The strategic-contingencies model implies that subunits that contribute to the critical resources of the organization will gain influence in the organization. Their influence presumably is then used to bend the organization's activities to the contingencies that determine its resources. This idea may strike one as obvious. But its obviousness in no way diminishes its importance. Indeed, despite its obviousness, it escapes the notice of many organizational analysts and managers, who all too frequently think of the organization in terms of a descending pyramid, in which all the departments in one tier hold equal power and status. This presumption denies the reality that departments differ in the contributions they are believed to make to the overall organization's resources, as well as to the fact that some are more equal than others. . . .

CHANGING CONTINGENCIES AND ERODING POWER BASES

The critical contingencies facing the organization may change. When they do, it is reasonable to expect that the power of individuals and subgroups will change in turn. At times the shift can be swift and shattering, as it was recently for powerholders in New York City. A few years ago it was believed that David Rockefeller was one of the ten most powerful people in the city, as tallied by *New York* magazine, which annually sniffs out power for the delectation of its readers. But that was before it was revealed that the city was in financial trouble, before Rockefeller's Chase Manhattan Bank lost some of its own financial luster, and before brother Nelson lost some of his political influence in Washington. Obviously David Rockefeller was no longer as well positioned to help bail the city out. Another loser was an attorney with considerable personal connections to the political and religious leaders of the city. His talents were no longer in much demand. The persons with more influence were the bankers and union pension fund executors who fed money to the city; community leaders who represent blacks and Spanish-Americans, in contrast, witnessed the erosion of their power bases.

One implication of the idea that power shifts with changes in organizational environments is that the dominant coalition will tend to be that group that is most appropriate for the organization's environment, as also will the leaders of an organization. One can observe this historically in the top executives of industrial firms in the United States. Up until the early 1950s, many top corporations were headed by former production line managers or engineers who gained prominence because of their abilities to cope with the problems of production. Their success, however, only spelled their demise. As production became routinized and mechanized, the problem of most firms became one of selling all those goods they so efficiently produced. Marketing executives were more frequently found in corporate boardrooms. Success outdid itself again, for keeping markets and production steady and stable requires the kind of control that can only come from acquiring competitors and suppliers or the invention of more and more appealing products—ventures that typically require enormous amounts of capital. During the 1960s, financial executives assumed the seats of power. And they, too, will give way to others. Edging over the horizon are legal experts, as regulation and antitrust suits are becoming more and more frequent in the 1970s, suits that had their beginnings in the success of the expansion generated by prior executives. The more distant future, which is likely to be dominated by multinational corporations, may see former secretaries of state and their minions increasingly serving as corporate figureheads. . . .

MISTAKING CRITICAL CONTINGENCIES

One thing that allows subunits to retain their power is their ability to name their functions as critical to the organization when they may not be. Consider again our discussion of power in the university. One might wonder why the most critical tasks were defined as graduate education and scholarly research, the effect of which was to lend power to those who brought in grants and contracts. Why not something else? The reason is that the more powerful departments argued for those criteria and won their case, partly because they were more powerful.

In another analysis of this university, we found that all departments advocate self-serving criteria for budget allocation. Thus a department with large undergraduate enrollments argued that enrollments should determine budget allocations, a department with a strong national reputation saw prestige as the most reasonable basis for distributing funds, and so on. We further found that advocating such self-serving criteria actually benefited a department's budget allotments but, also, it paid off more for departments that were already powerful.

Organizational needs are consistent with a current distribution of power also because of a human tendency to categorize problems in familiar ways. An accountant sees problems with organizational performance as cost accountancy problems or inventory flow problems. A sales manager sees them as problems with markets, promotional strategies, or just unaggressive salespeople. But what is the truth? Since it does not automatically announce itself, it is likely that those with prior credibility, or those with power, will be favored as the enlightened. This bias, while not intentionally self-serving, further concentrates power among those who already possess it, independent of changes in the organization's context. . . .

16 COMPARING ORGANIZATIONS

==

Relatively little has been written about the *differences* to be considered in diagnosing organizations. Important differences might include:

1. environments
2. task orientations
3. goals
4. functions
5. degrees of structure needed

Each of these factors will affect each of the boxes, often in ways not well understood or completely predictable. The following article elaborates on these issues by contrasting academic medical centers with industrial firms. The general analysis would also apply to colleges and universities.

WHY ORGANIZATION DEVELOPMENT HASN'T WORKED (SO FAR) IN MEDICAL CENTERS

Marvin R. Weisbord

Understanding and helping improve medical organizations has become a passion for many behavioral scientists, including me. It is a passion matched only by that of health administrators to have their organizations improved. On my pessimistic days, our mutual frenzy reminds me of a story the late Saul Alinsky liked to tell. It concerns a bitch in heat parading up and down behind a screen door, while a neighbor's hound scratches to get at her.

"That's a laugh," says the bitch's owner. "Your hound's fixed. Even if he got in here he couldn't *do* anything."

Reprinted by permission from *Health Care Management Review* 1, 2 (Spring 1976). Copyright © 1976 Aspen Systems Corporation. All rights reserved.

"You don't understand," replied the neighbor "My dog's a consultant!"

Though many of us have pawed through the screen door, we find medical centers peculiarly impregnable, at least with our present equipment. On the one hand there's a vast descriptive literature of health organizations.[1] On the other, there exists little practical data on how to use this knowledge effectively. In my interviews with health center managers, I note a mounting despair over trying to organize what seems, increasingly, a bottomless pit.

If those who are not "hands on" providers of health services wish to have useful impact on the functioning of health delivery organizations, we must start by owning up that certain management methods, no matter how valued in other settings, are—by any standard of scientific objectivity—not working very well in medicine.

In this article, I want to provide, from the standpoint of a student of organizational behavior, a new diagnosis of what ails medical centers. Using this diagnosis, I will explain why one elixir for which I have had high hopes—organization development (OD)—is, for now, not even a good placebo. My central thesis is that medical centers, unlike industrial firms, have coordination problems not subject to rationalization even by "state-of-the-art" administrative practice. I think advocates of other management technologies will find this explanation relevant too.

I see three major reasons OD works better for industry than medicine:

1. Medical centers have few of the formal characteristics of industrial firms, where OD, like all management science, was first recognized, tested, and developed.[2]

2. Physicians and scientists are socialized to a form of rational, autonomous, specialized, expert behavior, which is antithetical to the organization of any but the most narrow individualized pursuits.[3]

3. Medical centers, therefore, require three different social systems, not one, as in industry. The links among the *task* system which administrators manage, the *identity* system which undergirds professional status, and the *governance* system, which sets standards, are extremely tenuous.

Therefore, it is hard to achieve a "good fit" between individual and organization. Medical centers represent what the late psychologist A. H. Maslow called "low synergy institutions"[4]—that is, while the systems are extremely interdependent, people do not act that way. This is the opposite of business, where productivity improves measurably when people learn to work together better.

OD is hard to use in low-synergy situations, because it is based on an assumption not widely shared in our culture: that it is possible, through trial and error, to discover *organizational* procedures that enhance both productivity and self-esteem. In industry, people recognize a common stake in this discovery, even while skeptical of its worth. In medicine, professionals believe in their bones that procedures an organization needs for its survival will be inimical to theirs.

We need a new, non-industrial model for what constitutes a good individual/organization fit in medical centers. Industry has not been a very good teacher, for professionals experience "business-like" methods as threatening to their self-esteem. Why should coordination be more threatening in medical centers than in business firms?

OD IS INDUSTRY SPECIFIC

Nearly all organization development theory and research derive from industry, which sponsored the seminal work of Argyris, Beckhard, Blake and Mouton, Herzberg, Lawrence and Lorsch, Likert, McGregor, Trist and many others. Firms like Esso Standard Oil, Texas Instruments, TRW Systems Group, Union Carbide provided clinical test sites for theories about the relationships between human satisfaction and productivity.[5] This is probably because OD is intended to help organizations balance, better than they often do, the need for structural constraints and the need for creativity. Such constraints exist to a greater degree in industrial organizations than elsewhere.

Structure is important because it is the creation of rational, systematic relationships which constitute the essence of an "organization." Organizations make it possible for people to do things they value and cannot do alone. But, no matter how innovative, organizations perform if—and only if—they achieve a balance among four key structural features, which restrain individual behavior:

• Task interdependence

- Concrete goals
- Performance measures
- Formal authority.

The co-existence of these structural constraints makes an organization sensitive to improvement through focus on its informal system, for people either carry out or subvert goals through their normative behavior.

Historically, industrial firms were structured following the theories of church and military thinkers. To them, authority, goals, and interdependence were central; today, bureaucracy as a structural mode pervades our society. In the 19th Century technologies and performance measures made possible the marriage of bureaucracy to production. Management, as a profession, was born.

Bureaucracy's strength lies in certainty and order. However, its practices, like many industrial products, do not age well. In no time managers discovered that bureaucratic processes have built into them an intractable rigidity. This works against optimal performance. More, at some point the constraints of order outweigh the benefits, restricting personal judgment so that output suffers —and along with it people's self-esteem and morale.

In industry, behavioral scientists using OD provide exactly the right medicine. We introduce counterbureaucratic values and practices, making it legitimate to do things not a part of everyday work. This includes examining group problem solving, how people express and act on feelings ("personal style"), norms, policies, ways of handling conflict—anything that might conceivably impact on the performance of work.

Organizational development methods go under names like "teambuilding," process consultation, intergroup problem solving, survey, data feedback. All of them help people understand, express, learn about, and free themselves from their more irrational constraints. They can then achieve a better balance among goals, authority, task inter-

dependence, and measures. Having done it together, they are more likely to feel committed to making things work, and given recognition for their efforts, their morale improves.

HEALTH CARE PROFESSIONALS ARE SOCIALIZED DIFFERENTLY

Science-based professional work differs markedly from product-based work. Health professionals learn a rigorous scientific discipline as the "content" of their training. The "process"—not explicit—inculcates a value for autonomous decision-making, personal achievement, and the importance of improving their *own* performance, rather than that of any institution.

In consequence physicians identify much less with a specific institution and more with the culture of medical science. This constitutes a set of values, skills, and knowledge quite independent of any work setting. The rewards of major significance to them—respect, reputation—may come more from this larger arena than from their institutional affiliation.

MEDICAL CENTERS: THREE SYSTEMS, NOT ONE

Both health care and industry require financing; both have customers; each has inputs and outputs, environmental constraints, physical facilities, technologies, employment contracts, managers. At the same time, much important medical center activity does not seem connected to its administrative machinery.

Professionals are enmeshed in the three social systems—Task, Identity, Governance— that pull and tug at each other. Health administrators operate the least influential of the three, quite the reverse of the situation of the industrial manager.

The Task system refers to a specific work organization, which seeks to coordinate three tasks: patient care, education and research. The Identity system refers to the professional development, or career track, in medical science, on which the status and self-esteem of health professionals depends. The Governance system is the network of committees, boards, and agencies, within and without task systems, which set standards for the profession.

Each system has its own ground rules and membership requirements. Each is necessary to the others. Health center professionals belong to all three. Yet the Task system is, in many ways, at odds with the Identity and Governance systems, and vice versa.

THE TASK SYSTEM

In industry the Task system is called "management". In health care it's called "administration". I use the generic term Task system to mean either one.

Health care professionals do one or more of four tasks requiring coordination: (1) Patient Care; (2) Education; (3) Research; (4) Administration. Each task is independently valuable to a reasonably complete health care system. These tasks constitute the work of medical centers, hospitals, clinics, and health maintenance organizations.

Patient care, education, and research superficially resemble business functions like production, marketing, or research and development. These superficial similarities encourage the use of industry-based technologies, like program planning and budgeting, management by objectives, and organizational development.

These create an illusion of rationality that disappears quickly when scrutinized, for there are radical discrepancies between industrial and medical Task systems. They lack commonality *exactly* on the four features that make industry such a fertile laboratory for OD.

In industry, management attempts to obtain organizational support for a common definition of interdependence, authority, goals, and measures, while avoiding financial loss. But as Figure 1 shows, in complex medical centers goals tend to be abstract, authority diffuse, interdependence low, measures few and controversial. Since there are three systems, not one, it is extremely hard to achieve organizational support, and even harder to avoid financial loss. Let us discuss each of the four features in turn.

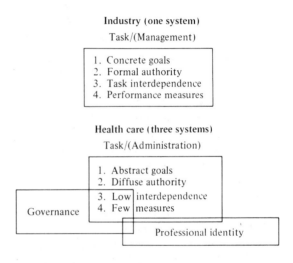

Overlapping Identity and Governance systems function to thwart the application of goals, authority, interdependence, and measures in the Task system.

Fig. 1. Differences Between Industrial and Health Care Systems.

Task Interdependence

Industrial managers each do one task at a time in an enterprise of any size. A person works in production, marketing, sales, or finance, for example, and while a manager might build a sequential career in various functions, none would conceive of trying to perform these tasks all at once. Nevertheless, the functions are interdependent. The organization requires all to be performed well if it is to be successful. This mixing requirement—called "task interdependency"—rests on two concepts: the differentiation of function, and the integration of functions towards specific goals.

Lawrence and Lorsch demonstrated empirically how these two concepts complement each other in high-performing business.[6] They showed that people need different social/emotional orientations for different tasks. Differences that make a difference include time horizon—how fast the feedback?; interpersonal relations—how important?; goals—how precise?; and so on. Such matters seem to vary with environmental complexity and rate of change. Successful managers recognize this.

Of course these differences, however necessary, create conflict because different groups in the organization have necessarily different goals. The more productive managers were found not only to differentiate skillfully, but also to integrate or manage effectively conflict between diverse functions. Examples of integrative mechanisms, as opposed to people, include information, cost control, budgeting, and planning systems.

Now, consider problems of differentiation and integration in health centers. First, health centers are differentiated primarily by specialty. Each specialty runs its own little "business" called a service. Within each service, several tasks may go on simultaneously: patient care administration, teaching and research. Moreover, these tasks are *all* performed by people wearing multiple hats. Few health center professionals do only one of the major tasks, for to do a single task seriously hampers status and mobility in the other two systems. The most complex example is a one-person entity called a "department chairman" in a medical school, whose title masks the fact he is often not only doing all four major tasks, but managing many other people who also do two, three, or four things at once.

To make sense out of this reality, Lawrence, Charns, and I found we had to turn Lawrence—Lorsch theory upside down.[7]

Imagine the organizational confusion when task differences exist not only between functions, but also with each individual. As Figure 2 demonstrates, coordination is often left to the whim of the individual.

How can one manage such a system? With difficulty. The reason it runs at all is because individuals are so adept at differentiating and integrating what they do. Health professionals identify much more task conflict "in general" than they do "in my own work."[8]

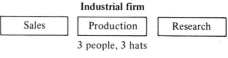

Industrial firm

| Sales | Production | Research |

3 people, 3 hats

Problem: Integration. What's the strategic goal?

Medical center

| Patient care | Teaching |
| Research | Administration |

One person, many hats

Problem: Differentiation. Who's doing what?

Are the goals compatible?

Fig. 2. Two Different Task and Organization Problems.

To me this means multiple hats are not so much a personal problem as an *organizational* one. Task system managers do not know what to do if they can not predict how much of each task is being performed on a given day, the strategic goals this work supports, how much it will cost, and who will pay for it.

This fact accounts for much conflict between administrators and professionals. The one tries to coordinate towards institutional goals, and the other sees this effort, given their personal goals, as bureaucratic constraint which hinders, not helps, their performance and reduces their autonomy.

Concrete Goals

Setting priorities, upon which rational resource management depends, is central to industry. "Only if targets are defined," writes Peter Drucker, "can resources be allocated to their attainment, priorities and deadlines set, and somebody held accountable for results."[9]

Health priorities are hard to set, for everything seems equally urgent. Hospital managers consider patient care central, medical deans education, clinicians their own specialty. For many teachers research matters most, because academic advancement, peer recognition, and personal satisfaction are wrapped up in it.[10]

THREE-LEGGED STOOL

The famous "three-legged stool"—equal commitment to service, research, teaching—permits each person to defend whatever he does as high primacy of one or another task at any point in time. Besieged on all sides to accommodate every social and political need, a service institution, writes Drucker, "cannot concentrate; it must try to placate everyone." Thus, the critical question for medical centers is: Can we pay for it? The organizational question is: Does it make sense for us to do it?

One way out of this intolerable goal dilemma is to specify which services or customers come first. Narrowing goals makes coordination with existing technologies more feasible. This strategy has made limited-service private hospitals a successful growth industry while local medical school affiliates are going broke.

It is much easier to run a "businesslike" operation when profit is predicated on treating selected diseases, while limiting or eliminating teaching and research entirely. At the same time, there is a professional cost in this. Physicians attracted to academic medical centers wish to choose for themselves which mix of tasks they need to do to remain at the cutting edge in their fields. They resist the implication they could learn, grow, create, and contribute if limited to working on one task at a time.

This obstacle, however, is not insurmountable. Task differences are subject to rational analysis, even without forcing people to take off some hats. For example, it is possible to write separate contracts for each hat a person wears, instead of lumping tasks into one undifferentiated person labelled "Professor and Chairman."

Performance Measures

In industry, accountability hinges on managing to a set of numbers. Having goals, dividing up and coordinating work, seem pointless unless you can track progress and make course corrections. Business firms use three major indices: Costs, productivity, and profitability.

Customers are the judges who enforce accountability. Their behavior affects the numbers by which managers manage. Customers can go elsewhere, lobby Congress, write Ralph Nader, picket, boycott, in short make life as miserable for a firm as its faulty products do for them. Health care customers—patients, students—have fewer options. They can do the above, but they are fighting three systems, two of which have cultural/international roots, rather than a single entity with offices somewhere.

The health care Task system uses three major indices, each measuring quite different dimensions: (1) size of budget; (2) space; (3) salaried "full-time equivalents." More of each is held to constitute good performance, and less equals bad, because, as Drucker says, "No institution likes to abandon anything it does."

Quality control, while an issue for administrators, is very difficult for them to manage; for quality standards come not from customer to manager to organization, but from the Governance system to the manager to the customer. Given the nature of medicine, public expectation, and physician training, it is physicians who set and enforce quality standards.

Until recently this has been an extremely individual, rather than organizational, act. "Such evaluation," writes the Joint Commission on Accreditation of Hospitals, "isn't done systematically . . . in a way that reflects the bulk of care given in a hospital." Therefore, the "onus is on the reviewer rather than the system," making it hard for the institution to learn and perform differently.[11]

Thus, while most physicians have and practice high standards, there are few organizational procedures for connecting standards, good or bad, to dollars, space, and staffing decisions. The JCAH's new focus on outcome audits (how well did the patient do?) is a step in the direction of better organization—if such data can be linked to Task system decisions, and not just to physician competence. But so long as the two sets of standards are managed independently of each other, health costs will continue to spiral.

Formal Authority

To enforce and link Governance with Task system measures requires not only a cognitive act but decisiveness. Industrial managers are acknowledged to have the right to decide, even when people question their good sense. The marketplace, in the long run, determines whether they are right or wrong.

In industry, it requires formal authority to sanction "teambuilding," a democratizing process which spreads influence to those who have had too little. In addition, the formal boss-subordinate relationship provides a setting that permits the scrutiny of dynamics important for task accomplishment: anxiety; group collusion to maintain problems; unrealistic expectations for the boss, and vice versa; intolerance of mistakes; reluctance to speak candidly; and the impact of interpersonal feedback on working together.

Health administrators are not exempt from these dynamics. Many have legal responsibility for the consequences. Their formal authority, though, extends in practice only to nurses, aides, technicians, service employees, and other administrators. It excludes physicians and scientists. In this situation business tools and training have limited utility. Health administrators find themselves more often playing the political game of engineering consent rather than the managerial game of implementing decisions.

Lawrence, Charns and I have asked hundreds of medical school faculty to whom they were responsible when wearing each of their medical task hats. From 20+ percent for undergraduate education, to 55 percent in patient care, to 70 percent on research have said "no one," or left the item blank, or named a person or group outside their medical center. While accountability is a much discussed and much valued concept, when applied to others, a great many medical faculty cannot imagine Task system accountability at all. For them, it is purely a Governance matter, based on setting standards for the identity system.[12]

THE IDENTITY SYSTEM

It is the salience to the doctor of the physician Identity system that is key to understanding why health care is so hard to organize. There is a complex interplay of forces: The medical personality, how doctors are socialized, what society expects of physicians. All of these forces reinforce a physician self-concept based largely on the technical expertise needed to diagnose and treat disease, and the mental toughness to make life-and-death decisions alone. This symbolic system exists inside each physician. It is based on public recognition of professional credentials which confer status and a sense of self-worth. Four binds result from this emphasis.

The Self-Concept Bind

The scientific definition of knowledge relevant to disease is extremely limited. All data outside a medical model of life are difficult for many doctors to internalize, let alone act upon. This in no way denies the impressive achievements of modern medicine. It does result in doctors paying a high price, internally, to maintain identity. Most consider task-related feelings, for example, as irrelevant. Some grow quite emotional at the suggestion emotions constitute "scientific" data worthy of study, codification, understanding, and integration with whatever specialty they practice. Many share, in the extreme, a common cultural belief that to show feelings is an unprofessional retreat from reason and a sign of weakness.

They tend to see no middle ground of choice between uncontrolled, hysterical catharsis and extreme self-control. Yet few people do work that continually stirs up so much anger, fear, and helplessness. Thus, physicians have few ways of using their emotions constructively toward the solution of problems, in the same way they use their expertise. This seriously limits the degree to which they can invest in joint work with others, and in the utility of their contributions when they do.

This bind extends to positive feelings too. To a great extent trust, in such a disorderly system as health care, is a valuable commodity. Often one's good feelings about another provide a reliable indicator of relevant expertise; many physicians use personal relationships and intuitive trust as important variables in their professional judgments.

Medical theories cannot easily accommodate this fact. Unless your conceptual frame includes (a) a sense-making view of the interplay among feelings, behavior, and relationships, and (b) the impact of these on medical practice, you cannot utilize such data systematically. In fact, a high percentage of important medical decisions are made from such a framework—which constitutes, by formal standards, an extremely unscientific view of medicine.

The Accountability Bind

Doctors do not judge each other's work publicly. However valued the concept, it is difficult to practice it. This makes sense where identity is so closely linked to narrow expertise. Only those with equivalent specialized knowledge are presumed to be able to judge one's work. Moreover, at least until recently, such judgments—even when made formally, as part of a hospital audit—were based on "How I would have handled this case," rather than the result for the patient and the impact on the hospital.[13]

Paradoxically, each physician has strong opinions about health system goals, and what roles *all others* (non-physicians) should play in achieving them. They "often regard themselves as expert in medicine at large," writes a public health school dean, which "includes all parts of the hospital . . . and, beyond that, the community, since so many aspects are 'health related.' "[14]

"CATCH-22" OF MEDICINE

Accountability is the Catch-22 of medicine. The demonstration of expertise in one specialty, which is critical to self-esteem, is taken as admission of incompetence in all other areas. Thus, physicians accept medical administrator claims to management expertise—so long as no clinical matters are involved.

The trouble is that in hospitals nearly everything is health related. Yet accountability—for the system as a whole—is extremely fragmented. Though most physicians care very much about quality, they have few procedures for linking this concern to institutional management.

The Knowledge Bind

Identity hinges on state-of-the-arts skills and knowledge. Yet nobody can keep up any more. "If I did nothing but read journals all day," one doctor told me, "I'd just fall behind at a slower rate." To maintain status, doctors must maintain an illusion of keeping up. Knowing the impossibility of doing this, they do the next best thing. They narrow their focus and become sub-specialists.

This has a curious organizational consequence. It cannot be predicted when a new technique, piece of equipment, or care concept will be developed. It *can* be predicted at what point in time physicians will pressure their medical facility to acquire an innovation: at once. From an Identity system perspective this makes sense. Whether it makes sense from a patient care or teaching or institutional management standpoint varies considerably from place to place.

To put it another way, knowledge is piling up at a rate beyond the ability of anybody to assimilate it—and it is easier for physicians to blame bureaucracy for their inability to keep up than to accept their own human limitations.

The Task Interdependence Bind

The only reason to be organized is that the problems you are trying to solve require it. Certainly this is true of complex health facilities. At the same time, organizations, for optimal performance, require some cooperation—which implies give and take. Physicians, caught in their other binds, feel compelled to direct, control, decide and be responsible for every patient and patient decision within their purview. It is hard for doctors to share life-and-death risks with anybody, even the patients themselves. What is more, this bind is growing tighter. A growing number of malpractice suits seem based on the premise that infallibility, rather than best effort, should be the minimum standard.

Physician identity has serious consequences for medical organizations. It is the department, rather than an institution, which undergirds Identity. Medicine is organized by specialty to a greater degree than generic tasks like service, teaching, research. Specialty is so pervasive that without the label it is difficult to achieve status in a medical center. Budgets tend to flow through departments. Programmatic activity—integration of knowledge around patient problems—often suffers.

Except for science-based R & D, there is nothing in industry remotely comparable to the medical Identity system. To a remarkable degree industrial managers measure self-esteem and organizational achievement together. They feel good about themselves when the numbers improve, and badly when they do not. The needs of Task and Identity systems work hand in glove. Enhancing one will also enhance the other. It is this chance that makes organization development valuable and welcome.

THE GOVERNANCE SYSTEM

The Governance system sets and maintains health and medical practice standards. It is the "appreciative" mechanism, in Vickers' phase, which performs the valuing function that makes the Identity system so potent.[15]

Governance exists both in and outside institutions. Inside, it includes trustees, hospital and medical boards, audit committees, and—in medical schools—faculty senates, executive faculty (chairmen), task forces, and committees on everything from admissions to curriculum and grading. Outside are professional societies, specialty boards, accrediting groups, granting agencies, and government. These influence admission to the field, ethical practice, funding, and educational, clinical, and research criteria.

Governance, in its own terms, is the best organized of the three systems. From the standpoint of health care systems, however, Governance mechanisms tend to have three flaws:

Licensure by a Governance group, not an employment contract, undergirds Identity. It is not necessary to demonstrate competence in working with others, nor an understanding of organizational complexity, to achieve status in medicine. Moreover, it is not necessary to demonstrate achievement in a particular Task system. Once technical competence is certified, all else is assumed.

Governance systems tend to be more closed than the Task system, which requires daily interaction with patients, students and the public. There have been few pipelines into health policy which lay people can use, although this is changing.

In addition, links between Governance and Task systems are spotty, rather than well-institutionalized. In most hospitals, for instance, utilization review, under cost pressure from third party payers, is an important Task problem. Meanwhile, hospitals are also under pressure to phase-in outcome audits, as a means of insuring uniform, high quality care. The latter is a Governance function. As hospitals are presently structured, whether physicians will have an opportunity to analyze with managers the relationship between both sets of data and their impact on goals and costs is questionable. Another result of this is that administrators are called upon to implement standards which they are not considered competent to judge. This exacerbates still more the inherent conflict between physicians and managers.

Governance systems work against interdependency. Internal committee meetings, by far the most frequent type in medical centers, tend to be long, frustrating, and often nonproductive. Departmental loyalties are more intense than loyalty to the whole which Governance represents. Without concrete institutional goals, it is hard to favor anything except what will be least restrictive of one's own freedom of action.

THE HIGH COSTS OF POOR LINKAGE

Throughout, I have tried to show the significance of the lack of links between Task, Identity, and Governance systems, and to demonstrate how this works against rational management and incurs costs.

This lack of links among the three systems requires more Task system administrators. This drives up fixed costs, which are then squeezed from professional budgets as a sort of "coordination tax." Despite this, integration remains elusive. It takes place in a vacuum. Toward what ends is the system being integrated? If ever there was a cat chasing its tail, it is the addition of administrative systems in the absence of goals that professionals share.

Second, is cost in alienation. An anomaly of medical centers is the degree to which the Task system so slavishly imitates industry's least appropriate bureaucratic mode. Functional specialization defines status in health, despite a crying need for programs integrated on behalf of whole people—patients, students, communities, the professionals themselves.

To cite one example, consider a connection between deteriorating doctor-nurse relationships and rising hospital costs. There are in the main three things hospital patients need: Clinical care, personal attention, and help in getting a complex system to focus on their own case. Doctors provide the first service. Increasingly, aides do the "hands-on" care, clerks the paperwork, allied technicians the clinical tests, and ombudsmen the patient advocacy. Nurses, who might provide a link between clinical and administrative tasks, are being squeezed out. RN's often don't want the narrow jobs, for they are trained to greater responsibility.

They cannot use their knowledge well in the present setup, despite the fact they spend more time with patients, and often understand better than anyone the complex relationship among physical, emotional, social, and administrative problems.[16] With clinical and administrative training, they might make excellent hospital integrators—much better, in fact, than doctors or administrators. Instead, they are opting for the Identity game—seeking to become nurse practitioners—because nobody, themselves included, can visualize a more appropriate use for their training.

WHY OD HASN'T WORKED—SO FAR

Since face-to-face interdependence is so important for solving medical center problems, it seems plausible that applied behavioral scientists, with OD skills, would have some useful procedures. Alas, we have our binds too.

First, our knowledge is inadequate. Though we have some ideas about how to coordinate the major tasks, industrial theories shed no light at all on how to link the three systems in ways so that both individuals *and* organization are enhanced. They do not, in particular, account for the consequences of a highly competitive Identity system, based entirely on individual achievement.

Second, our structure-reducing, interdependence-enhancing technologies do not work where there is no organizational payoff for interdependent behavior. To practice structure reduction in such a competitive environment is to raise professional anxieties even higher, for these technologies seek to improve a set of conditions physicians do not value to begin with.

The OD repertoire needs structure-*creating* interventions, consistent with our humanistic values. Yet we share with health professionals a profound mistrust of mindless bureaucracies.[17] To the extent we can find no middle ground between free-flowing "organic" relationships and industrial constraints, we may resist the persistent—not intermittent or temporary—commitment that the invention of innovative structures calls for.

THE HEALTH MANAGER'S BIND

The risk for all of us is falling prey to what Maslow called "the dangers of unrealistic perfectionalism."[18] It is this syndrome which probably accounts in part for the short half-life of deans, chiefs, chairmen and administrators. Knowing the scene firsthand, many go into management believing they, unlike their predecessors, will avoid the big mistakes.

They see the pitfall—there is little evidence to the contrary—as personalities, not systems, and soon discover they can not easily change others. Instead, they seek to change themselves, in the same mode that made them competent physicians or scientists—by acquiring new skills and knowledge. They study MBO, PPBS, and the more adventurous OD, as if these were anatomy courses through which the system, once understood, can be manipulated. However, the courses are based on industrial practice and deal with a very different anatomy.

Where their industrial counterparts use technology strategically, they use it *ad hoc*, to patch up this situation, to damp down that one. They find themselves constantly saying No to people they like, rejecting ideas they value, holding the creativity of others at bay, unappreciated for the good things they have done, attacked for the numberless things others think they *should* have done. Only a few redefine the problem as something beyond technology: how to discover/translate/invent wholly new modes.

How can this be done? The paradox is profound. Though the Identity system names the game, and the Governance system makes the rules, the Task system is the playing field. Those who play by technical expertise alone win only at the expense of many others, jeopardizing an already fragile system. A critical variable is cognition of the missing linkages, for managerial changes which lack Governance sanctions or threaten Identity are not likely to be stable.

Paradoxically, to introduce a new management practice sensitive to all three systems requires, in the absence of relevant organization theory, innate political and interpersonal skills. These skills, though in short supply, are not lacking entirely. Some administrators with whom I have been privileged to work over the years are doing things worth studying:

- Budgeting both by department *and* program to encourage integrative activity
- Clarifying the center's institutional and departmental goals

- Involving professionals in managerial tasks
- Planning resource management more deliberately
- Bringing physicians and scientists into institutional budget discussions
- Educating others to the complexity of these tasks.

Judging the efficacy of these efforts by "all-or-nothing" medical standards seems inappropriate, for no one knows what "all" looks like, and "nothing" is unacceptable in a system strangling for lack of organizational innovations equal to those of medicine.

A sensible goal for health managers, it seems to me, is to try to make small improvements, say 10 percent, in the congruity of goals, interdependence, authority, and measures. Small rationalizations, sanctioned by Governance, mindful of Identity, contribute importantly to more humane medical centers.

Figure 3 charts the complex interdependencies I think must be taken into account in any new theory of individual/organization fit in medical centers. Present technologies seek

to rationalize the Task system (solid lines). Whether they also can be used to link the three systems is one test of their practicality. Those unwilling to experiment with new structural relationships cannot facilitate change, for the changes called for may be the very ones they resist. If that is an exaggeration, the changes called for are certainly structures of a different sort than any of us know much about. They are structures that encourage, support, and utilize creative, individualistic, and idiosyncratic behavior for socially desirable ends.

If we can own up to our ignorance, and to our values in such matters, then I believe we are ready to have the "right" problem: how to create, in health-care-specific situations, a better fit between people and work.

REFERENCES

1. Georgopoulos, Basil S. (Editor), *Organization Research On Health Care Institutions.* Institute For Social Research, The University of Michigan, Ann Arbor, Michigan, 1972.
2. Friedlander, Frank, "OD Reaches Adolescence: An Exploration of Its Underlying Values." *The Journal of Applied Behavioral Science,* Vol. 12, No. 1, 1976.
3. Freidson, Eliot, *Professional Dominance: The Social Structure of Medical Care.* Aldine Publishing Co., Chicago, Illinois, 1970.
4. Maslow, A. H. "Synergy in the Society and in the Individual," Chapter 14, *The Farther Reaches of Human Nature.* The Viking Press, New York, 1972, pp. 199–211.
5. French, Wendell L., and Cecil H. Bell, Jr., "A History of Organization Development," *Organization Development.* Prentice-Hall, Inc., Englewood Cliffs, New Jersey, Chapter 21, pp. 21–29, 1973.
6. Lawrence, Paul R., and J. W. Lorsch, *Organization and Environment.* Homewood, Illinois: Richard D. Irwin, Inc., 1969.
7. Lawrence, Paul R., Marvin R. Weisbord, Martin P. Charns, "The Organization and Management of Academic Medical Centers: A Summary of Findings." Unpublished Report to Four Medical Schools, Organization Research & Development, 1974.

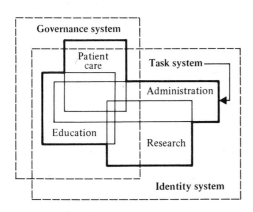

1. **Task system** itself requires coordination of major tasks—the target of management technologies.

2. In addition, links are needed with **Governance** and **Identity** systems. Theory is inadequate to this.

Fig. 3. Systems Link-Up Needed in Medical Centers.

8. Lawrence, Weisbord, Charns, op cit., page 7.

9. Drucker, Peter F., "Why Service Institutions Do Not Perform," *Management—Tasks—Responsibilities—Practices.* Harper & Row, 1974, Chapter 12, pp. 137–147.

10. Lawrence, Paul R., Marvin R. Weisbord, and Martin P. Charns. *Academic Medical Center Self-Study Guide,* Report to Physicians' Assistance Branch, Bureau of Health Manpower Education, National Institutes of Health, 1973.

11. Jacobs, Charles M., J. D. *Procedure for Retrospective Patient Care Audit in Hospitals,* Joint Commission on Accreditation of Hospitals, Third Edition, 1973.

12. Lawrence, Weisbord, Charns, op cit., page 6.

13. Jacobs, op cit.

14. Lynton, Rolf P., "Boundaries in Health Care Systems" (Backfeed Section), *Journal of Applied Behavioral Science,* Volume 11, No. 2, 1975, page 250.

15. Vickers, Sir Geoffrey, *The Art of Judgment,* Basic Books, New York, New York, 1965.

16. Charns, Martin P., "Breaking the Tradition Barrier: Managing Integration in Health Care Facilities," *Health Care Management Review,* Winter, 1976.

17. For a sensible, humane statement see, Culbert, Samuel A., *The Organization Trap and How to Get Out of It.* Basic Books, Inc., New York, 1974.

18. Maslow, A. H., op cit., p. 217.